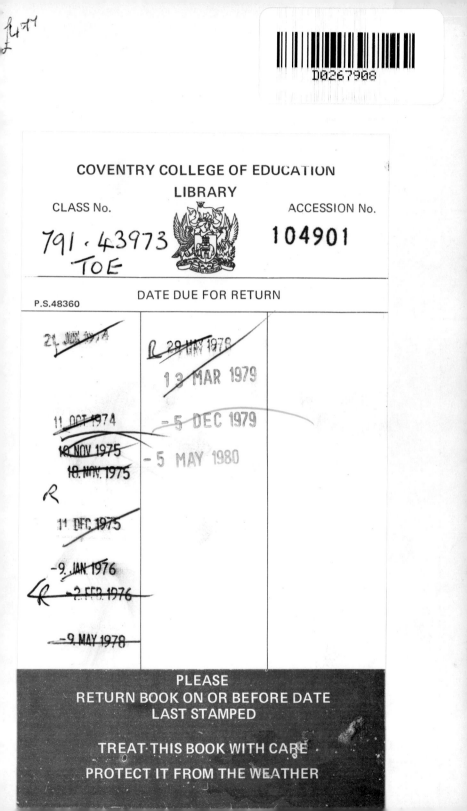

Hollywood and After

Hollywood and After

The Changing Face of American Cinema

JERZY TOEPLITZ

Translated from the Polish by Boleslaw Sulik

LONDON · GEORGE ALLEN & UNWIN LTD
Ruskin House · Museum Street

ISBN 0 04 791032 1

Printed in Great Britain
by Cox & Wyman Ltd,
London, Fakenham and Reading

ACKNOWLEDGEMENTS

The author and publisher wish to thank the Motion Picture Association of America and the British Film Institute for their assistance in providing stills for this book and the following distributors for permission to reproduce the stills used in this book: American International Pictures, Inc. for the still from *Bloody Mama*; Cinema International Corporation for stills from *Love Story, The Godfather, Uptight, Once Upon a Time in the West, Catch-22, Medium Cool, Lonely are the Brave* and *Airport*; Cinerama Releasing (U.K.) Ltd for stills from *They Shoot Horses, Don't They* and *Straw Dogs*; Columbia-Warner Distribution Ltd for stills from *A Clockwork Orange, Five Easy Pieces, Getting Straight, Easy Rider, Woodstock, Bullitt, The Green Berets, Bonnie and Clyde, Funny Girl, The Liberation of L.B. Jones* and *In Cold Blood*; Contemporary Films Ltd for the still from *Putney Swope*; Metro-Goldwyn-Mayer, Inc. for stills from *2001: A Space Odyssey, Doctor Zhivago* and *Gone with the Wind*; Sherpix Inc. for the still from *The Stewardesses*; Twentieth Century-Fox Film Company Ltd for stills from *Little Big Man, M.A.S.H., Tora, Tora, Tora, Butch Cassidy and the Sundance Kid, Hello, Dolly, The Boston Strangler, The Detective, Pretty Poison, The Sound of Music, The Bible* and *Cleopatra*; United Artists Corporation Ltd for the still from *Alice's Restaurant*; and Vaughn Film Distribution Ltd for stills from *Lonesome Cowboys* and *Trash*.

CONTENTS

ILLUSTRATIONS

1

The New Pattern

Hollywood: The Symbol and the Reality

The name of Hollywood is frequently applied to the entire American cinema. Hollywood is responsible for this and that, Hollywood is evolving, Hollywood has lost its dominant world position – we say it often, having in mind not the single district of the great city of Los Angeles, but the film industry of the United States. Tradition speaks more forcefully to us than reality. What was undeniably true in the twenties and thirties, and still had some grounds at the half-century mark, has no basis in the facts and statistics of the 1970s. Today the American cinema and Hollywood represent two different things, by no means synonymous, and only marginally and to a diminishing extent overlapping.

Let us start with topography. Way back in the old days of the cinema, during the First World War and in the immediate years after it, all the film-making activities became concentrated in the Hollywood district of Los Angeles. Here the studios and laboratories were situated, here the film-makers, producers, directors and stars of the screen set up house. But soon, before the twenties ended, the exodus began. The companies were looking for more suitable locations for their studios, with ample back lots to build monumental sets on. Actors were emigrating to more secluded and exclusive places, like Beverly Hills, Bel Air, or Santa Monica. Hollywood could no longer be contained by the actual city of Los Angeles; it moved out to Los Angeles County. On 22 September 1937 the city council of Los Angeles, taking pride in having an undisputed film capital of the world under its jurisdiction, formally created a separate district of

Hollywood, allowing it, however, no real autonomy, no self-government. Many of the studios found themselves within the new district. Adolph Zukor, Samuel Goldwyn, Charlie Chaplin, the partners from RKO Studio, had their base here, as well as some less important production companies. But Universal, for instance, had its headquarters outside Hollywood proper, though almost next door to it. Warner Brothers were situated in Burbank, a different part of the city, and the Metro-Goldwyn-Mayer empire extended over a considerable acreage of Culver City. In 1940 Walt Disney quit his small and restricting studio in Hyperion Street and moved to Burbank, setting up a new studio near Warner Brothers. Twentieth Century-Fox chose a site in West Los Angeles, five miles north of Hollywood.

After the Second World War, with further migration and the acquisition of outlying territories for projected future studios fifty or more miles from the old capital of the cinema (Twentieth Century-Fox in Malibu, Metro-Goldwyn-Mayer–Thousand Oaks in Conejo Valley), little was left of the traditional Hollywood.

Already some people have argued that there is no good reason for retaining a name that has lost all geographic and cinematic validity. A significant discussion on this took place in Los Angeles in November of 1967 at the meeting of the City Council Planning Committee. One of those present, Councillor Paul H. Lamport, proposed that the boundaries of Hollywood should be extended to include the neighbouring territories of Universal City. The reaction of his colleagues was immediately hostile. They not only refused to support the proposal but counter-attacked, requesting that the original order of 1937, setting up the separate district of Hollywood, be annulled. Why persist in something which long ago lost all point, ran the argument. The counter-proposal was voted in. Councillor Lamport declared that he would appeal to the plenary session of the City Council. Perhaps the threat was effective, perhaps some counter-moves were made behind the scenes, but within a week the Planning Committee withdrew its new measure, pronouncing that the order of 22 September 1937 still held good.[1] Traditional sentiments prevailed and

Hollywood remained on the map, but inside its old boundaries, without Universal City.

Topographic changes reflect only the formal and, in a sense, external aspects of the problem. Of greater significance are the transformations that have taken place inside all the studios – those few remaining within the postal district of Hollywood, and those that have moved to other parts of the city or outside it. These changes are of fundamental importance.

Of course, it wouldn't be true to say that there is no more shooting on studio stages. Work is continuous, but it is mostly on television serials rather than on full-scale productions for cinema circuit distribution. And altogether this work takes up no more than a part of the available studio space. In the old days, in the thirties, the annual output fluctuated between 300 to 400 features; now it barely reaches 100 to 150.

All the big studios stood in vast grounds known as back lots, suitable for location shooting and the erection of sets. These tended to become a permanent feature, so that whenever the cinematic action moved to ancient Rome, a medieval German township or an African village, a superficial dressing up of the existing edifices sufficed to produce the required effect. London, Paris, Peking, Moscow – all were there within easy reach. But as time passed the method of work and – more importantly – the fashions and expectations of the public changed. Audiences now insist on authenticity and refuse to accept Parisian streets made of hardboard. Back lots are becoming deserted and useless, only occasionally coming to life when the studio mounts a rare, expensive, blockbuster like *Cleopatra*.

They are not, strictly speaking, useless because in most cases acreage occupied, until recently, by fictional worlds, is being transformed into building lots. In place of Pharoah's palaces and walled fortresses, housing estates, hotels and supermarkets have sprung up. Twentieth Century-Fox pioneered this development, selling in 1962 to Alcoa (Aluminium Company of America) its 260 hectares (about 640 acres) bordering on Beverley Hills for the sum of $43 million. A flourishing, affluent Century City came into existence, interspersed with pointed skyscrapers and with a typically luxurious Century Plaza Hotel as a focal point of the new estate. The success of the operation induced others to follow suit.

In July of 1967 MCA, with a controlling interest in Universal Studios, began building a hotel on the south-western outskirts of Universal City. The hotel rises to twenty-one storeys and comprises five hundred rooms. It was christened Sheraton Universal Hotel of the Stars in honour of its joint partners: Sheraton Hotels and Universal. And the reference to the stars represents a tribute to a proud past. It is only the first stage of a long-term project, designed to transform completely what was one of the oldest studios in Los Angeles. Carl Laemmle acquired the site in 1915 from a farmer, a Mr Taylor, who had been running a chicken ranch there. For the next fifty-two years Universal City was producing films. Thousands and thousands of movies, distributed all over the globe. Now an entire complex of hotels and motels is going to rise here, 1,800 apartments all told, at a cost of $40 million. *Sic transit gloria* . . .

Paramount, which has kept the tradition alive longer than anyone else, decided in 1970 to close down its studio near Marathon Street and Gower Street, at Melrose Avenue. It is a large cluster of buildings and back lots including the old RKO Pictures (later the Desilu Studios). Its northernmost part borders on the Jewish cemetery, which, needing to expand, would be quite willing to buy a part of the site; but the existing building regulations effectively prevent it. Gulf and Western, which has a controlling interest in Paramount, is offering the entire site for $30 million to anyone who – like Alcoa – would transform the old scene of Cecil B. De Mille's, Gloria Swanson's and Gary Cooper's greatest triumphs, into a housing estate.

The old film fortress with a roaring lion as its famous screen landmark – in other words, Metro-Goldwyn-Mayer – doesn't want to be left behind. In October of 1970 68 hectares (around 165 acres) of its Culver City grounds changed hands. Lovitt and Sons acquired the site for $7¼ million, to erect on it an estate of luxury flats. A further 72 hectares await a prospective buyer. Thus in a few years there will be no trace left of the cinematic empires and the screen legends; unless as a museum, which is also possible and profitable and thus of real interest to the studios.

Studios are no longer inaccessible fortresses, jealously guarded from the curious eyes of outsiders, enchanted and mysterious story-book castles. On the contrary – they have opened their doors wide to all visitors, seeing in the policy clear-cut gains, both commercially and in terms of public relations. Leon Wasserman, the chief of MCA, pioneered it. It was his idea to organize, in July 1965, the first guided tours of Universal City. The prices in 1970 were $3.75 for adults and $1.75 for children below the age of 11. A ticket buys a two-hour trip in pink trams around the vast terrain of this kingdom of films and television. Courteous guides come forth with profuse information on all subjects of interest. Taking photographs is allowed, as is peering into shooting stages. In the 1968–9 season there was a special attraction in the form of a meeting with live TV stars – James Drury and Doug McClure, leading personalities of the popular NBC series *The Virginian*. Conducted tours of the studios are held every day, including Sundays, from 10 a.m. to 3 p.m.

Twentieth Century-Fox is at home to the public only on Saturdays and Sundays, 10 a.m. to 5 p.m. There are no pink trams here; instead, visitors are greeted by an army of girl guides, dressed in red, white and blue uniforms, with badges in their lapels exhorting people to 'think twentieth'. Young men in mini-cars, equipped with 'walkie talkies', direct the heavy traffic in narrow streets among studio buildings and sets erected in the open air. A festive mood is generated. Fancy hats, souvenir albums of photographs and soft drinks are on sale. In 1968 the visit would reach its climax towards the end, with the sudden appearance before the admiring crowds of Adam West, the legendary Batman, who would, at an auspicious moment, lean out of his fantastique Batmobile car. William Fox would, no doubt, turn in his grave if he conld see how, in the sixties, swarms of intruders are treating his sanctuary.

Conducted tours of the studios brought to Universal a far

from negligible income: in 1969 $5½ million. There were over a million visitors. The success of this 'tourist' scheme has encouraged MCA, the parent company, to undertake and develop similar ventures. In 1969 a subsidiary company, registered as Landman Services Inc., was set up to organize conducted tours of the federal capital, Washington, for a price of one dollar per head. Furthermore, another joint stock company was created – Minibus Inc. – to produce and market minibuses especially designed for excursions in Los Angeles and Washington. And this is not all: far-sighted and provident MCA directors set up a market research unit known as Action Research Center Inc. Of course, there are many such units in the United States analysing the trend of the market, advising producers on what commodities are likely to be in demand and how to advertise them. But the distinguishing feature of the Center is that it is using as its research sample the Universal City visitors – a representative cross-section of the American public. Uncle Carl – as the old pioneer, Carl Laemmle, used to be affectionately called – could never have dreamt of this new part, that of counsellor for a wide variety of business ventures, played by his beloved film city.

To behold with one's own eyes the very spot on which some famous old picture was shot – *The Hunchback of Notre Dame*, or *Phantom of the Opera* – proved a considerable attraction, but Metro-Goldwyn-Mayer is offering its visitors even more powerful excitements. In Culver City, in February 1970, the first sale of cinematic souvenirs was held: of costumes, props and remnants of all kinds. Collected and carefully preserved for half a century, these cinematic treasures are now leaving the vast and inaccessible vaults. No longer needed, they seem eminently suitable for clearance. Fastener Research Corporation was put in charge of the operation.

The sesame gates have been thrown open to the public. Accessories from over two thousand films are being sold by auction, and what items there are! Elizabeth Taylor's wedding veil, Clark Gable's torn frock-coat, Judy Garland's dancing shoes, and even Ramon Novarro's helmet from the silent *Ben Hur* of 1927. And also fragments of interiors and pieces of furniture, and even an entire Verona courtyard – the meeting-place of Romeo (Leslie Howard) and Juliet (Norma Shearer) in the old Shakespearean adaptation of George Cukor (1936). At the eleventh hour Debbie Reynolds, who started her career in Culver City, tried to save for history and future generations a part of the collection; at the very least the costumes of Greta Garbo. But the board of directors rejected her offer. A contract with Fastener Research Corporation secured them greater financial rewards. These auctions in the dream factory, according to a *Newsweek* reporter, are sad and somewhat distasteful occasions, as if an old friend's wedding-ring, his Sunday suit and fishing rod were being sold to pay for his debts.[2] A clearance sale of Hollywood is being held by companies with old and famous names. Not just to repay the old and recent debts, but to survive, to keep in the swim, to exist. But for how long?

Loss of Independence

The names are the same: Paramount, Metro-Goldwyn-Mayer, Universal, Twentieth Century-Fox, United Artists, Columbia, and Walt Disney Productions. Only RKO Pictures and Republic are no longer with us. Outwardly everything remains as of old. The roaring lion, the Statue of Liberty with a flaming torch, and a mountain peak wreathed by stars – they all still appear on the screen. But it is merely a disguise, because that façade of old signs and trade-marks hides other names with genuine attributes of power, capital, initiative. An ordinary mortal, encountering on his occasional visits to the cinema the same, familiar companies, has no way of telling who really stands behind them, who owns and directs them. But for people with a professional interest in the cinema, the façade no longer counts, and the old names are only used colloquially, out of long habit. In financial, banking and industrial circles, the Hollywood past has left hardly a trace. Universal means Music Corporation of America; Paramount is Gulf and Western; United Artists is the Transamerica Corporation, and Warner Brothers is now, as

Warner Communications Corporation, a part of National Kinney Corporation. In January 1971 only Twentieth Century-Fox and Columbia have still retained a single identity, while Metro-Goldwyn-Mayer is controlled individually by Kirk Kerkorian from Las Vegas, rather than his own Tracinda Investment Company. In principle, however, almost the entire film industry, as represented by the traditional 'Big Five', or 'Big Eight', is undergoing, in a different degree and at various stages, a similar process of transformation. And the final, inescapable conclusion is always the same, however varied the disguise: loss of independence.

Perhaps the most typical instance of the trend is the absorption of Paramount into the operations of Gulf and Western Industries Inc., situated in Houston, Texas. In 1957 it was still a small company, producing and marketing motor-car accessories. Its annual turnover reached just $6½ million. Then came a period of expansion: taking over other companies, moving into all possible fields of interest. In ten years eighty joint stock companies came under the Gulf and Western banner, among them New Jersey Zinc (a zinc mining and processing concern), and South Puerto Rico Sugar (sugar cane plantations). In 1972 the turnover reached $1.67 billion.

In 1966 Gulf and Western bought Paramount and, a year later, Desilu Productions. This was done in strict accordance with the company's tenets, stipulating that a controlling interest may be acquired in any trade or industrial unit which (a) is not threatened with overseas competition, (b) is not competing at home against gigantic corporations, and (c) is not producing commodities which could be easily forced out of the market through the technological superiority of competitors. By these standards Paramount represented an attractive proposition. No unequal competition threatened it either in the United States or from abroad. The old film fortress was neither weaker nor stronger than other cinematic potentates. Given a dollar injection from Gulf and Western it could become a leading power. To underline the importance of this acquisition the chairman of the parent company, Charles G. Bluhdorn, himself headed the new board of

Paramount, and he invited to serve on it two of his closest associates: David S. Judelson, the President of Gulf and Western, and Martin S. Davies, the director of the Leisure Time Division.

Analysis of the entire field of operations covered by Gulf and Western is of no concern to the cinema. Relevant here is only one of the twelve trade sections, known as the Leisure Time Division, comprising various lines of the entertainment industries. It includes companies producing films for the cinema and television, the production of records and magnetic tape, of complete systems for cable transmission of TV images (CATV) and, last but not least, an electric guitar factory, with a subsidiary branch in Japan (Sega Manufacturing Co.). Operating outside this section is Chicago Thoroughbred Enterprises which manages two race tracks in Chicago: Arlington Park and Washington Park, and also the Arlington Park Towers Hotel, frequented by racegoers. The Leisure Time Division by no means provides the chief source of Gulf and Western's profits. Its share comes up to just 12·17 per cent of the entire sum. Reducing that percentage to its primary elements we find that the income from the production and distribution of films amounts to 5·17 per cent of the income from all other sources. It is a significant count, showing that within an industrial giant like Gulf and Western, the proud Paramount Studios, with so many costly multiple million dollar productions to its credit, has become just a small cog in a large and elaborate mechanism. In the general accounts of Gulf and Western, loss or profit on Paramount operations is of no crucial importance. That 5 per cent represents a small proportion of a multi-million dollar profit and a turnover of thousands of millions of dollars. The new chief of Paramount (and of Gulf and Western), Charles G. Bluhdorn, views the performance of the film studios in a very different kind of perspective than Adolph Zukor, the founder of the company, used to do. For Zukor the production of films was a matter of livelihood and pride, of life and death, to put it in terms of an over-dramatic cliché. Yet, even in the year of the great box office triumphs of Paramount, in August 1972 Charles

G. Bluhdorn, in a Reuter's interview, stressed very clearly that Gulf and Western were being divided into twelve operating groups, so that no one part of the company 'can make or break it'. He added: 'We are very thankful to Paramount for *Love Story* and *The Godfather* . . . but at this point we'd still be viable without them.'[3]

When in August 1969 Messrs Bluhdorn and Judelson were called before the Senate anti-trust sub-committee to explain the nature and scope of Gulf and Western operations, Judelson talked stirringly of the company he was heading as a 'federation of small, medium and large companies, each of which joined of its own accord'.[4] He added later, not before the sub-committee but at the shareholders' meeting in December of the same year, that the 'aim of the federation is to demonstrate to the Nation that there is nothing wrong in the American way of life'.[5] Thus a policy of incorporating various different companies, with nothing in common, has found its philosophy. In 1970 all the twelve sections made profit which, according to Judelson, furnishes the best proof that the flexible and realistic policies of diversification, as practised by Gulf and Western, have passed the test. One of these steps was the decision to close down the Paramount Studios in Hollywood.

The New York company of Kinney National Service, later known as National Kinney Corporation, which (since 1969) controls Warner Brothers, is not an industrial giant on the scale of Gulf and Western, but it operates the same principle of diversification. The concern, until the middle of 1971, consisted of three sections: (1) leisure time, (2) building, and (3) financial. The first one included, apart from Warner Brothers, *Mad Magazine* (the famous comic strip and cartoon publication), a publishing agency – National Periodical Publications, the Independent New Company, the Licensing Corporation of America and Panavision. The last item is of key importance: it is a factory providing lenses for wide-screen productions. Most of the studios employ the Pana-vision system. The only serious competitor is Techniscope, owned by the Technicolor company. In July 1971 the company split into two, both under the same financial control.

The old name, National Kinney Corporation, is reserved for building and financial operations; the leisure-time section has been transformed into an autonomous company, Warner Communications Corporation. The two companies are closely connected and Warner Communications Corporation has shares in National Kinney Corporation and also in an important National Kinney Corporation's subsidiary, Garden State National Bank in New Jersey.

In view of the existence of the two separate companies it is difficult to assess how the production of films is faring in comparison to profits from parking lots and funeral parlours. Compared to the turnover of National Kinney Corporation before the take-over, the studio operations of Warner Communications Corporation probably accounts for about 20 to 30 per cent of the two sister companies.

Directors of National Kinney Corporation, contrary to the Gulf and Western practice, did not intervene directly in film matters. They have put loyal people in key positions, but they themselves kept their distance. As the chairman of the company, William V. Frankel, said at the annual meeting of shareholders: 'We leave initiative and management to the professionals, and I believe that we have got the best in the business . . .'[6] All the directors of National Kinney Corporation solemnly declared that they would not try to write the scripts or pronounce on studio matters requiring professional expertise. Furthermore, they are to refrain from judging the box office potential of films, seen or unseen by them, and – perhaps the most difficult promise to keep – resist the temptation of playing at casting directors. Splitting the National Kinney Corporation into two companies has not brought any changes into the direction of the newly created Warner Communications Corporation. The 'big shots' of the Kinney enterprise remain, as before, the key figures in the film company. After the death of William Frankel in 1971 his close friend and financial right hand of many years' standing, Steven J. Ross, never directly connected with the film industry, became President and Chairman of Warner Communications Corporation.

A parent company, owning 98·38 per cent of all the United

Artists shares, goes by name of the Transamerica Corporation and operates from San Francisco. It also comprises diverse kinds of enterprises. It deals in the building and management of hotels and motels, selling various lines of insurance, in investment loans and real estate. It owns Trans-International Airlines, which specializes in charter flights. The company's latest acquisition is a chain of commercial TV stations – Metromedia. As the range of operations gradually increases, the interest in film production recedes further and further into the background. Sometimes, at the shareholders' meetings, John R. Beckett, chairman of Transamerica Corporation, omits any mention of its subsidiary, United Artists.

Chronologically, the latest outsider to gain control of film studios is Kirk Kerkorian, the Armenian millionaire, now in his fifties. Kerkorian owns two large hotels and gambling casinos in Las Vegas, The Flamingo and The International, and is the largest shareholder in Western Air Lines. A few years ago he also owned Trans International Airlines, but sold them to the Transamerica Corporation. He controls his companies, including Metro-Goldwyn-Mayer, through Tracinda Investment Company Ltd, with offices in Las Vegas. He himself owns all the shares of this company, which takes its name from his daughter – Miss Tracy Kerkorian.

Kerkorian won practical control of M-G-M in two stages. In the summer of 1969 he bought 24 per cent of all shares, and in November increased his holding to 40 per cent, which gave him a dominating influence over the board. The old management, Edgar J. Bronfman and Louis F. Pol Jr, were soon forced out, and new people, appointed by Kerkorian, took over the studios. James T. Aubrey Jr, till 1965 a programme director for Columbia Broadcasting System, became the director of production in M-G-M. The entire operation was accomplished with tremendous speed and skill. No one would believe that the outsider from Las Vegas could out-manoeuvre such powerful rivals as the Canadian company Seagram (spirit distilleries, makers of the world-famous gin), and the American publishing concern, Time Inc. (the *Time* and *Life* weeklies). These two respected companies supported the management of Bronfman and Pol, but failed to move in time to prevent the acquisition of shares by the Armenian and – before realizing what was happening – lost control.

To carry out this transaction Kerkorian contracted considerable debts in European banks. Comparatively small and young, founded in 1955, the Burston and Texas Commerce Bank Ltd, based in London, loaned 22 million Eurodollars, Burkhardt and Co. from Essen, 50 million. Interest is extremely high: 12·7/8 per cent a year in the first case, 13 per cent in the second. In other words in 1970 Kerkorian had to find $9 million just to pay the interest. In this light the clearing operations, like the sale of grounds in Culver City, or the auction of valuable props from the fifty-year-old history of Metro-Goldwyn-Mayer, may appear as necessary measures. In September 1972 Kerkorian bought 170,000 shares, increasing his holding from 40 per cent to 44·8 per cent. His old rival, Edgar J. Bronfman, became his ally at the end of 1971, and together these two gentlemen are the uncontested masters of the company. M-G-M is at present more interested in hotel-building than in film-making. The new Metro Grand Hotel in Las Vegas, the largest resort of this kind in the world, will cost around $90 million.

In two companies – Columbia Pictures and Twentieth Century-Fox – there were, until early 1973, no take-overs by any stronger outside interests. No one knows what is going on behind the scenes. The only oasis of peace, so far apparently quite immune from all outside threat, is Walt Disney Productions. But this is the result of the specific kind of operations run by the company. It makes its millions not out of films, but out of the magic playgrounds known as Disneyland and Disney World.

The process of absorption of the film companies by the great corporations with diversified interests is making a strong and lasting impact on the structure and policies of the entire American cinema industry. The principle of diversification can be applied over a wide field of trade and industrial operations, but it can also be put to use in the cinema. Following the example of the presidents and directors of Gulf and Western, National Kinney Corporation, or

Transamerica Corporation, the management of the studios adapt the system to their own needs. Structural changes are accompanied by a change in priorities. And not towards the recognition of the value of films, the necessity of producing them, but towards the logic of profit and loss. The income counts, not films.

Main Product and By-products

Why should giant concerns, dealing in real estate and airline management, want to buy film studios? What induced, in the final count, the financial potentates from Gulf and Western, Kinney National Service and Transamerica Corporation to move into the cinema? It is obvious that where millions of dollars are at stake, where the level of dividends is of decisive importance, the magic of Hollywood, a fascination with stars and a gambler's risk inherent in any production project started in the hope of scoring a spectacular box office success, cannot be considered an inducement. Businessmen were motivated by the material, calculable advantages they saw in the film companies. William V. Frankel, explaining to shareholders of Kinney National Service the reasons for the acquisition of Warner Brothers, quoted the following factors determining the commercial viability of the transaction: (1) the market value of the music section of the company which publishes scores and records; (2) the potential value of equipment, installations and the whole production capacity for cinema and television; (3) 110 hectares (250 acres) of ground in Burbank; (4) a well-stocked film library. Significantly, films currently in production in the studios were not included in the list.[7]

Let us, to clarify the picture, try to assemble and itemize all the varied activities and interests, and thus all the assets of the big Hollywood companies. There are others beside the four basic advantages specified by Frankel. Theoretically, films for theatre distribution remain the staple product of the companies. In second place are films made exclusively for the television market. Third, the scores and records of old and recent film music. Fourth, the marketing of various by-lines and by-products, or the sale of advertising rights (i.e. cartoon film characters, employed by grocers to stimulate trade). Fifth, the film libraries, an accumulation of negatives of all past productions plus a mass of unused material, also, to a certain extent, marketable; all the rejected takes, scenes edited out of the final print, etc. Sixth, shooting stages, available on hire to other producers. Seventh, film laboratories, supplying home needs but also taking outside orders. Eighth, cinemas, studios, and other assets overseas. (By the Supreme Federal Court order, based on the anti-trust laws, film companies are allowed to own cinemas only outside the U.S.A.) Ninth, own commercial TV stations. Tenth, sites in Los Angeles or outside the city. And eleventh, production of films for TV cassettes. The final point is, at present, a speculative one, based on an appraisal of forthcoming developments, but already here and there the first preparatory steps have been taken towards this new, potential market. The list, as we can see, is sufficiently long to back up the assertion that the concept of 'diversification' existed inherently in the film companies before it became fashionable among the American industrial giants.

Land is, of course, the most substantial of assets, it often becomes the last sheet-anchor, and saves the battered companies from going under. All the Hollywood companies, with the exception of United Artists, can boast of being land-owners. Their holdings vary in size, with the two greatest potentates being Twentieth Century-Fox – owner of 2,738 hectares (around 6,700 acres) in Malibu, and Metro-Goldwyn-Mayer with 1,850 hectares (around 4,600 acres) in Ventura County. Their distance from the city makes these grounds, for the moment, unsuitable for housing, but they could become the future centres of production. Darryl Zanuck of Twentieth Century-Fox announced in 1968 that within five years (other spokesmen for the studio say six to ten years) all the studio buildings, workshops and offices situated in West Los Angeles would be closed and pulled down, with the vacant site earmarked for new office blocks, hotels and shopping centres. A new studio is to be erected in a deep canyon in Malibu, already extensively used for location shooting. The site is thirty-one miles from the city centre and six miles from the ocean shores. Metro-Goldwyn-Mayer is planning a move to the Thousand Oaks settlement in Conejo Valley, Ventura County, forty miles from its present residence in Culver City – which the studio has graced for forty-five years.

The second tastiest bit for a potential buyer is item number five: film libraries. For a long time it had been accepted that an old film, exhibited and exploited to the full in cinemas, becomes, after a time, a celluloid waste. The fact that occasionally some forgotten old hit would be fished out of the vaults for a film society or other specialized screening was of no commercial account. But television – the insatiable moloch – has radically transformed the situation. Old films have found a real market.

The turning point came on 25 September 1966, when David Lean's *The Bridge on the River Kwai* went out on ABC TV network. For the right to show twice this Columbia production, nine years old at the time, the Ford Motor Company paid $1,200,000 just to interrupt the screening a few times – in accordance with the American practice – with fleeting advertisements extolling the virtues of new Ford models. David Lean's work was watched on that memorable day by an audience of 60 million Americans – according to reliable figures published by Arbitron Ratings Inc. A record of records!

Sponsors – industrialists and tradesmen who buy television time to advertise their product – were persuaded that the showing of feature films was the best way of gaining the viewers' attention. Good, old movies. Viewers prefer them to thirty- or sixty-minute instalments of television serials. Towards the end of 1966 licence agreements were signed between the main television networks and the film production companies. ABC and CBS concluded deals with Twentieth Century-Fox, Paramount and M-G-M. Ninety-three million dollars were paid for the right to show 112 films. ABC paid $5 million for *Cleopatra* – for the right to show the film twice, not earlier than 1971. Three other films were priced at $2½ million; many others at half a million.

CBS concluded an agreement with Metro-Goldwyn-Mayer for forty-five films for a sum total of $52,800,000, and – a point to note – eighteen of those films were still to be produced. The old sales technique of 'blind booking', prohibited by the Supreme Court in 1948, is gaining a new lease of life through television. The agreement between CBS and M-G-M has another significant feature: it includes not only future productions, but also old films, already seen on television. Unlike some of their rivals, the directors of M-G-M proved far-sighted, by only loaning their films rather than selling them. Their wise policy was now bearing fruit. Each group of new productions was to be complemented with re-issues of old films, at least six, at $400,000 a film. Here again, the condemned practice of block booking was resuscitated.

There are no more old films. Every production, no matter how well exhibited on cinema circuits, gains another span of life on the small screen. The blessing of television has prolonged the commercial life of a film. By how many years – five, ten, fifteen? Who can tell? What is clear is that the period of exhibition has been considerably extended, perhaps doubled, or even trebled. The wealth of a studio is now measured by the number of negatives stored in its vaults.

Land and films preserved in the vaults thus comprise the most attractive assets of a film company. One would expect to find that the shooting sets and other studio buildings are of comparable value. In fact the position is now reversed: the studios are becoming a liability rather than a source of profit. There are several reasons for this, the most important being that facilities created thirty or forty years ago no longer meet the current requirements and cannot be readily adapted to modern production methods. The giant shooting sets and supply departments were designed for the simultaneous production of a dozen or more medium- and large-budget features. Those days are long gone and nowadays a studio considers itself lucky having two or three films in simultaneous production. The remainder of the studio floor is given over to television serials, but demand for them now is also declining. The maintenance of a studio with a dozen or more shooting sets costs annually around $3 million. The figure refers to a slack period, when administrative duties are reduced to hardly more than cleaning, opening and locking up. In order to lessen the operating costs of the studios, in September 1972 Columbia Picture Industries and Warner Brothers pooled their resources and created a jointly owned new company, Burbank Studios Inc., containing all the studio facilities of both companies. Each partner participates on an equal basis in operating costs and profits. Only laboratories continue bringing in a steady income.

An extremely profitable sideline is item number three: the exploitation of the musical aspect of cinematic productions through the issue and sale of scores, records and magnetic tape. In 1970 Universal earned almost as much from the sale of its musical bylines as from the distribution of films (21 and 22 per cent respectively of the total income). Gulf and Western, seeing the profitability of the operation, moved to separate the music enterprises from the film company and to bring it directly under the Leisure Time Division of the parent company. Thus the income from records and scores is now flowing directly into the Gulf and Western coffers and cannot be used, as in the past, to mend the shaky balance sheets of the studio. This is another instance of the general policy to contract the field of operations of the once independent and self-sufficient film-producing units.

An increasing part in the commercial life of a studio is played by departments or subsidiary companies especially created to trade in the various by-products of the main industry. An excellent example of the trend is provided by the M-G-M Merchandizing Corporation, set up in 1968 and wholly owned by the company. In two years the turnover of the new enterprise has increased twelvefold, and its profits tenfold. After the music and TV film production, it is the third division to bring the studio clear-cut profits. The M-G-M Merchandizing Corporation is proving tremendously energetic and incredibly ingenuous in uncovering additional sources of profit. For example: the price for a still photograph from any old film, to be reproduced for advertising, or to illustrate a book or a magazine article, is $50. The company does not confine its operations to exploiting the studio treasures but tries its luck independently. Its greatest success so far was the record *First Man on the Moon* (the Apollo 11 exploit). It was sold at 25 cents to self-service grocery stores, which in their turn offered it at 39 cents to customers with a minimum $5 purchase. Two million of those 'lunar' records found their way into private homes, bringing a healthy margin of profit to the supermarkets as well as to Metro-Goldwyn-Mayer.

The M-G-M Merchandizing Corporation, brilliantly successful as it is, cannot claim to be a real originator and pionner in this field. The promoter and past master of merchandizing was the creator of Mickey Mouse and Donald Duck, the late Walt Disney. The current safe and solid position of Walt Disney Productions and its subsidiary companies is based on the clever commercial exploitation of the master's prolific cinematic imagination.

Walt Disney realized early in his career that merchandizing could safeguard his artistic freedom. This knowledge would have probably availed him little if it was not for his irreplaceable and irresistible brother – Roy Disney. It was he who supplied for the partnership – if not a genius – at least an uncommon commercial ability. In the early thirties, following the original success of Mickey Mouse, under the guidance of Roy a separate company was set up: Walt Disney Enterprises Inc. It was to form the basis of the future tele-cinematic entertainment empire.

Sixty publications in the United States and twenty in foreign countries print strip cartoons of the extraordinary adventures of Mickey Mouse. In many countries of the world there are weekly magazines devoted exclusively to the popular Mouse. The French *Le Journal de Mickey* has a circulation of 700,000. In North America alone eighty of the toy-producing companies have concluded licence agreements with Walt Disney Enterprises.

In 1955 Disneyland opened, for the fanciful millions, its gates to Fairyland. Up to the beginning of 1972 over 110 million people have viewed the display pavilions, open parks and streets of the unique exhibition complex, which contains

B

the essence of the popular American tele-cinema culture. The Wild West myth lives here next to space travel, and distinguished guests are shown round by guides wearing Mickey Mouse or Donald Duck costumes. One can fly to the moon, take a dive into the ocean depths in a modern submarine, or take a trip in an old nineteenth-century Mississippi steamer. A record of admissions, both for a day and for a week, was set up in the summer of 1967: 67,228 and 383,000 respectively. Income from Disneyland reached, in the same year, 35·6 per cent of the total for the entire company. The distribution of films and television brought in the remainder, with only 5 per cent contributed by the master's old favourite – animation. In March 1972 a new part, covering thirty-five acres, was added to Disneyland. It has the romantic and promising name of Bear Country.

But to Walt Disney his land of magic seemed no longer good enough, either in terms of commerce or of prestige gained. The empire-builder dreamt of a grander capital and new millions. On the other side of the United States, on the Atlantic coast, another fairyland city has been planned, even more fabulous and carrying an even prouder name – not Disneyland but Disneyworld. In central Florida, between Orlando and Kissimmee, 27,400 hectares (about 65,000 acres) of land were purchased – an area twelve times larger than Disneyland. Two new companies, set up for the purpose, WED Enterprises Inc. (Walt Elias Disney) and Mapo Inc., were made responsible for erecting and organizing the gigantic playground. A glass roof is to cover the central part of the area, and the initial cost is estimated at $165 million. The entire enterprise is budgeted at about $500 million (Disneyland with all the refinements and annexes cost $135 million). The work is expected to take twenty-five years to complete and is to proceed in stages, but the first set of attractions was opened to the public in October 1971. In the first year of its existence Disneyworld was visited by almost 11 million tourists.

Disneyland and Disneyworld are not everything. The most recent advertising–cum–commercial move is the setting up, under the management of Walt Disney Productions, of a great theatrical–circus–cinematic spectacle, *Disney on Parade*. Their partner in this gigantic enterprise is the NBC TV network (National Broadcasting Corporation). On a large scale, or in a circus ring, actors play popular Disney characters. From time to time the action moves on to a giant cinema screen. *Disney on Parade* is based loosely on *Alice in Wonderland*, but another spectacle, already in preparation, is to be woven around *Snow White and the Seven Dwarfs*. The success of the spectacle can be gleaned from the fact that in Salt Lake City, at the beginning of 1970, 77,000 people, or one-third of the city's entire population, saw the spectacle in the course of nine days.

In a period of dynamic expansion of the American cinema Hollywood magnates have acquired many overseas possessions: cinemas, studios, houses – anything that promised to strengthen their hold on new commercial territories. Of those possessions little is left now, but nevertheless they form a valuable asset, occasionally being used to plug holes in the balance sheet. Thus in 1970 Metro-Goldwyn-Mayer could boast of $1½ million profit only because losses incurred on the production and distribution of films were made up by the sale of land in Culver City and of cinemas in South Africa. A similar kind of operation – the sale of a chain of cinemas in South Africa – brought Twentieth Century-Fox $11 million of additional income. Darryl Zanuck has set up within the organization he is heading a special real estate department for the management of properties in Great Britain, Australia, New Zealand, Canada, Latin America and the Middle East. Those foreign assets become an important surety against all possible setbacks. Paramount owned, until 1970, over 50 per cent of the Famous Players Canadian Corporation, with 368 cinema halls in Canada and interests in television companies. In accordance with Gulf and Western policy this enterprise was transferred, as a separate unit, to the Leisure Time Division of the parent company, which meant a further decline in the film company's own assets.

On the wide spiral of side-lines and by-products we descend gradually to its actual centre: the production of films. It is, after all, a fundamental reason for the existence of a film company. Ever since the entrance of television, the previously homogeneous production has split into two primary streams: films for cinema exhibition, and films for the small screen. The first cause no end of trouble, and usually bring only losses; the second, until recently, were bringing profits. We say 'until recently' because in the years 1969–70 the situation has deteriorated. Television programme trends, from the companies' point of view, took an undesirable turn. Live sport is taking up considerably more viewing time, light entertainment and variety shows are becoming more popular, and feature films, designed for cinema exhibition, appear to be forcing out half-hour or hour-long serial instalments. What film libraries have gained, the production departments of television films are now losing.

This leaves us with what would appear to be a crucial problem concerning the production of films for cinema exhibition. Films of a kind which, screened all over the world, have made the names of Paramount, Metro-Goldwyn-Mayer and Twentieth Century-Fox famous, have glamourized Hollywood, the American cinema and the American way of life. For Zukor, Louis B. Mayer, Jack Warner, Harry Cohn, cinema was their whole life. Can the same be truthfully said about their successors, Charles Bluhdorn, William Frankel, or Kirk Kerkorian? The new magnates, unlike the old, do not talk freely about films. They would obviously prefer to say nothing, but as this is neither possible nor politic, they confine themselves to slogans and generalities. After the bitter experience of 1969, when all the big-scale projects proved expensive failures, their production announcements betray one common quality: a modesty, unheard of in Hollywood and contrary to all Hollywood tradition. They are all planning only a small number of films, carefully and modestly budgeted. Some put the limit at $2 million, others, without specifying it, swear never to allow another expensive block-buster to reach the screen. What would the venerable Adolf Zukor, the originator of Paramount and still its titular, honorary president do if he had a right to intervene in the company's affairs, after Martin S. Davis put the studio's annual production target at ten to twelve films? He could not be pleased, either, with the definition of Paramount as a 'mini-major'. The epoch of 'majors' – of the giant film corporations which operated in the golden age of Hollywood – has gone for ever, according to Martin S. Davis, a deputy President of Gulf and Western and a deputy President of Paramount in charge of production.

There is no point in deluding anyone: the big companies, having burned their fingers in ambitious production projects, will do nothing to increase their present targets. Large bank credits, negotiated to finance those projects, have left them with heavy liabilities. They can rather be expected to limit the number of films produced still further, giving ground to foreign competitors and independent home producers. Television cassettes, in the early stages of their development, cannot greatly affect the situation, because they will initially be made up of available, old material. That was the agreement signed by Darryl Zanuck with CBS in March 1970, giving EVR (Electronic Video Recording) cassette system access to the Twentieth Century-Fox film library on condition that a film cannot be loaded into a cassette earlier than five years after the end of its commercial exploitation in cinemas.

Prospects

Life does not tolerate a void. It is true that at the beginning of 1970 the number of cinemas in the United States fell to 13,600, the lowest so far, as compared with 22,000 at the time of the Second World War; and it is also true, that 16 million weekly admissions represents a new low in the history of the American cinema. But those cinemas and cinema-goers, whatever their number, demand new films and if they cannot be provided by the old, Hollywood companies someone else is going to profit: namely, the foreign film distributors, or independent home producers. This is precisely what has happened. Amazingly and incredibly Hollywood – the 'big five' or the 'big eight' – can no longer claim the monopoly of the American screens. The restrictive, repressive policies, only partly caused by past production excesses, have borne fruit.

Early in December 1970, at a film employees' meeting in the Hollywood Palladium, in the presence of Governor Ronald Reagan and John V. Tunney (the Republican senator from California), a leaflet, claiming that 70 per cent of screen time in the U.S.A. is now taken up by foreign films or films produced abroad, was widely circulated. Even if we should agree with the trade weekly *Variety* that foreign import figures were exaggerated, the balance has clearly been disturbed and the American cinema has lost dominance over its own home ground.[8] After all, in 1946 only 19 per cent of films were of foreign origin, or produced abroad.

An opposite aspect, of the American capital invested in production, gives us a different set of figures. Towards the end of November 1970 there were, altogether, 221 American-financed films in production (two more than in 1969) but only 131 of them at home and 90 abroad. In 1972, due to the box office successes of several home-made films, *Love Story*, *The Godfather*, *The French Connection*, the number of run-away productions decreased in comparison to 1968 to represent a figure of 28 per cent.

Production statistics are equally emphatic about the partial decline during 1969–70 of the big Hollywood companies. In 1969 the real Hollywood accounted for over three-quarters of all the Hollywood films, as against fifty independent productions. In 1970 the independents increased their product by 90 per cent, with ninety-five films, while the old companies lost 25 per cent, reducing their production to 126 films. In consequence, in 1970 the independents represented 43 per cent of American production, and the Hollywood companies 57 per cent (the overall number of independently produced films grew from nineteen in 1968 to 107 in 1972!) The difference is no longer wide, and with the addition of foreign imports a situation has developed where the big companies are no longer in a position to dictate the programme policy to home cinemas.

Retreat of the old companies causes serious repercussions, not only on the American screens. Its impact on the employment situation in the Californian film industry is quite painful. In Los Angeles and its environs, towards the end of 1970, unemployment in the industry reached 40 per cent of all those qualified for work. The situation of so many thousand jobless people is exerting pressure on the political leaders to save the American cinema by rescuing Hollywood. The presence of Reagan and Tunney at the meeting which was called by a film section of the AFL (American Federation of Labour), provides ample evidence that those appeals have reached the ears of the top Californian politicians.

The meeting called for the Federal Government to help Hollywood. Reagan agreed to submit a demand that 20 per cent of all gross receipts from the exhibition of home-made American films should be freed from tax. Should the government refuse to heed this suggestion, or prove reluctant to act on it, the meeting threatened to boycott all cinemas showing foreign films, or runaway productions. Producer-director Robert Wise, present at the meeting, said that Hollywood can recover its rightful place only with government help. In September 1972 the Screen Actors Guild submitted to the White House a recovery programme for the American film industry, asking among other items for the exclusion from taxation of a certain percentage of the gross of a domestically produced motion picture, curtailment of returns on TV and, finally, for cessation of government film-making.[9] In reply to the SAG memorandum and to similar demands made by Barry Goldwater Junior, Republican member of the House of Representatives from California, President Nixon ordered, in October 1972, government department chiefs to 'better utilize the motion picture industry'.[10]

Undoubtedly, government subsidies and tax reliefs, or customs barriers which were also discussed, would strengthen the film industry's defence against the foreign invasion. But this would not be enough to return Hollywood to its old fame and fortune. The structural changes are too deep and too comprehensive, the new developments in the system and technology of production too radical, to be returned to *status quo ante* by mere administrative or legal measures.

Most of the unemployed are studio workers and camera

crew technicians. Independent producers are not keen to shoot on studio stages, preferring locations and natural interiors, and they try to cut down the size of a crew as far as possible. Trade unions, which for a long time have insisted on respect for the old regulations with their absurdly inflated number of obligatory technicians and assistants, in 1969 relented somewhat, seeing that defence of this particular fortress was unrealistic. On productions below a million dollars budget a 'mini-crew' was allowed. Actors agreed to accept lower rates of pay for work on even cheaper films – costing no more than $150,000. However, the concessions are likely to result in only a slight improvement in the employment situation, since small crews on cheap productions can never absorb the legions that used to work on large productions for the old companies.

Technological developments and new production facilities are moving the opposite way. In Los Angeles a 'Cinemobile' enterprise, known to the trade as 'a studio on wheels', operates a most successful business. The company offers producers a long, train-like coach, with dressing-rooms and accommodation for technicians, fully equipped for sound, image and lighting. The coach accommodates comfortably a crew of fifty. In 1969 Cinemobile provided facilities for thirty-five productions, in 1970 for seventy. On demand it can provide a full, technical crew, sharing in the production and accepting a part of the financial risk involved. Cinemobile will certainly find imitators, and the number of willing customers for the old studios will be reduced still further.

The siting of a film production centre is also becoming an issue. The crowd at the Hollywood Palladium meeting assured unquestioningly that any Federal help to the film industry would profit Los Angeles. However, it is not all that certain because other cities, in other States, are now trying to attract producers with a view to developing their own centres of the film industry. For San Francisco and Chicago those wishes may still lie at a pious hope stage, but for New York the existence of a dynamic, developing production centre is no longer a design for the future, but a present-day reality. It was due, in no small measure, to John Lindsay, then mayor of the city, who spared no effort in attempting to create favourable conditions for film-makers. A special squad was set up by the mayor to remove all administrative obstacles to facilitate the issue of licences to film, and to gain the co-operation of all office and public services, including the police. The consequences of this policy were not long in coming. In 1965, before the election of Lindsay to the post of mayor, thirteen feature films were being shot in New York but only two of them were completed. In 1968 there were thirty film crews at work, and fourteen of the films were purely local projects. In 1972 fifty-three feature films were shooting in New York. Governor Nelson A. Rockefeller emerged in November 1972 as a powerful ally of film-makers, allowing them to shoot in national parks and other previously reserved areas. New York State's Commerce Department was designated as the Central Office for film production information and use. Sometimes there were more film-makers at work here than in Hollywood, the traditional capital of the cinema. Is it possible to reverse the trend, and attract the crews from the Atlantic coast back to the other side of the Continent? It seems doubtful.

The future of the American cinema does not depend on where the films are to be made but on the kind of films that are made. Perhaps Otto Preminger, the ostensible cynic, was right when he tried to bring the entire discussion from the sentimental and nostalgic regions down to hard, cinematic fact: 'What does all this Hollywood patriotism mean? What is Hollywood? It's just a studio. It's here today, and there tomorrow.'[11]

2

The Blockbuster Syndrome

From Cecil B. De Mille to Cleopatra

The super-spectacle has a long screen history. Before the First World War the Italians had been the masters of the genre. Later D. W. Griffith took over the baton from them, making the gigantic *Intolerance* but this ambitious and enormously expensive production did not originate a series of similar works, as is frequently the case in the film industry, especially in America. The box office disaster of this philosophical treatise in an expansively spectacular shape could not encourage anyone to similar explorations. The honour of producing a popular formula for a cinematic super-spectacle went not to D. W. Griffith but to another pioneer of the cinema, Cecil B. De Mille, who by the beginning of the 1920s had already won a high reputation as a director of successful drawing-room comedies. De Mille, however, was suddenly seized by a missionary and apostolic zeal, and in 1923 proposed to the Famous Players–Lasky Company (now Paramount) the making of *The Ten Commandments*. It was to be the story of Moses (no less) and the Jewish migration from Egypt, across the Red Sea, to the Promised Land. The initial budget was set at a round figure of $1 million. For that time it was an astronomical sum, sufficient for the financing of a dozen quite well-made films.

At first the project met with resolute opposition which was, however, gradually eroded. De Mille explained to his New York and Hollywood backers that his interest in the story was aroused by the box office success of *The Covered Wagon*, James Cruze's great epic Western, the opening run of which extended to fifty-nine weeks! His ambition, De Mille said, was to create 'a different Western and a spectacle in the same exciting package'.[1] The argument convinced the businessmen and they agreed to the production of this extraordinary Western in biblical costume. There was, of course, continued heart-searching during the production, when – as almost invariably happens – the budget was being swelled by unforeseen, mounting costs, and the shooting was running over the original schedule.

At one point De Mille even wanted to pay off the studio, but Messrs Zukor and Lasky providently refused to accept his offer. Their business instincts proved to be sound. The lucky day of the opening came on Christmas 1923, and *The Ten Commandments* promptly broke the record of *The Covered Wagon*. The first run lasted sixty-two weeks.

The cinematic formula for the super-spectacle became a fact; it subsequently produced an entire tradition of filmmaking, with its masters and years of continuous success. It was of course success measured predominantly but not exclusively in commercial terms. During the negotiations and arguments with the studio about *The Ten Commandments*, De Mille declared: 'I believe it will be the biggest picture ever made, not only from the standpoint of spectacle but from the point of humanness, dramatic power, and the great good it will do.'[2] This grandiloquent assertion could serve as an original model for the publicity campaigns of all the great, the greatest and the unique, cinematic spectacles. They have all been based, in a greater or lesser measure, on the tried methods and ideas of the Master. Throughout his long career De Mille has only twice (out of seventy completed productions) failed to give the studio the profits it was hoping for. It has been said about him that like Midas he changed everything he touched into gold, transforming celluloid into a continuous flow of dollars. According to a Paramount boast De Mille's films have grossed $750 million on the world market and have been seen by well over four thousand million people (not counting television screenings). Those dizzy figures make clear the reasons for De Mille's privileged position within the Hollywood set-up, and why his legend has outlived him (since his death in 1959), continuing, until quite recently, to exert a real influence.

Referring to the Western tradition, the maker of *The Ten Commandments* twice over (the silent in 1923 and the sound version in 1956), has, in effect, spelled out what is, to him, of supreme importance in a super-spectacle: action. Dramatic conflicts, fights, tense physical confrontations, chases, natural disasters or disasters of human doing. A spectacle is not just a series of *tableau vivants* of dazzling splendour (though that, too, has its proper place in it), but a vivid drama. In this human drama love is playing a far from negligible part. Not the idealized love of Griffith's *Broken Blossoms*, but earthly love, full of sexual passions. The Bible, according to De Mille, offers numerous opportunities in this field and ready-made screen ideas if, of course, you know how to read the Old Testament stories. Take *Samson and Delilah*, for example. De Mille offers two alternative interpretations of his own film: 'We'll sell it as a story of faith, the story of the power of prayer. That's for the censors and the women's organizations. For the public it's the hottest love story of all time.'[3]

The originator of the cinematic super-spectacle believed that the rise of the film would be vindicated through the production of motion pictures of grand, epic sweep, with action of absorbing interest and ... designed to serve high ideals. De Mille was not treating the Bible simply as a useful fund of stories; he saw in it a source of inspiration and an original departure point for all of his activities. He believed in his own apostolic mission, was taking it seriously and, discounting false modesty, used to compare his work with the effort of medieval builders and artists. 'I am doing with my films more or less what the medieval artists and architects have done; I am interpreting the Bible in the manner of my own time.'[4]

In 1951 a journalist asked De Mille for his list of the ten best films of all time. Not too original a question, but the answer it produced is worth quoting. De Mille's list was made up of the following titles: the Italian *Cabiria*, D. W. Griffith's *The Birth of a Nation*, the silent *Ben Hur*, the silent

The Ten Commandments, the silent *King of Kings*, King Vidor's *The Big Parade*, De Mille's *The Sign of the Cross*, *Gone with the Wind, Going my Way* with Bing Crosby and *Samson and Delilah*.[5] Out of ten films four were his own: *The Ten Commandments*, *King of Kings*, *The Sign of the Cross* and *Samson and Delilah*; out of ten films only one could not be included in the super-spectacle genre, a comedy with Crosby as a Catholic priest; and out of ten films there is only one, *The Sign of the Cross*, which cannot boast of more than $4 million in distributors' takings. Produced in 1932, at the height of the Depression, it broke no records but incurred no losses.

No doubt 'the best' was for De Mille synonymous with the most popular, which in turn translates as the most commercially viable and profitable. It should not be held against him. His films were designed for an audience of many millions, and he could not be fully satisfied unless his work reached the masses. A comparison of De Mille's 1951 list with the box office statistics published twenty years later by *Variety* shows that most of the pictures picked out by the Master as the best found their way into the roll of the biggest commercial successes of all time. The two earliest titles, *Cabiria* and *The Birth of a Nation*, are missing because the figures of their box office takings are not available. But it is well known that these works of Pastrone and Griffiths were the great popular hits of their time and the profits they brought must have been enormous. Of the other eight *The Sign of the Cross* is out – for reasons stated above. Three titles are among the first five of the record-breakers: *Gone with the Wind* (No. 1), the new, 1959 version of *Ben Hur* (No. 4), and De Mille's new, 1956 version of *The Ten Commandments* (No. 5). The other films are to be found lower down the list, with the distributors' earnings from the United States and Canada ranging from 5\frac{1}{2}$ million (*The Big Parade*), to 11\frac{1}{2}$ million (*Samson and Delilah*).[6] Accepting new versions for old films, included in De Mille's list, I am not trying to cloud the issue. For the sake of this argument the actual films are less important than titles and screen stories proving to be, in a sense, timeless. It only underlines the effectiveness of the super-spectacle formula, first launched almost fifty years ago.

Returning, once again, to the box office statistics, let us consider the top twenty of the several hundred films listed in *Variety* of 1973 (the bottom limit is the figure of $4 million earned for the U.S.A. and Canadian distributors) in 'All-time Box Office Champs'.[7] We find that three of the record-breakers are films in De Mille's style, including one of his own, namely, William Wyler's *Ben Hur* (1959), De Mille's *The Ten Commandments* (1957) and Joseph Mankiewicz's *Cleopatra* (1963), occupying eighteenth position. One could add one other film as having an obvious affinity with the Master's formula: Victor Fleming's *Gone with the Wind* (1939). Including the last one it comes to 20 per cent of the top twenty. Doesn't this figure explain that Hollywood is gradually abandoning the formula which has served it so well for so long?

It seems significant that chronologically the last film made in the De Mille manner and placed among the winners opened in 1963, more than ten years ago. It was *Cleopatra*, the super-super-production of Twentieth Century-Fox, occupying the twelfth position on the *Variety* list. The trouble that beset the making of *Cleopatra*, and the returns which came some way short of the high expectations, helped to cool the producers' ardour and led them to adopt a restrained and cautious attitude. It appears that *Cleopatra* may have been the last chord of that Ancient-cum-Biblical symphony, initiated by De Mille's silent *The Ten Commandments*. This is probably the end of the super-spectacle in the classical (if we may call it that) manner, as worked out and perfected by the director of *King of Kings* and the early, sound *Cleopatra* (with Claudette Colbert, 1934). It is conceivable that a super-spectacle, undoubtedly in decline in the early seventies, may yet return to splendour; but surely in a different form. Certain devices and conventions have aged and no longer elicit a response from the modern audience.

Had it not been for the abnormal circumstances surrounding the production of *Cleopatra*, the 'ageing' of De Mille's formula would not have been, perhaps, highlighted in such a dramatic manner. As it happened, the film, wrapped up in a web of outrageous gossip, became notorious well before the opening. Impatient expectations and hopes ran well ahead of what could actually be put on to the screen. It had to be a masterpiece, the eighth wonder of the world. And meanwhile . . . But don't let us anticipate events. The idea of making this film first surfaced in 1958. Walter Wanger was to produce it, with Rouben Mamoulian directing. The budget was initially set at $5 million, later to be reduced to $4 million. Towards the end of 1959 Elizabeth Taylor was signed up for the title role. But as soon as shooting started in September 1960 the star fell seriously ill. In January 1961 Rouben Mamoulian left the director's chair and was replaced by Joseph Mankiewicz. The new director considered all that had been done of little value, and promptly submitted a new screenplay for the studio's approval – the tenth in succession. By this time the budget has swelled to $10 million, and a few months later (in September 1961) to $14 million, to be reduced by the studio heads to $12½ million. It proved to be a short-lived saving, and only four months later the budget stood at almost twice that sum – $24 million. In June 1962 Spyros Skouras, the President of Twentieth Century-Fox was dismissed by the shareholders. He was succeeded by the dynamic and high-handed Darryl Zanuck, who at once applied himself to the problems of *Cleopatra*. Dismissing Walter Wanger, the producer, he took personal charge of the editing, keeping Mankiewicz away from the cutting room. It provoked a veritable storm of protests and threats of law suits, but Zanuck rode it all and at last, on 12 June 1963, 'the most expensive film of all time' was publicly unveiled in the New York Rivoli Cinema. *Cleopatra* ran there for sixty-three weeks, taking $2½ million from the first-run, New York audience. Up till January 1971 the film has earned $26 million for Twentieth Century-Fox from the United States and Canada alone. The takings from foreign markets have not been made public, but it is known that in Great Britain, Italy and France the Twentieth Century-Fox blockbuster has not come up to the producers' expectations. Adding $5 million to be paid by television for the right to screen the film twice, it still seems doubtful if all the income from it came anywhere near the ceiling of $62 million needed, according to Darryl Zanuck's authoritative statement, to make the production pay its incredibly expensive way.

It appears that the critical judgement of Bosley Crowther who, in *The New York Times*, described *Cleopatra* as 'one of the great epic films of our day'[8] was further off the mark than that of his *New York Herald Tribune* rival, Judith Crist, who summed up the Twentieth Century-Fox blockbuster with the sentence: 'It is at best a major disappointment, at worst an extravagant exercise in tedium.'[9] The 243 minutes of screen time were embellished with some memorable lines from Elizabeth Taylor, such as: 'A woman that cannot bear children is like a river that has run dry,' or, 'I will bear many sons – my breasts are filled with love and life.' The publicity value of the scandalous gossip surrounding the star's affair with Richard Burton, her screen partner, availed them little. Critics did not thrill to the screen passions of the former Mrs Eddie Fisher – later Mrs Richard Burton.

Had De Mille lived he might have realized his life-long aspiration, and transferred the Bible itself to the screen. It was achieved by the Italian producer, Dino de Laurentis, mainly backed by Twentieth Century-Fox money. *The Bible* was to be a super-production in colour, shot for the giant screen of the new, single-camera Cinerama system. The film which opened in 1966, can be seen as an epilogue to the entire 'School of De Mille', and a tribute of sorts to its departed Master.

Christopher Fry, the dramatist, and the director, John Huston, accepted the task of providing a visual digest of the twenty-two chapters of Genesis. It proved all the more difficult because they were obliged to respect many often contradictory views and attitudes towards the Scriptures, from unbelievers through various Churches inside and outside the Christian Faith. It resulted, predictably, in a compromise, rather vague, if in spirit fairly close to the position of American Fundamentalists and their literal reading of the Scriptures. In effect the over three-hours-long spectacle, showing little of Christopher Fry's *'esprit'*, found itself anchored firmly in Cecil B. De Mille's tradition. Vaseline generously coated over the lens gave the images of Paradise with its golden trees a 'poetic' aura, and cleverly placed plastic leaves both covered and excitingly enhanced the nakedness of Adam and Eve. Over Sodom, condemned to destruction, rose a wholly contemporary nuclear mushroom, and the panic at the Tower of Babel, caused by the confusion of languages among the builders, was shot in the classic Hollywood manner, leading us back to the memorable Babylonian sequence in Griffith's *Intolerance*.

The producers wanted it to be another super-spectacle, perhaps the biggest so far. That much is clear. But what was it that John Huston, the distinguished maker of *Battle of San Pietro*, *The Treasure of the Sierra Madre* and *The Red Badge of Courage* wanted to convey through it? He was drafted to direct *The Bible* only after all the earlier choices – Robert Bresson, Luchino Visconti and Orson Welles – had declined. How was Huston interpreting the subject? At a press conference, given before the start of the shooting, he declared, firstly: 'I take the Bible the way it is,' and, secondly: 'I believe in the essential unity and love among the human kind.'[10] A noble creed, undeniably, but rather broadly worded. Did he get that message across to the millions who came to see God creating the Universe, and Eve treating Adam to an apple? One has doubts. Only one sequence of the cinematic Bible stays in mind – the Deluge. And it is the one in which the film-makers allowed themselves to take liberties with the text, discarding for once the dutiful respect for each word and phrase, and treating the story of the extermination of the human race with tongue in cheek. Here only, for some fifteen minutes of a three-hour spectacle, the creative personality of John Huston, who cast himself in the part of father Noah, was given full rein.

In 1966, for the last time, a film in the De Mille manner, *The Bible*, won a place on the annual list of top successes. In subsequent years the biblical and antiquity stories disappeared completely from the screen, and the number of other costume films was markedly reduced. The surviving projects were all being made not in Hollywood but in Great Britain, backed with American finance, but flying the Union Jack. In 1967 the Hollywood Academy awarded its Oscar for the best film of the year to Fred Zinnemann, the director of *A Man for All Seasons*, adapted from Robert Bolt's stage play. It was also one of the top box office films of the season, fourth on the annual roll of money-spinners. In 1968 no historical film could boast of any success, artistic or commercial.

In 1969 a minor success (fourteenth on the annual box office list) was gained by Anthony Harvey's *The Lion in Winter*, another theatrical adaptation, from a play by James Goldman. Remarkable acting by Peter O'Toole as King Henry II and Katherine Hepburn as Eleanor of Aquitaine transformed this rather static and wordy film into an absorbing, tense drama. The same cannot be said of *Anne of the Thousand Days*, another stage adaptation, produced in Britain with Universal backing. This story of Ann Boleyn, based on Maxwell Anderson's drama, had been turned by Charles Jarrott into a dull and pedestrian film, only partially redeemed by Geneviéve Bujold's playing of the unhappy Queen, and Richard Burton in the part of Henry VIII. Admittedly, *Anne of the Thousand Days* could boast of holding the sixteenth place on the box office list for 1970, but in the Oscar stakes it met with a sharp setback. Jarrott's film gained no less than ten nominations, including all of the most representative classes (the best film, the best actor, the best actress, the best screenplay, the best camera, etc.), but in the event the only Oscar it won was for the best costumes . . . Cold comfort for over-inflated hopes and expectations.

Thus the super-spectacle as conceived by Cecil B. De Mille is fading from the Hollywood stage. After *Cleopatra* no one is keen to go back to ancient Roman splendours; after *The Bible* books of the Old Testament seem less cinematically attractive. The Italians have turned to the New Testament, but in a different vein. The British, backed by the American studios, seek inspiration in history via the stage, and not at all in the spirit of De Mille. After fifty years of a developing tradition, of its rise and fall, the formula appears to have run to a full stop.

Vicissitudes of a Hero

Films do age – it is an undeniable and unqualified truth. But there are exceptions to this rule, as to most others. Occasionally films happen along which seem to render time impotent. Take *Gone with the Wind*, a screen version of Margaret Mitchell's best-seller produced over thirty years ago. It is not resting, like most of its contemporaries, in the dark privacy of the archive vaults, to be sporadically resurrected for a late night TV show for a red-eyed minority of cineastes. On the contrary, it goes repeatedly through new 'first night' unveilings in the full blast of publicity. In 1967 and 1968 *Gone with the Wind*, in direct competition with new hits, made the top twenty of current box office winners. It was the seventh successive re-issue of this Civil War story.

In 1967 the film appeared in a new, 70 mm version, designed to make it fit the wide and giant screen. The Metro-Goldwyn-Mayer technicians performed a difficult and complex operation, transferring the image on to a negative double the original width. Sound was also enhanced to produce stereophonic effect, and the fading colours corrected through special filters and printing frames. This beauty treatment, designed to satisfy the expectations of a new generation brought up on Cinerama and stereo sound, reputedly cost over $350 thousand. Commercially speaking, the operation met with full success, the new box office millions spelling out the public approval. Admittedly, there were some complaints about the grainy print, or close-ups of Clark Gable with the top of his head cut off, but the grumblers represented only a tiny minority of the satisfied masses.

What is the explanation for the continuing success of this film, produced in a different epoch for a different generation of cinema-goers? An absorbing plot, full of tense incidents, complying with De Mille's recipe, is one obvious quality. Sets, crowds of extras, colour are the other. But perhaps most important is the fact that Margaret Mitchell, in her story from the past, was describing a woman who in temperament, mentality and way of life seems contemporary through and through. It makes for an easy contact between the screen and the audiences. As Pauline Kael puts it in her blunt and pungent way: '*Gone with the Wind* was entertaining largely because of that scheming little vixen Scarlett who cared more for land than for love.'[11] In other words, she was not an idealized, romantic heroine. In that sense she differed greatly from the demigod heroes and heroines of De Mille's tradition.

The most evident contemporary element in a super-spectacle is a tendency to debunk the hero, or at least to move him down a peg or two into a more realistic dimension. Producers take it for granted that a modern cinema-goer is a naturally critical and sceptical creature, unwilling to believe in people presented as walking paragons of virtue. He no longer views a film as an enchanting fairy-tale. Hence the birth of a new kind of super-spectacle hero, an anti-hero in a sense. He is still the central character, he leads and motivates the action, but he has now become a person of complex psychological make-up, with controversial attributes. In accordance with modern ways he is no longer monolithic in his attitudes and qualities. The conduct of a new hero can be interesting in itself because he does not subscribe to any rigid rules of the game, as in old folk tales, or legends of chivalrous knighthood. Such an unconventional protagonist can be found in two films of the David Lean–Robert Bolt partnership: *Lawrence of Arabia* and *Doctor Zhivago*; and also, though in a different vein, in George Roy Hill's *Hawaii*, adapted from James A. Michener's bestseller.

In all three cases the unconventional character of the hero was inherited from a literary original. It was safeguarded by the integrity of scriptwriters: in Lean's films Robert Bolt, in *Hawaii* Dalton Trumbo with Daniel Taradash. They did their best to reconcile water with fire, that is, the super-spectacle formula with penetrating psychological insights into the motives of the leading characters. There is no reason to question the goodwill and seriousness of their intentions, but on most counts the screen results fell some way short of their goal. The hero of *Lawrence of Arabia* (a British production, backed with American money) is a mysterious character with many a secret in his soul, riddled by some deep-seated complexes. But cinema-goers, stunned and deafened by cavalcades of galloping Arabs, by bangs and explosions, never really find what sort of secrets he carries, and what particular complex is troubling him. And so, perversely, what sticks in mind is yet another knight errant in the service of some important cause. The importance of the cause can be gleaned from the production values, the effort and expense unsparingly lavished, rather than from the interpretation of historical events. Unless one has read *Seven Pillars of Wisdom* it is almost impossible to make out the subtleties of British diplomacy half a century ago.

The film of *Doctor Zhivago* (the sixth position on the *Variety* 1973 list) uses the October Revolution as a simple background to the vicissitudes of a private fate. In this way Boris Pasternak's novel was deprived of its philosophical backbone and, perhaps more, of its *raison d'être*. The writer, on practically every page, faces the hero with the process of social change, which demands rethinking and revaluation. Of course one doesn't expect millions of dollars to be spent on propagating revolutionary ideals, or even to set them out objectively, but it is difficult to accept the reduction of a rich, if controversial novel, to the banal dimensions of a love triangle, played out against the background rumblings of a revolutionary storm. And that was, by his own admission, how David Lean approached *Doctor Zhivago*. He said in an interview: 'The film has no political message. It is the story of people caught up in the drama of historical change. The political background will be suggested – as it was in *Lawrence of Arabia* – but as in the novel we concentrate on the personal fate of individuals.'[12]

In *Hawaii* there are somewhat different problems with the hero. The screen-writers strive to make it clear that the Reverend Abner Hale, who came from Boston to Hawaii in the 1840s to convert the natives, was not really an evil man – just exceedingly stubborn and tactless in conduct. These attempts to whitewash the missionary do not succeed, simply because in accordance with the spirit of the original, not the Protestant minister but the white colonizers should have been put in the dock. And that would hardly fit in with the super-spectacle formula. That is why the criminal conduct of newcomers to the happy islands is veiled by the lovely, Technicolored landscapes and charming, half-naked dancing 'hula hula' girls. It is disguised, in short, by all the tourist attractions of the place.

Real progress in debunking a hero was made in Twentieth Century-Fox's *Patton* (1969), directed by Franklin J Schaffner. The film was planned as a big, war spectacle. Shot in colour on 70 mm stock (a new system christened Dimension 150) it describes the military career of General George S. Patton Junior who commanded the VIII American Army in North Africa and Sicily, and the III Army during the Allied invasion of the European Continent. The plot takes in three years, 1943 to 1945, and pictures numerous battle scenes, field councils and scenes of military life. But the dominating feature is a creation of George C. Scott in the title part, both talented and passionate. As a British critic, John Gillett, says: 'Here is an actor so totally immersed in his part that he almost makes one believe he is the man himself.'[13]

What was he really like, this by now half-mythical Patton? A hero, a noble soldier, a military leader of genius? Or a neurotic, a psychopath, a man revelling in battle slaughter, recklessly sacrificing the lives of others in the cause of his personal glory? The film refrains from an explicit answer, leaving a lot to the interpretation and moral sense of the cinema-goer. This should be counted as an advantage rather than a flaw. At the same time the character of the general who cannot survive without a war, who only in war is able to find the meaning of his existence, comes across clearly enough. It is made explicit in Patton's line: 'I love the war. Peace is going to be a veritable hell.' After the victory over the Germans he is dreaming of a new confrontation, with the Eastern Allies.

Several reviewers described the character and attitudes of

Patton as anachronistic. The general had an unshaken faith in himself as a providential knight, a Holy Crusader. Believing in re-incarnation he saw himself, in olden times, leading great armies to famous victories. A pathological case? Undoubtedly. But also – which cannot be denied – a clever strategist and tactician responsible for driving a wedge into Normandy, or the relief of the besieged Bastogne. The problem is reduced to the question: is it legitimate to employ people of Patton's mould in order to win an armed confrontation with an enemy? Do their natural talents for the game of war justify their enormous 'Lust for Glory'? (This was the second title added by the British distributors. Originally the film was simply called *Patton* in the States.) For the *Newsweek* critic, Schaffner's film, although somewhat contradictory, in the end does glorify a madman.[14] The reviewer for the French journal, *L'Express* draws a different conclusion, believing that the public would leave the cinema with a new awareness of the anachronistic stupidity of militarism.[15] The *Neue Zürcher Zeitung* disagrees, reading into George C. Scott's creation a romantic treatment of the soldier's profession.[16] One can conclude from all those diverse voices that it was a conscious design of the authors (the screen-writers, Francis Ford Coppola and Edmund H. North, the director and the actor playing the title part) to create a disturbing and controversial character, close to the perceptions of the 1970s public. How easy it is, watching an African, or a Normandy battlefield, to relate it immediately to Vietnam. In *Patton* both 'doves' and 'hawks' could find food for some very contemporary thoughts. The film, which cost over $20 million, is most certainly going to pay its way. In the initial year of exhibition Twentieth Century-Fox has earned $21 million from the United States and Canada, and in the list of All Time Box Office Champs of 1973 Patton occupies the fifteenth position.

A different kind of a war super-spectacle is Twentieth Century-Fox's *Tora, Tora, Tora* (1969), the American–Japanese epic about Pearl Harbor, an enormous production, reputedly costing more than the actual Japanese attack on this American Pacific base. It was directed from the

Hollywood side by Richard Fleischer, and the former war antagonists were represented by directors Toshio Masuda and Kinji Fukasaku (replacing Akira Kurosawa, who withdrew after the shooting started). *Tora, Tora, Tora* (the thrice-repeated Japanese for 'tiger', which was the coded signal for the start of the attack on Pearl Harbor) is a 144 minutes-long description of the events leading up to the attack, and of the actual action. In the first and longer part we are shown the diplomatic activity between the United States and Japan, not yet at war but preparing for it. In the second part, we see squadrons of Japanese bombers, sowing death and destruction – a great spectacle, an impressive technical and cinematic feat.

And a hero? There are many, and so there isn't one. *Tora, Tora, Tora* is a reconstruction of true historical events, and all the characters are based on authentic people. The cast list is endless, so that one easily gets confused watching the parade of uniformed and civilian '*dramatis personae*'. They appear fleetingly to disappear for good, or to return for another moment, after a long absence. It is difficult to recognize those people, let alone to get to like, or to hate, them. They are just extras in the monumental struggle of the great powers. War becomes impersonal, an affair outside conscious human actions and human judgement. Why bother to rationalize, to give counsel, when we are faced with an elemental, unrestrained, destructive force? It is pointless to look in this armed combat for heroism in the traditional De Mille meaning of the term. At least, not on the American side.

Here we come to a strange paradox: the makers of *Tora, Tora, Tora* were apparently so determined to be objective that in the end they overcompensated and overbalanced. The American politicians and generals are pictured as a bunch of ignorant amateurs, lacking in foresight or the ability to influence the course of events. The shrewd American officers and civil servant characters of lower rank appear on the screen, but they can do nothing. The Japanese General Chief of Staff and the ministries are ruled by black forces driving forward towards the confrontation, but the gallant admirals are wise and opposed to war, while the Air Force officers possess all the Samurai qualities of fearless valour. They are willing to trade their lives for victory. The Squadron Leader, Fuchida (played by Takshiro Tamura), in charge of the air attack on Pearl Harbor, expresses all these high fighting qualities.

Thus, in an American war film, there is no room for heroes of one's own side. The honour is conceded to the valiant and noble adversaries. It seems not much of a consolation that Admiral Yamamoto, in the last line spoken from the screen, sounds a warning to his compatriots: Pearl Harbor is going 'to awaken a sleepy giant and fill him with a terrible resolve . . . '. Go home in peace, Richard Fleischer comforts his audience. We are going to win that war, in spite of the Pearl Harbor disaster. How we do it . . . is a matter for other films.

A morally ambiguous and controversial hero, like Patton, and a film lacking a hero, like *Tora, Tora, Tora*, are different aspects of the same phenomenon: a tendency to retreat from idealized concepts, to debunk romantic myths. A yet different aspect of this is illuminated by the marvellously poetic film creation of Stanley Kubrick, *2001: A Space Odyssey* (1968), a super-spectacle of the increasingly popular science fiction genre. Interviewed in the course of production, Kubrick was quoted as saying that looking for a likely formula he had been struck by the affinity of the story to Homer's *Odyssey*: 'It occurred to us [he is referring to the screen-writer, Arthur C. Clarke, as well as himself] that for the Greeks the vast stretches of the sea must have had the same sort of mystery and remoteness that space has for our generation and that the far-flung island Homer's wonderful characters visited were no less remote to them than the planets our spacemen will soon be landing on are to us. *Journey* also shares with the *Odyssey* a concern for wandering, exploration and adventure.'[17]

So much for Stanley Kubrick. In the finished film the great cosmic adventure found a fascinating visual shape. It is a genuine vision of the inter-planetary odyssey of the twenty-first century. But minus the heroes, in spite of the fact that in the imagination of the young cinema-goers, in their secret dreams and aspirations, it is surely the space-conquering astronauts who are the classic heroes of our times. Disinterested, courageous, representing universal, victorious humanity. Clarke and Kubrick have ignored all this, depriving the astronauts of their human features. Admittedly Bowman (Keir Dullea) and Poole (Gary Lockwood) are gallant, dedicated and likeable enough, but also quite faceless. They are just perfect subordinates, competent only at carrying out their particular tasks in an incomprehensibly complex mechanism. The most assertive and developed 'ego' is displayed, appropriately enough, not by a human being, but by a computer known as Hal 9000, able to speak with a 'human' voice. Thus *2001*, a marvellous, fantastic odyssey to the stars and beyond them, has to get along without a living, full-blooded Odysseus.

The more serious, dramatic development of a cinematic super-spectacle breaks radically with the traditional concept of an outstanding, noble hero. It substitutes either a 'flawed' hero, or discards him altogether. But isn't there a 'golden mean' between those two extremes? Isn't it possible to show conventional, unidealized people, but without stressing pathology, without aberrations? George Seaton's *Airport* (1969) offers an answer of sorts to this question. Not a full and definite answer, but nevertheless worth considering.

Is it, however, right and proper to categorize *Airport* as a super-spectacle? It is a contemporary film whose action takes place either inside a passenger jet or at the airport. There are no monumental sets, no crowds of extras. The public is not being seduced with the usual display of wealth. It all seems to point to a negative answer. At the same time the film was shot in an expensive multi-screen Todd AO system, and in colour. The scenes inside the aircraft and of the forced landing in a blizzard represent an impressive technical feat by the adept and experienced production crew. The not-so-trivial sum of $10 million spent on the film is clearly evident on the screen.

Another aspect of *Airport*, which allows it to be classed as a super-spectacle, is its cast. Ross Hunter, the producer, known for his smooth productions streamlined both in content and form, and the director, George Seaton, a competent craftsman without much originality, have resurrected an old thirties formula of star hits, successfully used by Metro-Goldwyn Mayer. In *Grand Hotel* for instance, directed in 1932 by Edmund Goulding, the cast included Greta Garbo, John and Lionel Barrymore, Wallace Beery, Joan Crawford and Lewis Stone. George Cukor's *Dinner at Eight* (1933) had Marie Dressler, John and Lionel Barrymore, Wallace Beery and Jean Harlow. In the Depression years it was such star-studded dramas that drew people into the cinemas.

It may seem that the great stars' era is long past, but there are still actors of tremendous popularity and drawing power. Collecting them all in one film was an expensive operation, but in the final account well worth while. Burt Lancaster plays the airfield master, a man of energy and iron disposition who, in a single, dramatic night has to cope with many complex problems: to clear snow-drifts off the runway, to overcome sabotage by local politicians, to appease citizens protesting against jet noise. Dean Martin is the pilot, Jacqueline Bisset a beautiful air hostess, Van Heflin a psychopathic assassin who wants to blow up the plane, and that excellent dramatic actress, Helen Hayes, plays a charming lady stowaway. Jean Seberg, George Kennedy, Lloyd Nolan and Barry Nelson are also in the cast. No wonder the *Variety* critic described *Airport* as 'This jet age *Grand Hotel*.'[18]

As in the star-studded films of the thirties everyone carries a problem and a subplot of his own. The task was made simpler by the decision to transfer to the screen the structure and motivation of Arthur Hailey's novel. But it was the achievement of George Seaton, the director who wrote his own screenplay, that one never gets lost in the thicket of plots and subplots, that the characters seem plausible and their fate of genuine interest. Moreover, one's emotions are deeply touched, and occasionally even one's intellect.

Curiously enough, the *Variety* critic was very sceptical about the box office potential of the film. He declared *Airport* to be an anachronism, an epitaph to the long outdated style of production. He criticized Seaton for under-rating the speedy perceptions of the modern audience, for boring it with tiresome explanations. Concluding, he doubted if Universal could recoup its multimillion outlay. The opinion dates from early February 1970. In January 1971 *Airport* turned up at the very top of the annual box office list, after an incomplete year's exhibition. The winner's worth varies from year to year, but the success of Seaton's film was quite incredible. In 1969 the top place fell to R. Stevenson's comedy *The Love Bug* which grossed $17 million. *Airport* took $38 million, with the runner-up, *M.A.S.H.*, R. Altman's black war comedy, earning $22 million. In 1973 George Seaton's film advanced to the seventh position on *Variety's* All Time Box Office Champs list, preceding the two De Mille's super-spectacles, *The Ten Commandments*, eighth place, and *Ben Hur*, ninth place.

The American cinema-goer is a mysterious creature – that seems to be the moral of the *Airport* story. He rejects the naïve formula of De Mille, refuses to thrill to romantic heroes, preferring anti-heroes, and after all that he jumps at the chance to see an old-fashioned drama using worn-out story and dramatic ploys, offering the supposedly out-of-date attractions of famous stars. What sort of a public went for it? Teenage, or middle-aged, the afternoon family audience, big city, or out in the country? All across the States, coast to coast, cinemas playing *Airport* have been doing great busi-ness. It appears, therefore, that Seaton's film pleased all audiences, despite the grumbling and fussing of the critics. It was liked by all who have retained the belief that cinema can be a pleasant way to pass the time, and that no disgrace comes from watching an interesting, conventionally well-made spectacle.

The Sound of Music

Variety readers had been so used to seeing *Gone with the Wind*, the same, ageless, box office champion of all time, that it was a shock to find out that in 1968 (returns till the end of December of that year) it was displaced in favour of *The*

Sound of Music. It took $72 million in only three years of exhibition, compared with $70 million earned by the old-timer, in almost thirty years of screen life. 'An extraordinary phenomenon' – that was the most frequent comment in the press and in private discussions.

How does one explain the unexpected, unique success of Robert Wise's film? No one claims it to be an outstanding artistic achievement, or even much above the average. On the contrary, everything in this work is based on known and tried conventions. *The Sound of Music* represents a triumph of faultlessly efficient direction, employing skilfully a variety of sentimental devices, guaranteed to elicit an easy response from the public. The effect is enhanced by music and enchanting views of nature. After all, for the tourist-minded Americans the far-away charms of Switzerland and Austria are a considerable attraction. All sort of things were, in fact, packed into the film: a singing nun and a children's choir, a conflict of earthly love and a spiritual obligation, parental love and a sense of duty, a patriotic resistance against the Nazi occupations of Austria at the time of the Anschluss in 1938 – in fact an abundance of evangelical virtues and high feelings. You name it and you can have it, and everything (or at least most of it) set to music by the incomparable partnership of Richard Rogers and Oscar Hammerstein II. Pauline Kael describes the film-makers and their feat pungently: 'They're the Pavlovs of movie-making: they turn us into dogs that salivate on signal. When the cruel father sees the light and says: "You've brought music back into the house," who can resist the pull at the emotions? . . . But it is the easiest and perhaps the most primitive kind of emotion that we are made to feel.'[19]

The musical trend in the super-spectacle range was begun by *West Side Story* at a time when the screen musical seemed in a serious decline. According to Fred Astaire television was mainly responsible, saturating the public demand with six to eight permanent musical programmes. Fred Astaire was wrong. *West Side Story* furnished the proof that a big screen musical is one of the most effective ways to combat the influence of television.

Late musicals copied the *West Side Story* formula, changing only the emotional tone. Of course, sentimentality remained, but tragic references were replaced by comedy. Material was provided by stage spectacles of proven success: *My Fair Lady, Camelot, The Sound of Music* or *Funny Girl*. In one exceptional case, *Mary Poppins*, the spectacle was adapted not from a stage original but from P. L. Travers' novel of wide appeal about a magical nannie.

A book, already tried and proved in a different medium, a star-studded cast, a carefully selected production crew with expert professionals from the field of cinematography, ballet and music and, most importantly, taking advantage of all the opportunities afforded by the screen to extend and enrich the spectacle – this is the success recipe of the modern, multi-million dollar musical. But in the end the female stars are of most importance. They carry the main expectations and influence decisively the public's interest and emotional response. Without Julie Andrews there would have been no *Mary Poppins* and, had somebody else been cast in the part of Maria, perhaps the public would not have been quite so madly enthusiastic about *The Sound of Music*. The worth of a star is most clearly evident in Wyler's *Funny Girl*, a film not conspicuous for artistic invention or spirit. Here everything is held together by the sensational Barbra Streisand. Whenever she is off the screen – luckily a rare occurrence – the colour spectacle becomes colourless and tedious. The importance of the star in a musical has been recently confirmed by the great success of *Fiddler on the Roof,* due principally to the splendid performance of Chaim Topol as milkman Tevye. Norman Jewison's film was the second best box office champion of 1972, only being bettered by *The Godfather.* Similarly, *Cabaret's* success is largely attributable to the incredible Liza Minnelli.

It might seem that in the super-spectacle family the big screen musical can be assured of a permanent place. The ancient and biblical giants might collapse and turn into dust but the musical would survive all storms and crisis. In the top twenty of the all-time list in 1973 there are four musicals, including two in the top ten (*The Sound of Music* at No. 3

and *My Fair Lady* at No. 10). In the second ten, *Mary Poppins* at No. 12, and *Funny Girl* at No. 19 have won a place. That was the favourable balance of the past decade, but the opening of a new one soon revealed dark spots on what has hitherto seemed a bright perspective. Big musicals, produced at a cost of tens of millions, can no longer pay their way. Twentieth Century-Fox, hoping to repeat the success of Julie Andrews in *The Sound of Music*, and of Barbra Streisand in *Funny Girl*, has backed *Star!* and *Hello Dolly* to the tune of over $20 million in each case. The studio looks to have little chance of recouping the outlay. Most probably it will have to write off considerable losses. Joshua Logan's *Camelot* and *Sweet Charity* directed by Bob Fosse, with Shirley MacLaine, have already met with a similar fate.

The causes of failure are always the same: basically they can be reduced to the excess of spectacular effects and the loss of essential balance. Blind, mechanical copying of earlier successes cannot guarantee a repeat performance. Julie Andrews may have been excellent in *The Sound of Music* but it doesn't follow that she is equally irreplaceable as Gertrude Lawrence in the biographical *Star!*, directed by Robert Wise. Barbra Streisand shone as Fanny Brice in *Funny Girl*, but *Hello, Dolly* was not suited to her talents to anything like the same extent. But there are other factors. After all, in Hollywood experience, follow-up copies of earlier successes have paid off many times. The heart of the matter lies elsewhere: in the stubborn refusal to part with a super-spectacle formula for a musical. Despite appearances, despite the evidence of fairly recent triumphs, one is asking timidly whether the formula is not, if not actually anachronistic, at least in need of urgent overhaul.

The modern cinema-goer is expected to be dazzled by the reconstruction of New York's 14th Avenue, *Anno Domini* 1890, in *Hello, Dolly*, or of London during the twenties in *Star!*; he is expected to be enchanted by group dancing and thrill to the anthology of old and new songs. But all this is supposed to be only the setting and background to the star performance, which inevitably diminishes in size, overwhelmed by the architectural, singing and dancing display.

The public wants more of Julie Andrews or Barbra Streisand, and the film-makers offer dressed-up parades, and ask us to admire the background, choreography, and the quality of Technicolor, or colour de luxe. In the thirties Busby Berkeley sought cinematic solutions in dancing formations, in the seventies Michael Kidd only reproduces and multiplies on the big screen the Music Hall stage. Isn't it possible to produce modest musicals, affording greater acting opportunities to such popular stars as Barbra Streisand and Julie Andrews, asks Pauline Kael coyly. And she herself provides an immediate and discouraging answer, quoting the great tycoon of the cinema: 'D. F. Zanuck says you can't make little musicals and the rest of the industry seems to concur.'[20]

It is difficult to be a prophet in the film industry. The losses on big screen musicals in the sixties could give credence to Pauline Kael's arguments, but the recent box office success of *Fiddler on the Roof* may signify that, after all, not the critic of *The New Yorker*, but the experienced producer, D. F. Zanuck, is right. Norman Jewison directed *Jesus Christ Superstar*, released by Universal in June 1973, and Columbia prepared the production of another musical, *Godspell*.

The Future of a Super-spectacle

The American cinema is now sailing between Scylla and Charybdis. You can make a fortune out of a single blockbuster, but in case of failure the spectre of bankruptcy looms large. To make, or not to make, blockbusters – that is the question. Statements by the companies' presidents and chairmen responsible for production plans in the early seventies seem to indicate considerable restraints on large investments. No studio at the moment can boast of a project with a budget of over $10 million, or even $8 million. The cost of an average film should not exceed $2 million, says Robert Evans of Paramount, and his colleagues from Columbia, Metro-Goldwyn-Mayer or Universal appear to concur. In 1972 Gordon Stulberg, President of Twentieth Century-Fox, was slightly more generous, allowing $2·6 million to be spent on the average production. A super-spectacle, even a modest one (which is, of course, a contra-diction in terms) cannot be made for that kind of outlay.

The reasons for the sudden economies arise not only out of the chastening past experience and the take-over of the film industry by the great corporations with diversified interests but out of a detailed economic analysis of the block-buster phenomenon. Difficulties and obstacles pile up at every step and it takes a true giant to crash through them to success. Let us look at those problems in turn.

Firstly, the enormous productions dragging on for many months and sometimes years, such as *Cleopatra* or *2001*, can result in the freezing of bank credits. A studio with five or six blockbusters scheduled gets up to its neck in debt and has to find tens of millions just to pay the interest charges. The $20 million guarantee, which the exhibitors agreed to pay Twentieth Century-Fox for *Cleopatra*, have just about covered the bank interest. The redemption of a super-production extends over several seasons while debts pile up. Cheap films, by contrast, can be exploited quickly, and bank loans repaid much earlier. This is a strong argument in favour of production economies and a shift of interest towards smaller, less costly films.

Secondly, there is the problem of exhibition. In the good old days, before the separation of production and distribution from cinema exhibition, there was a simple system. A big film was known as an engine, pulling through, as 'coaches', several B and C productions. Cinemas were obliged to book the lot, especially in the case of a parent studio. In deals between different studios it was a reciprocal arrangement: X would buy from Y a complete 'train' (engine and coaches) and vice versa. But from the time of the so-called 'divorce' at the turn of the forties a studio has to handle its films separately. Block booking is now an illegal transaction.

In order to re-coup the outlay quickly a system of 'road showing' was devised – pre-release runs of a blockbuster in selected venues (sometimes in theatres adapted for film projection) with considerably higher admission charges, from $3 to $5.50. The run is unrestricted, often extending through many weeks and only after a film has come off those premiere screens can it be generally released. In theory a sound and promising system; in practice increasingly disappointing. Cinemas in the United States usually fill on three week-end evenings: Friday, Saturday and Sunday. An extended run with empty weekdays can jeopardize the profitability of road showing. And more and more the audience is prepared to wait patiently until the big film comes down to a small cinema, to be seen for two dollars, or less.

Road shows, very popular in the late sixties, with every studio obliged to show off its most important ware in this way, lost a lot of their attractiveness when the two Twentieth Century-Fox musicals, *Doctor Doolittle* and *Star!*, unexpectedly failed. Metro-Goldwyn-Mayer has suffered a similar experience with two of its productions, *Ice Station Zebra* and *Shoes of the Fisherman*. In 1967–8 only two of eight road shows, *Gone with the Wind* and *2001: A Space Odyssey*, have really proved themselves. Not every expensive production, not even every super-spectacle justifies a special treatment of this kind. Not the size of the budget alone but the character of the work and kinds of techniques used should be decisive factors. If a film has been shot in Todd AO, Dimension 150 or Cinerama it has, of course, to be shown in theatres equipped with all the proper facilities. But there are new difficulties here.

The introduction of 70 mm film stock, at the time, encouraged the studios to embark on giant productions. The new gauge allowed them to intensify the effects of size and to reproduce them to the best advantage on the big screen. In 1968 there were in the United States about 730 cinemas equipped with 70 mm projectors. But this potential for exhibition is not fully employed, mainly because of the high print costs – a 70 mm print is ten to fifteen times the price of a standard one. Distributors now consider that only 'certainties' are worth the expense of a few 70 mm prints. All the other big films go out on 35 mm.

Thirdly, there is the problem of where to shoot the big productions. It is much cheaper to base them in European studios where extras, building materials and technicians are available at half the Hollywood price. The drain away from Californian studios meets with understandable protest from the American trade unions, supported by certain government and political circles. This, like it or not, cannot be entirely ignored. Spyros Skouras had a lot of trouble with the unions during the entire *Cleopatra* episode. Not one take of this super-blockbuster originated in an American studio. But had the Twentieth Century-Fox boss listened to good advice, or succumbed to the threats and called the production back from Rome to Hollywood, the cost of the most expensive film of all time would have been increased at least by another 25 per cent.

Producers defending the principle of 'runaway productions' argue the need for authentic backgrounds, and a realistic treatment of the story. Sometimes those arguments are substantiated, but more often they are used to camouflage purely economic factors. The case of *Patton* illustrates it perfectly: the story takes us to Africa, Sicily, France and Germany, and is intended as a true biography of the American general, of genuine historical and documentary worth. And where was *Patton* filmed? In Spain, of course, where regiments of Generalissimo Franco's army can be hired for a very reasonable fee to serve in turn in American and German uniforms. The battle of Bastogne was shot around Segovia, scenes from the French and German theatre of war near Pamplona, the Tunisian and Sicilian campaign not far from Almeria. Four days of English locations and one in Morocco added the finishing touches. All the interiors were shot in Madrid studios. And in this way a representative American film was born.

The wasteful system of financing the super-spectacles, difficulties in exhibition, and increasing political pressures on 'runaway production' all works against the continuation of the formula. There is a gradual withdrawal, often reluctant, but clearly perceptible and continuous. How can it be any different when statistics say that only one of every three films produced in America is paying its way? In this situation a new project is looked at from all sides, checked and double-checked, and obviously, when the financial risk involved is smaller, the proposition becomes more attractive. It can more easily pass through the needle's eye of bank credits and exhibition guarantees.

A far cry from the good old days when, in the thirties, Cecil B. De Mille asked the Paramount studio for information on the average return on a film after five years of exhibition. The answer was that each dollar brings 80 cents of clear profit. No wonder they were so ready to invest in a big spectacle. A statistical guarantee of 80 per cent profit over a period of five years! Today it is a lottery, with a one in three chance of winning anything. To re-coup the costs of production a film has to take many times the original amount of the box office, or receive two and a half times the outlay from distributors. How many super-spectacles can hope for that? Statistics show that it is preferable to produce, not super-spectacles, but less costly films with human interest. The year 1972 will be remembered for many years to come as the turning point in Hollywoodian traditions and habit, bringing total upheaval to the hierarchy of all-time box office champions. Francis Ford Coppola's *The Godfather*, after only a year of showings, took first place on the list, previously occupied for three decades by *Gone with the Wind*. It is impossible to call *The Godfather* a spectacular film: one doesn't see on the screen thousands of extras and costly sets. Still further away from De Mille's formula are films placed fourth and fifth: Arthur Hiller's *Love Story* and *The Graduate* of Mike Nichols. To dot our 'i's, three out of five films in the top category of all-time champions are not super-spectacles.

3

The Changing of the Guard

The Old Guard

On 2 March 1958 the solemn funeral of Harry Cohn took place. In Columbia studios, on the joint stages Number 12 and Number 13, a crowd of mourners gathered to bid farewell to the last of the great Hollywood tyrants. Throughout his long-lasting regime Harry Cohn wielded practically absolute power. Films with the world-famous sign of the Statue of Liberty holding a smouldering torch were made and exhibited solely on the basis of his judgement. He was a ruthless man, hated by many, principally by those who had failed to cross the threshold of success and put the blame for it on the dictator from Columbia; but those who had won through and accumulated fortunes held a different view of the deceased. They remembered him as a valiant ally in the struggle, a tenacious fighter in the common cause, never flinching, never yielding an inch of ground.

The age of despotism ended in Hollywood with Harry Cohn's death. Almost everybody must have felt that as they crowded tightly together on hurriedly assembled chairs or benches and listened to the funeral oration by the comedian, Danny Kaye, a representative of the successful ones. The eulogy had been prepared by Danny Kaye in collaboration with the dramatist, Clifford Odets. Reputedly, in his early play *The Big Knife*, Odets had modelled the character of a ruthless and vain studio director on no one else but Harry Cohn. Now he was painting him in different colours, almost in a halo of greatness. In the proud and high-minded words of the funeral oration: 'We sit here on this great stage of the studio that Harry built, in itself a monument to some of his most remarkable qualities. Without irreverence, this was Harry Cohn's cathedral. This is where he lived and worked and dreamed, and this where his energies, ambition, and vision gave reality to these dreams.'[1] More than fifteen years have passed since Harry Cohn's funeral. Who would dare today, unless altogether divorced from any sense of reality or a sense of humour, call a film studio a cathedral? Tributes and eulogies had been characteristic of the age drawing to its close on that March day in 1958. Cathedrals for their own glory had been built by Harry Cohn of Columbia, Carl Laemmle of Universal, and Louis B. Mayer of Metro-Goldwyn-Mayer.

They were the rulers and high priests at the same time. They gave orders and officiated in their temple fortresses at the solemn services of film production. It was a mixture of black magic and religious ritual, with its own liturgy worked out in thoughtful detail, and everything protected with the seal of papal infallibility. When a rash lady journalist dared to make a critical observation about a film marked with a roaring lion, Louis B. Mayer scolded her benignly from his high throne, pointing out that 'Every M-G-M picture is a good one. Some pictures are better than others, but there are no really bad pictures, at any rate there are no bad M-G-M pictures.'[2]

The high-priests are gone. Some still inhabit our globe, living now in the privacy of their homes, of no further interest to the once so inquisitive journalists. Adolph Zukor, born in 1873, was reported to have been dead, in common with many pioneers, in a supposedly expert book about the film industry. In fact, Zukor lives in his New York apartment, surrounded by his grandsons, great grandsons and great-great grandsons. Occasionally he even shows up at the board meetings of Paramount, created by him half a century ago. He still retains the position of a Chairman Emeritus of the Board, and is enjoying excellent health. Of course, he has no say in the actual running of the studio, but his junior colleagues and ex-pupils listen gladly to his sound pronouncements that 'The film business can only thrive on good films.'[3] Self-evident truths sound better when voiced by the man who opened the first permanent cinema in New York. When? In 1904! On 7 January 1973 in the International Ballroom of the Beverley Hilton Hotel Adolph Zukor celebrated his 100th birthday. Hundreds of guests, representing the Hollywood world of film and television, were present at this memorable event. The guests paid $125 per head for the privilege of being there. (The money went to assist the charitable activities of Variety Clubs International and Friar Club of California.) In a personal message President Nixon said that 'the creative vision and ingenuity of Adolph Zukor inspired the growth of an art form that entertains, informs and enriches the lives of millions around the world.'[4] The dynamic pioneer of the motion picture industry, deeply moved by the celebration of his centenary, made the following statement, 'I would work in pictures today if I were a young man.'[5]

Sam Goldwyn strolls the Beverley Hills promenades, or, to be precise, the alleys of the gardens surrounding his private residence. Hard of hearing and not in the best of health he hasn't attended any film festivities for years. In 1969 he entrusted the reins of his enterprise, Samuel Goldwyn Productions, to his wife, Frances Howard, a former actress, who has shared his life in apparent harmony for the last fifty years. The old man, one of those who have built up the film capital, is no doubt aware that today Hollywood is no longer what it was. How naïve now seem the Goldwyn homely truths from the opening of the fifties, before the television boom: 'The creators of motion pictures, the producers, writers, the directors, the actors, and all the other artists and technicians involved, have always been interested in all the same things which interest most Americans – telling stories, making money, owning cars, having families, talking, singing, dancing, loving, history, sports, laughter – the entire catalogue of interests and emotion that is America.'[6] Films of the seventies speak about another kind of America, and present a different catalogue of problems and emotional experience.

Jack L. Warner – Colonel Warner as he liked to be called – proved the most durable of the old guard. When in 1966 he sold his own and his family's studio, Warner Brothers, to a Canadian company, Seven Arts Productions, he retained the position of an independent producer for himself. But after two years the company was taken over by the Kinney National Service Corporation, and Jack Warner had to leave for ever the Burbank studio where he had spent so much of his life. He at first turned his attention to stage productions, but then went back to his own field of activity – the production of films. In 1972 Columbia released two Jack Warner productions: a modest Western, *Dirty Little Billy*, describing in realistic mood the career of the legendary outlaw, Billy the Kid, and a spectacular musical film version of a Broadway hit, *1776*. The second of these films was shot in Hollywood, described by Warner as: 'What has always been and always should be the capital of the motion picture art.'[7]

The last of the movie tycoons to depart from the major companies is Darryl Francis Zanuck. Of course he is a bit younger than the other surviving pioneers, Goldwyn and Zukor; Zanuck has only just turned seventy. He has been concerned with the cinema for almost half a century, having spent the best years of his youth in the Warner Brothers studios. When the sound revolution came and Warners led off with *The Jazz Singer*, Zanuck helped to consolidate their predominant position on the market, producing some of their gangster hits, as well as social dramas. Some filmmakers, especially the directors, blamed him for ruthlessly cutting their finished product. He was known, by no means fondly, as a film butcher. Zanuck defended himself, arguing that many a grandly conceived spectacle suffers from lack of pace, from too much celluloid. Such pictures can be made 100 per cent better by intelligent re-editing. 'Now Warner Brothers pictures', he used to assert, 'are recognized for their tempo, speed, and direct continuity of thought and action.'[8]

In 1933 Darryl Zanuck left Warner Brothers where he had played an important, almost a key part, but still in a position subservient to that of Jack Warner. Supported by Joseph Schenck, another Hollywood magnate, he set up a new studio, Twentieth Century Pictures. A year later it merged with an old firm of Fox Films, becoming Twentieth Century-

Fox, which is still in existence. In fact the post of the President was held by the Greek, Spyros Skouras (resident in New York), and Joseph Schenck became the Chairman of the Board, but Zanuck, as the Chief of Production, ruled sovereign and unhindered in his Hollywood studio. On his own territory he was just as much a law-maker and an arch-priest as L. B. Mayer or Harry Cohn were on theirs.

For the next twenty years Twentieth Century-Fox and Darryl F. Zanuck were perfectly synonymous, easily interchangeable. But in 1954 the Zanuck era came to an abrupt end. The move came from the Chief of Production himself, with no outside pressure. Zanuck blamed his decision on changes in the production set up, commenting: 'Hollywood drove me out. That's my story and I'm going to stick to it. Actors are now directing, writing and producing. Actors have taken over Hollywood completely, together with their agents. The producer hasn't a chance to exercise authority.'9 Zanuck moved to Europe to produce films as an 'independent' partner of his old firm, Twentieth Century-Fox, in which, incidentally, he remained one of the largest share-holders and an official adviser. The voluntary exile lasted for eight years, until 1962 when Spyros Skouras was forced to resign as the President and the Chief of Production. Members of the Board asked Zanuck to help them find a suitable successor to Skouras – someone young, full of drive and with proven ability. Zanuck's calm answer was that the only man he could recommend with a clear conscience was himself. Thus came about the return of the prodigal son, to a higher position than the one he had held before.

Darryl Zanuck made his son, Richard, the Chief of Production in Hollywood while he stayed in New York to take charge of all the complex business affairs. Initially he was successful, leading Twentieth Century-Fox into a box office boom. *The Sound of Music* became even, if only for a year, the box office champion of all time, nosing out the legendary *Gone with the Wind*. But the auspicious beginning did not last. Too much money was invested in expensive productions which the public did not take to. The bankers and other backers with seats on the Board began hinting at the reckless policies of both the father and the son. In 1969, acting before the storm actually broke, Zanuck senior performed a chess operation known as castling the king: he asked to be relieved of the post of the President, retaining for himself the chairmanship of the Board and the title of the Chief Director. He proposed for the vacant position of the President his son Richard. The Board acceded meekly. The success of *The Sound of Music* seemed still an irrefutable argument, much more persuasive than the distant rumblings of the approaching storm.

The lightning struck late in 1970. The two main creditors, Chase Manhattan Bank and Morgan Guaranty Bank, demanded a radical change in the policies of the company, seeing that its current annual deficit exceeded $80 million. The most urgent warning came with the catastrophic fall of Twentieth Century-Fox shares on the New York exchange. Early in 1970 the quotation was $20 a share; ten months later it was only $8. Faced with the gravity of this situation, Darryl Zanuck sacrificed his son, accepting unblinkingly his ostensibly voluntary resignation from the posts of the President and the Chief of Production. Elmo Williams, the producer of *Tora, Tora, Tora*, has been put in charge of production and Denis C. Stanfill, till then a Deputy President representing the financial interests of the banking houses, has taken over as President. But the real *eminence grise* was William T. Gossett, the chairman of the Executive Committee, for many years (1947–62) the Deputy President and the Chief Legal Adviser of the Ford Motor Company. In reality Zanuck has been removed from the helm, having lost to Gossett the chair of the Executive Committee, and keeping the rather nominal post of the Chairman of the Board. Even the chairmanship of the board did not last long. Six months after his son's dismissal Darryl F. Zanuck faced a new drama. His enemies mobilized their forces to evict him. Zanuck was clever enough to avoid pointless fight and the prospect of outright defeat. On the eve of Twentieth Century-Fox shareholders' general meeting, which was to take place on 19 May 1971, the last movie tycoon issued to the press the following statement: 'I have decided not to request re-election as chairman of the Board . . . It is my desire to be free of all corporate administrative responsibilities . . .'[10] The new bosses of the company, representatives of New York City financial interests, were thoughtful enough to nominate Darryl F. Zanuck chairman emeritus of the board. An honorary title sounding important, but having no practical value.

Dennis C. Stanfill was promoted to the post of chairman of the new board, and Gordon Stulberg assumed the key promotion of President of the Company. Stulberg came from the cadre of top executives and had gained the reputation of an energetic and gifted producer as head of Cinema Center Films Corporation (films for television). So ended the long reign of D. F. Zanuck in Twentieth Century-Fox. He is now an independent film producer, president of D.F.Z. Productions Inc. and all that is left to him is to plan future campaigns, and to confide to the public his hopeful projects or his thoughts about the state of the American cinema.

Zanuck is an old hand at the game, and he knows which cards to play first. He pays his dues to the all-powerful financial backers, but does not forget the creative talents. He declares: 'Our production program, while maintaining its creative freedom, will operate in much closer contact with our marketing needs and our financial capabilities.'[11] But the sly fox is aware that public tastes are changing, so he adds: 'The film-maker must reflect the tensions and frictions of our society.'[12] Still, a leopard cannot change his spots. Having dutifully stated that producers and directors must observe closely the changing aspect of the times and be sensitive to the needs of the day, Darryl Zanuck quickly passes on to anticipate that 'When the craze for monotonous eroticism overshoots the mark, we shall go back to the Bible, or to pure romantic love, or even to a new version of *Cleopatra*.'[13]

The New Bosses

A key figure in the Hollywood system of production has always been the chief of production of a big studio, whatever the company. Frequently he was given the title of a Deputy

President in charge of production, sometimes with the grandly adjectival 'World' added to stress that his power extended overseas, wherever films financed by the mother company were being made. When in the early fifties the ranks of the old guard began to crumble and the magnates faded away one by one their places were being taken over by young people, mostly in their thirties, coming from a different intellectual background and with different work habits.

These were not the immigrants from Central or Eastern Europe, who even late in life could not fathom the subtleties and intricacies of the English language, but American university graduates, men of refinement and, most importantly, rooted in the traditions and manners of the United States. They may have been sons or grandsons of the immigrants, but their world was very different from the world of their grandfathers who had settled in the American continent at the end of the nineteenth century, or early in the twentieth century. Undoubtedly in many cases the young ones learned the craft, in the business rather than in the creative sense, from their elders, but they realized that the era of the film potentates, of the absolute rulers, the monarchs of Hollywood, had gone for ever.

Richard Zanuck, widely known as the *dauphin*, the next in line, can be taken as representative of the new generation. He was twenty-eight when, on his father's return to Twentieth Century-Fox, he was made Chief of Production. He produced his first film at twenty-four. At thirty-five he became the President. The period of unemployment after his fall in 1970 lasted barely three months when Zanuck junior accepted the post of Deputy President in charge of production at Warner Brothers. This new chapter in the professional career of Richard Zanuck lasted only a bare seventeen months. Neither Zanuck Junior nor his friend, producer David Brown, felt happy in the Warner Brothers set-up as supervisors of a large, major studio film programme. They asked for release from their contractual obligations, and this was given them in July 1972 in order that they might become independent producers.

During his almost ten-year stint at Twentieth Century-Fox

the younger Zanuck revealed the qualities of drive, courtesy and single-minded application. He took an interest in everything, seeing every project through from the acquisition of film rights to the production of a screening print and the first preview. He personally supervised each item in the production plan through all the stages. He was in general control, he made the vital decisions but he never interfered, peremptorily, in other people's work. And this is where he differed from the old guard. Darryl Zanuck always felt free to kick out a director in the final stages of production and to sit down himself at the editing table. For Richard such behaviour would be unthinkable. One could advise, discuss things, argue, put pressure to bear, if need be, but not dictate, not act behind the others' back.

Richard Zanuck's main premise was to do away with the impersonal processes of production. The young Chief strived to make actual people responsible for the achievements or the failures of film-making – rather than the anonymous mechanism of the studio. Hence his attempts to build up the authority of individual producers and directors, while keeping himself in the background. 'There is no shortage of talent,' he says. 'The only shortage lies in the number of men who can courageously and knowledgeably evaluate it.'[14] In other words, the task of the chief of production in a big studio is to find people of talent, to ensure the best possible conditions for their work and to trust them to bring it to a successful conclusion.

Richard Zanuck realised that this kind of policy carried a considerable personal risk to the Chief of Production. Remaining in the background, dispensing laurels and honours to the others, he still has to accept responsibility for the general result, measured, not in artistic but box office terms. A man of talent can make more money and gain greater satisfaction as an independent producer than as a chief of production in a studio.

Zanuck junior learned to his cost, when he was asked politely but firmly to sign a form of resignation, that supporting other talents while refusing to advertise his own merit does not carry sufficient guarantee of security for his own interests. Did anyone care to remember that in the course of the previous seven years Twentieth Century-Fox achieved 112 Oscar nominations, winning more awards from the Hollywood Academy than any other studio? Nothing counted in the face of the financial losses incurred in the recent months. Although in the past he had made not a few dollars for the shareholders, Richard Zanuck had to pay with his position for the current deficit.

Could this be avoided? Had Darryl Zanuck decided to play 'va banque', rather than give way to the financial pressures, his son would probably have held on to his post. In 1967, while Zanuck senior was holding sway in New York and Zanuck junior in Hollywood, there was an ideal situation, without the conflict, typical of the American cinema, between the backers from the East and the producers from the West. This inherent, natural conflict was the original source of all the palace revolutions, all the shifts of power and structural changes in Hollywood. People who invest money in the film industry are not patient, they do not like to wait too long for an improvement in the situation. Producers and directors know that even the wisest, the most carefully plotted policies of the studio can never ensure an unbroken stream of successes. After the fat, the lean years are bound to come. When the East (that is, New York) shows sufficient confidence and patience to ride out the run of bad luck, the West (that is, Hollywood) can work on calmly. When the patience runs out in the East, the heads roll in the West. Darryl Zanuck acceded to the bankers' demands. The antagonism between New York and Hollywood flared up once again.

The Paramount Chief of Production since autumn 1966 is Robert Evans, born in 1931, nick-named, slightly disdainfully, the Blue-Eyed Boy of Charles Bluhdorn, the Gulf and Western potentate. It was Bluhdorn who discovered Evans and made him first the head of Paramount in Europe, and later the Chief of Production in Hollywood. The decision, rather unexpected and not too enthusiastically received in film-making circles, seemed mainly based on Evans' colourful biography.

He was born in New York, the son of a dentist, the director of a well-known clinic. From early youth he was attracted to an artistic career. At fourteen he was already deriving a fair income from radio acting and later became a disc jockey in Florida. But at the same time he managed to graduate in economics and to go into business. In the early fifties he became a partner and a director of Evan Picone, a prosperous company producing ladies' clothing. He might have stayed in the skirt and ladies' suits trade till the end of his days if it wasn't for an idea to spend a vacation in California. Robert Evans' subsequent career is extremely cinematic, rather like a Hollywood fairy-tale about a contemporary Cinderella, including even the characteristically simple moral.

One day Norma Shearer, the former star, saw Robert Evans taking a dip in a Beverly Hills swimming pool. Just then Universal was shooting *Man of a Thousand Faces*, a film biography of Lon Chaney. One of the characters there was the peerless Irving Thalberg who died in 1936, the greatest Hollywood chief of production of his time. Norma Shearer, who was his widow, saw in Evans almost a physical double of Thalberg, and the young businessman was promptly offered the part. One of the Los Angeles dailies printed the news about the unexpected engagement under the sensational heading: 'Youthful Clothing Tycoon Jumps into Swimming Pool and lands in Movies.'[15]

Evans' start in film acting was not markedly brilliant. *The New York Times* found the part of Thalberg 'unspeakably bad', and the playing rather amateurish. But already in the adaptation of Hemingway's novel, *The Sun also Rises*, directed by Henry King in 1957, the critics praised the young actor in the part of Pedro Romero. He accepted a five-year contract offered him by Darryl Zanuck. In 1962 Evans sold his holding in the clothing firm and resigned the directorship. He worked for a short time as a producer in Twentieth Century-Fox and in March 1966 he found himself under the Gulf and Western flag. Charles Bluhdorn told him: 'You have had business experience. You've proven yourself a success as businessman and executive. You've had theatrical background and you know how to function with creative people. If you can use all abilities, you'll do the best job in town.'[16]

Has Robert Evans passed the test and proved Bluhdorn's confidence in him to be well founded? After a couple of years in a key job he appears to be in a strong position. That is, of course, if anyone can ever be strong in Hollywood, where twenty-four hours' notice is often considered sufficient. But there are no signs in heaven or earth of any impeding changes in the cinematic kingdom of Gulf and Western. At the celebration of Adolph Zukor's 100th birthday, Charles Bluhdorn took the opportunity to thank Bob Evans. He said: 'Paramount couldn't be anything without him. He worked with me seven years – on *Love Story* and *The Godfather* and he deserves everything that's due to Paramount.'[17] Evans is tremendously hard-working. Day and night he lives, eats and sleeps film. Nothing but film. Deriders – and there are always many – suggest that he is more interested in signing contracts and buying film rights of literary originals than in the actual production of films. But this is not borne out by the Paramount Chief of Production's own pronouncements. When interviewed on the subject he declared that he believed in being close to the making of the screenplay, to the casting and the final stage of editing a film.[18]

Evans, unlike Zanuck junior, has been known to intervene personally in the processes of production. He proclaims the need for a greater measure of control over the directors' work. It has occasionally led to angry rejoinders and even to a court suit. Elaine May, a young woman director, has charged Paramount with unauthorized recutting of one of her films. But Robert Evans keeps repeating obstinately that the company he represents concerns itself not only with the financial, but also with the creative, aspects of production. The conflicts, more frequent at the beginning of the seventies than in the early stages of his rule, do not, however, normally escalate into open warfare between the creative film-makers and the administration. The door of the Evans office remains open to anyone prepared to argue out his case.

A new figure among the chiefs of production is James T.

Aubrey Jr, appointed by Kirk Kerkorian in October 1969 to the post of President and Chief Manager of the Metro-Goldwyn-Mayer studio. Aubrey is a *'homo novus'* in the world of cinema, but with a varied and even stormy television career behind him. Born into a rich, patrician family, educated in Princeton, he started work in ABC, moving on to CBS where for several years he had held the position of Programme Director. In March 1965 he was suddenly sacked from the job. The official reason was a difference of opinion between Aubrey and the other members of the management on policies to be followed. But this enigmatic statement could not hide the cruel reality of the diminishing popularity of programmes controlled by Aubrey. The television oracle, in the form of Nielsen's Ratings Agency, clearly revealed that an increasing number of viewers were turning to the rival networks of NBC and ABC. And it was irrelevant that in the past Aubrey was responsible for producing several extremely successful serials, like *The Defenders*.

Born in 1919, James T. Aubrey is a tough operator, never flinching from radical measures. As he said in his television days: '. . . ours is a very competitive business. You have to make decisions, and decisions aren't always the popular thing. Every time you make a decision you affect someone tremendously personally.'[19] But even the toughest and, to some, potentially painful decisions were transmitted with a smile, in the most courteous manner. This was how Aubrey has acquired his nick-name – The Smiling Cobra.

The new President manages Metro-Goldwyn-Mayer dictatorially, cutting down the staff, closing down the London studios, discontinuing the production of some films, setting the maximum budget for all future projects at $2 million. He also demands that the creative personnel – producers, directors, and especially actors – share with the studio the financial risk involved. Let them all have a stake in the hoped-for profits, that's all right, but not make money out of a film that brings only losses. Obviously, such reforms do not meet with an enthusiastic response from artists and technicians.

Yet at the same time Aubrey fully understands the necessity of a close working relationship with creative people. 'You can't make pictures by computer,' he says.[20] A clear-cut understanding with film-makers engaged on a project is needed, and an agreed policy, marked out in advance, for each separate production. From this procedure successful results should flow.

David Picker, from 1972 to 1973 the President and chief operating officer of United Artists, appears to have had an easier task. Born in 1931, he is the third in a line of film potentates. His grandfather and father held managerial positions in the distributive and trading sector of the film industry. He himself has been attached to United Artists since 1956. In 1962 he was appointed the Deputy President in charge of production, and since June of 1969 has been at the helm of the company's affairs. Compared to his opposite numbers in the rival firms his job is made easier by the fact that United Artists has no studios of its own and is thus free of all troublesome burdens of ownership. 'We don't make pictures ourselves,' says Picker. 'We are in the business of supporting those creators we believe in.'[21]

The new chiefs of production have none of the majestic aura of infallibility characteristic of their predecessors of the Old Guard, who believed in their sacred mission, entrusted to them, they thought, by the American people. They liked to be surrounded by an air of mystery, and when they did speak out they insisted that their pronouncements be accepted as dogmas, not to be argued with. In the last account, the Old Guard believed, the creative responsibility for all the films was lodged with them only. Louis B. Mayer once told Saroyan, striving to write something for the screen, that there were many precious pearls in his work, but they were not threaded together. Only the producer can make a necklace of the scattered pearls.[22] The reality of film-making is seen quite differently by David Picker. 'There is only one place,' he says, 'where American films are today and that's in the heads of the people who are making them.'[23] The best of the American cinema does not grow in the studio, nursed and pampered over by top management, but is born in the creative imagination of artists and film-makers supported by the chiefs of production with all the resources at their command.

The Producers

The American production system is pyramid-shaped, with a chief of production at the top, and film directors at the base carrying the main burden of transforming scripted projects into the finished screen product. But in the middle ranks, between the chief of production and the directors, a group of intermediaries and protectors operate: in other words, the producers.

In the past quarter of a century the producer's function has changed considerably. In the old days – with Hollywood at the height of success and power – the producer was an employee of the studio. The chief, responsible for the total output, would entrust to his charge a group of films. For seeing them through to successful completion the producer would receive, in addition to a permanent salary, an agreed percentage of any profits. Any dispute between the producer and the director (a rather infrequent occurrence) would be conclusively settled by the chief of production.

In fact, such producers employed by the studio no longer exist. It is true that some are still tied up by a contract to a single company, but the practice of overseeing several productions at once has been discontinued. The current principle is that a producer can be in charge of only one film on the floor at any given time, and from the loyal agent of the studio heads he is gradually becoming a close and trusted collaborator of the director. He helps the director to deal and negotiate with the studio. The emphasis has shifted 180 degrees: the producer and the director have become allies, held together by a common aim. No longer can a studio count on the producer's support in opposing the director's views.

What are the producer's duties, and what qualifications does he need for the job? In the old days Jesse Lasky of Paramount defined the producer's work and the qualities it takes to perform it in a poetic and almost religious vain: 'The producer must be a prophet and a general, a diplomat and a peacemaker, a miser and a spendthrift. He must have vision tempered by hindsight, daring governed by caution, the patience of a saint, and the iron will of Cromwell.'[24] In others words he needs to be a genius who just happened to find himself in the film business. Lasky's lofty and poetic descriptions can be contrasted with the rather prosaic views of L. B. Mayer. When Joseph Mankiewicz, the screen-writer, went to the Metro-Goldwyn-Mayer monarch with a timid request to let him become a director, the answer was: 'First – a producer, then – a director. You have to learn to crawl before you can walk.'[25] A producer has to see to all the every-day, earthly matters before a director can spread the wings of fancy.

Both the old definitions, the lofty as well as the prosaic one, seem too metaphorical, too imprecise. Jesse Lasky, himself a producer, saw his profession in an aura of reverence and mystery. L. B. Mayer, in his own eyes a king among the producers, looked down on his inferiors, the crawling, earthly creatures.

Much more can be gleaned about the real function of a producer, as it stands today, from the screen-writer Ernest Lehman, who wrote *The Sound of Music* and moved on to a new position in Twentieth Century-Fox when Richard Zanuck asked him to take charge of *Hello, Dolly*. Replying to the question: 'What does a producer do?' Lehman said: 'As far as I'm concerned he does four things. First, he says yes or no to a possible acquisition. There are thousands of books and plays that might be made into movies; a pro-ducer's first job is choosing the few that should be. Since each project is a potential disaster from the beginning, he has to be sure that what he selects has the greatest possible chance for success.

'Second, he must make sure that the screenplay is as good as it can possibly be. Naturally, not all screenplays can be equally good; all kind of factors come into play. But the producer must keep on the writer's tail so that his particular screenplay is as good as it can be. Third, he must do every-

thing he can to hire the most talented people in their field –
actors, directors, technicians.

'Last, and this is the hardest and perhaps the most important part of producer's job, he has to step back and let them
get on with their work.'[26]

So much for Ernest Lehman. He leaves out one essential
function of the producer if he operates independently: the
organization of financial backing for his productions. A
producer employed by a studio does not worry about this;
an independent, working for himself, usually takes a project
to a distributor which already has at least some financial
backing. The company, which is going to rent the film to
exhibitors and sell it to foreign contractors, usually advances
certain sums of money towards the production costs, becoming a partner in the enterprise. And no matter whether the
producer is employed by a studio, or working independently,
his duty is to keep to the limits laid down in the budget
estimates. As Al Ruddy, a Paramount producer, succinctly put
it: a producer is 'the guy who has to find the point at which a
film can be done for the best quality at the lowest price'.[27]

In Lehman's description of the producer's obligations one
notes especially the statement that his most important and
hardest task is to leave the freedom of action to creative film-
makers, led by a director. 'Don't intrude, don't intervene,'
is the maxim of a film producer of the seventies, a maxim
quite unacceptable to someone like Irving Thalberg in the
thirties. Then a producer was an overseer, or, to put it more
delicately, the director's own guardian angel; today he
clears the field, ensures the best possible conditions for
creative work. John Houseman, one-time collaborator with
Orson Welles back in his theatre days and later a Metro-
Goldwyn-Mayer producer of long standing, declares: 'The
creative producer's main job is to organize and guide a
production without interfering with the work of various
collaborators he has chosen.'[28]

This advice from a senior colleague is put into practice by
several young producers who have emerged in the last few
years. Joe Manduke, the producer of Arthur Penn's *Alice's
Restaurant*, says that his task is to ensure the greatest

autonomy for the director and the actors.[29] John Sturges, a director with many box office successes to his credit, describes his collaboration with the producer Harold Mirisch in these words: 'We decide together things like scripts, budget and stars. Then I'm on to make the picture and that's it.'[30] Larry Turman, a forty-year-old producer who graduated from the Los Angeles University's film department (U.C.L.A.), believes that it is his duty to clear the path for young talent, to accept the risk which the big studios prefer to evade.[31]

Changes in the producer–director relationship, which have been such a marked feature of the industry's evolution in the past twenty years, have led to a weakening of the tendency to combine the duties of director and producer in one and the same person. A director of high artistic ambition often finds it more convenient to have a collaborator and a trusted ally in a producer who takes upon his shoulders the thousand, thankless administrative, economic and legal problems, rather than, in the name of total autonomy, to run the entire, complex production machinery himself. Negotiations with agents representing writers or actors, especially, can consume an immense amount of time and energy.

Only a few experienced directors of the old generation who went through a tough training in the former days, and have no reason to recall nostalgically their collaboration with producers, still operate as producer directors. The younger ones prefer to share the duties and the responsibilities with producers. Characteristically more frequent are the instances of combining the work of screen-writing and producing. The writers believe that the power to choose a director and actors increases the chance to get across to the audience the original spirit and intentions of the screenplay. This was the motive behind Nunnally Johnson's advance to the producer's chair in the thirties and forties, and today Ernest Lehman is following the same trail.

The Directors' Elite

The change in the ranks of producers has been mirrored, if to a lesser extent, by the movement among directors. Of the veteran directors already active in the silent days, William Wyler, Henry Hathaway and Howard Hawks are still working, as is Alfred Hitchcock, who began his creative life in England. King Vidor and Fritz Lang have retired and now give lectures at universities or serve on international festival juries. The old master, John Ford, the peerless poet of the American cinema and maker of *Stagecoach*, was inactive from 1968 until the time of his death in 1973.

Of all the veterans Howard Hawks has kept his form best. He represents a traditional and, one might say, a classic school of a narrative cinema, and, surprisingly, is equally appreciated by viewers who want unpretentious entertainment as by the younger, discriminating film-goers, brought up on various 'new waves'. The old master's philosophy and his technique are simple. Hawks is a story-teller, and the plots he chooses must have strong and clear dramatic conflicts. Each film should have three or four moments of maximum tension, three or four scenes where the hero is shown in action, in a fight. When these climaxes have been properly managed the viewer swallows the rest of the story much more easily. One must also remember that clearly motivated characters define the course of action, while the action reveals the qualities of the characters.

Hawks resents all attempts to capture the audience through technical tricks, extraordinary camera angles, baroque effects of lighting and photography. He believes in the old principle, already proclaimed by Pudovkin, that the camera should be placed in a position which affords it the best view of the action. And the simplest way to register the screen action is also the best way. Perhaps there is some truth in the comparisons made between Hawks and Hemingway. Both of them espouse a simplicity, terseness, spareness of narrative, both know how to treat serious, and even tragic affairs without bombast, even, on the contrary, with an uninhibited sense of humour.

Andrew Sarris aptly defines the cinema of Howard Hawks as honest, direct, efficient and functional – perhaps the most essentially American, in the context of other directors' work.[32] One could add that the studios greatly value any association with this senior film-maker, because all his films make money. Howard Hawks simply does not know how to make an unpopular film.

A group of slightly younger veterans includes those who came to the cinema at the time of the sound revolution, often with some Broadway theatre experience. They were engaged because they were at ease with dialogue, and they could handle stage actors, then crowding into Hollywood. Not all the pioneers and law-makers of the sound period could maintain their dominant positions. Rouben Mamoulian, the maker of *Applause* and *City Streets*, is all but forgotten. George Cukor, on the other hand, the maker of once famous films such as *Dinner at Eight*, *Little Women* and *David Copperfield*, is still active and going strong.

George Cukor is rightly known as 'the actors' director'. In the course of his long professional life he has worked with all the great Hollywood stars, from Greta Garbo to Audrey Hepburn. In a sense he also employs a classic method, specializing in psychological portrayals of people. But where for Hawks the important element is action, for Cukor it is the reactions of his screen characters. Shot after shot, often in a quite conventional arrangement of close-ups, medium or long shots, explains to the audience what the heroes think and feel. The images are supported by pointed and carefully paced dialogue.

Cukor does not exaggerate the director's creative contribution or eulogize over its merit. His work is the opposite of what is known as the author's cinema. It follows naturally from his understanding of the director's position as 'one midway between the scripter and the actor'.[33] A director should be able to communicate to actors his own point of view, his interpretation of the story being filmed. And the proof that Cukor is a sensitive reader of screenplays and that he knows how to reproduce on the screen their mood, style and spirit in films as varied as *Romeo and Juliet*, *Camille*, *My Fair Lady*, *Travels with my Aunt*, or even the more difficult and not wholly successful *Justine* from Lawrence Durrell's *Alexandria Quartet*.

Directors who appeared in the American cinema during or immediately after the war can hardly be called veterans, but they do make up a senior group, accounting for a considerable part of the Hollywood directors' *élite*. Many names spring to mind – Otto Preminger, Stanley Kramer, Orson Welles, Vincente Minnelli, Robert Wise, Billy Wilder, Budd Boetticher, Don Siegel, Samuel Fuller. A film directed by any one of this group is always awaited with some interest. One expects at least a fairly absorbing story, told well, with a carefully selected cast. No serious complaints about the standard of craftsmanship. But new discoveries, artistic revelations, or even any other qualities of freshness and surprise are now, from this group, extremely rare. It appears the same once interesting and gifted film-makers, like Vincente Minnelli, Robert Wise or Billy Wilder, stagnate in the repetition of the same, rigid structures, the same tricks of the trade and stylistic mannerisms. More alive, perhaps eclectic, but keen to try new ways, to find new subjects, is Otto Preminger. His *Tell Me that You Love Me, Junie Moon* is an interesting attempt at a study of an invalid's life.

Undoubtedly, those names of senior directors belonging to different generations and with careers extending into different periods of the cinema are still representative of Hollywood. When one talks of the American cinema they spring to mind first, and take a prominent part in any evaluations and judgements. Tradition still weighs heavily, a habit of thought which even some American critics seem to fall victim to. And yet the sixties and the opening of the seventies have revealed a yawning – if not yet a chasm at least a gap between what is a representative label and what forms the reality of the American cinema today. To put it in a nutshell: the directors' *élite* may be representative of Hollywood, but not of what is shown on the American screens. A look at the box office statistics of 1968–72 shows clearly the difference between the honorary champions and the real winners.

Out of a hundred top box office films only four were made by the senior directors: in 1968 S. Kramer's *Guess Who's Coming to Dinner* and Henry Hathaway's *True Grit*, in 1969

William Wyler's *Funny Girl* and in 1971 *The Andromeda Strain* by R. Wise. All the other directors with top box office successes to their credit belong to the generation of film-makers that made its bow in the middle fifties, or in the sixties. And most of them came to film from television.

The Television Generation

The invasion of Hollywood territory by directors, producers and writers from television is closely related to the development of American television in the early fifties. At that time the live television theatre had reached a crisis point caused, paradoxically, by technical progress. When the registration of an image on magnetic tape was perfected, and the initial problems of transmission by cable were successfully solved, the live theatre became expensive and inconvenient outside the new format of the popular spectacle. Interesting productions from the theatre series *Playhouse 90* or *Texaco Star Theatre* disappeared from the programme schedules.

Quite apart from these technological and industrial causes, there were also psychological factors at work. After many years of continuous staging of plays for the small screen, week after week, directors felt worn out. It was becoming increasingly difficult to hit on fresh ideas, on new ways of treating the same themes. At the same time the circumstances in which they had to work changed: from pioneering conditions which allowed ample space for individual freedom, to rigid industrial controls. The sponsors – publicity-seeking firms buying programmes to advertise their product – had a bigger say and were making an increasing use of it. The Madison Avenue advertising agencies, acting as intermediaries in contract negotiations between the potential sponsors and the television companies, also felt entitled to join in on the act with advice and suggestions. In the hustle of big business art was pressurized into the background, if not out of existence altogether. Creative people of all sorts felt ready to leave. The exodus had began.

Between 1954 and 1957 a group of television writers moved

to Hollywood, with Paddy Chayefsky, Reginald Rose and Rod Sterling among them. Several directors came at the same time, people like Daniel Mann, Delbert Mann, Robert Mulligan, Sidney Lumet, Martin Ritt and John Frankenheimer. Tired of television routine and unable to continue their more adventurous work they looked for artistic opportunities in the cinema. A leading figure in this first wave of television immigrants was John Frankenheimer.

Frankenheimer had been working in New York and later in California in the Los Angeles television studios, first as an assistant director, and then directing independently. In 1955 and in the early part of 1956 he was responsible for staging over one hundred programmes, mostly plays, but also some live television serials.

He remembers his television work with a sense of gratitude, almost with nostalgia. 'I think that everything I am today I owe to it,' he declares.[34] Television, he believes, gave him a marvellous chance to grow and to develop. Interviewed by Gerald Pratley, the maker of *The Young Savages, The Train* and *Grand Prix* explains his debt to the other medium. Television teaches the discipline of working within a very tight schedule and to a precisely defined format. It helps one to distribute the emphasis where needed, to include all the important points within a constant and familiar framework. There is also the problem of retaining a television viewer's attention, more difficult than in the cinema where he buys a ticket and settles in for the entire performance. A viewer in front of the small screen has a choice so the tension has to be built up and the intervals placed in a way that would keep his interest alive. Andrew Sarris, not one of Frankenheimer's admirers, pokes fun at his habit of ending a sequence on a note of high drama, as if he was still afraid that the viewers might switch off before the commercial.[35] A rather undeserved piece of malice, even if the habit of interrupting a show for a commercial does play a part. What counts, after all, is the final effect, the ability to hold the audience's attention, whatever the means employed.

Frankenheimer specifies the factors in his television experience that have most helped him in making feature films.

First, staging a great number of productions gave him confidence in his later work with actors. A variety of parts and characters, continuously changing casts inevitably open up wider vistas, bringing a director into contact with differing temperaments and personalities. Second, the ability to communicate with writers, finding a common language with them – essential for a director like Frankenheimer who does not write his own scripts. 'If you're going to have any of your personality in a film or in a television show,' he says, 'it has to be there in the script. It just cannot be done with the camera.'[36]

Lessons learned by Frankenheimer in television have not only increased his basic skills, but have led to the development of a new, brisk and bustling narrative style. A similar background, often enriched with some experience of the Broadway theatre, formed the qualifications of the new group of directors, who came to Hollywood in the sixties.

Arthur Penn tried the theatre after a thorough training in live television drama. His stage production of *The Miracle Worker* was one of the most resounding successes in the New York theatre. In his cinematic method there are echoes of television in the way Penn employs close-ups and movements within the frame. He likes to be close to the actor, close enough to be able to read his mobile features. He understands the value of montage, and uses it, though instead of cutting 'live' pictures, as in the television studio, he now has to employ an editing table. But he knows that in both cases montage, changing the context and the dramatic values of a single shot, can shape the meaning of a screen work.

Characteristically the directors who have come to film from television, regard montage as a much more important part of their skills than did the film-makers of the thirties and the forties. They seem to be closer to the traditions of the silent screen.

Of course, television technique should not be transferred literally and mechanically to the screen. In a television show the set format and the need to keep viewers under constant pressure (recalling, curiously, Eisenstein's 'montage of attractions') often leads to a certain crowding of technical effects, the over-employment of the tricks of the camera. But a film director cannot submit to the temptation to dazzle with a display of his continuous, technical virtuosity. George Roy Hill, the maker of *Butch Cassidy and the Sundance Kid*, who also learned his craft in television, confirms that it takes time to overcome those temptations. 'When you first start', he says, 'you use TV techniques, slamming in close-ups, using crazy angles and dazzling footwork so the public won't notice how bad the script is. Then you learn that the great directors don't move their camera. They nail it to the ground and move the actors.'[37]

Former television directors who have managed the successful transition to film all corroborate the Frankenheimer view that television offers the best training ground for film-makers. Elliot Silverstein from the TV Alcoa Video Theatre, who directed the successful comedy *Cat Ballou*, employs a colourful simile in his praise of this practical film university: 'TV is like learning your craft in a pressure cooker. If you can survive that, you're ready for anything.'[38] Jack Smight (*Kaleidoscope*) agrees that television is the best place for the young starting out on their professional life. They have an immediate chance to put in practice what they have learnt, to test their growing skills.

Sydney Pollack, the director of *They Shoot Horses, Don't They?*, who spent his youth in a TV studio, draws attention to another influence of television. He has directed Chrysler Theatre productions and several episodes of the popular serials, *The Defenders*, *The Fugitive* and *Dr Kildare*. In his view television directors (and he is certainly an outstanding example of this) brought to film a new sense, and a new application of realism. They like to approach a subject in a documentary manner, to reveal the context in which events are taking place. This way of looking puts greater demand on the director's inventiveness and imagination, making, in effect, for a greater creative freedom.[39]

The television generation has changed considerably the artistic character and the content of the American cinema, breaking through its rigid routines, its blind adherence to conventions that were current twenty or thirty years ago. Perhaps the change would have come anyway, even without the impact of television, but the process would have taken longer and the outcome might not have been quite so decisive. In this sense film was helped by its arch rival, especially since it became an industrial giant in its own right. As John Frankenheimer has said: 'When I found that television was turning into a purely film and tape medium I started thinking about leaving. I thought, if I'm to work on film, I'll work in the real film.'[40]

Anyone Can Be a Director

Mervyn Le Roy, a veteran director with over fifty feature films to his credit, not counting those he has only produced, speaks disparagingly about the youngest generation of directors. 'We have guys making pictures who never saw a studio,'[41] he says. And it is true that today anyone with a little shrewdness, a bit of impudence and courage, and at least a suspicion of talent can make a film. Not just in the 'underground cinema' where the door is kept wide open to all, but officially, with expectations of a normal cinema release. Studios directed by the new bosses do not mind experimenting from time to time. The risk, as practice has shown, proves not infrequently worth while. Small-budget films, directed by young and unknown film-makers, have been known to pay handsomely.

These young, creative artists, youths in their early twenties eager to set out and conquer the world – where do they come from? The natural store of talent is provided by universities and colleges running film courses. In 1970 there were 301 of them, 100 more than in 1969. An army of teachers give lectures and direct practical exercises, while a 3,000-strong multitude of students prepares to take a university diploma or a degree on some aspect of film-making. Graduates from all those teaching establishments, representing variable standards and, on the whole, limited resources, for a long time found it impossible to cross the threshold of a major studio as independent film-makers. Mostly they were looking for, and getting, some work in educational television or short films. The feature film industry seemed an impregnable fortress.

The man who first achieved the breakthrough and actually entered the fortress was Francis Ford Coppola, a graduate of Los Angeles U.C.L.A. While still a student he was noticed by Sam Goldwyn who gave him a prize for a scripting exercise. Coppola worked as an assistant to Roger Corman and then directed his first feature film at the age of twenty-two, whilst still a student at U.C.L.A. He describes this first undertaking, *Dementia 13*, as 'a horror film, with a lot of people getting killed with axes and so forth. It had very good reviews and I made money on it. In England it was released as *The Haunted and the Hunted*.'[42] His next feature, *You're a Big Boy Now* (1967) was a fair success, both artistically and commercially. Coppola became a member of the narrow *élite*, directing big-budget musicals and other prestige projects, writing Oscar-winning screenplays (such as for Franklin Schaffner's *Patton*), organizing, from a San Francisco base, his own production set up. Success did not spoil this first American university-produced feature film director. On the contrary, it confirmed him in the belief that personal films, produced as cheaply as possible, but placing no restrictions on the director's need to express himself, are a viable proposition. The world-wide success of *The Godfather* made Francis Ford Coppola number one American film director. In September 1972 he formed, with two other highly successful film directors (William Friedkin of *The French Connection* fame and Peter Bogdanovich (*The Last Picture Show* and *What's Up Doc*) the Directors Company. The three bright young men, all under thirty-five, will produce and direct twelve films over a period of six years, being four for each them. Paramount Pictures Corporation is 100 per cent responsible for the finance and later for distribution of the production output: profits will be split fifty-fifty between Paramount and the Directors Company. Each director will have total control over his picture, once the project has been approved by a six-man board of the Directors

Company, this board to consist of the three directors and three delegates from Paramount.

One of the films supervised by Coppola in his capacity as a producer in his own American Zoetrope Production Co. was a science fiction film with the rather foreboding title of *THX 1138 4 EB*, directed by George Lucas, born in 1946. At twenty-one Lucas, a student at the University of Southern California, entered for the 1967 Los Angeles Festival of Student Films a fifteen-minute fantasy about a grim society of the future, run by computers and television monitors. This little exercise, shot on a Los Angeles location, showed not only familiarity with Orwell and Huxley but a remarkable cinematic talent. And then an extraordinary thing happened, unknown in the entire history of Hollywood. Warner Brothers offered the student a contract to make a full-length feature film on the same theme, under the artistic supervision of Coppola. *THX 1138* reached the screen in March 1970, getting a very sympathetic reception from the critics. *Newsweek* found *THX 1138* amazingly professional for a first film.[43]

Not every film graduate at the many American universities running such courses can meet with the same success, but the importance of Lucas is that a precedent has been created, and the leap from student exercise to professional feature is now possible. At the moment, Lucas is probably the youngest of the directors working for a big studio, but there are other film-makers of his generation, only a year or two older, directing or producing full-length features: for example, Paul Williams (*The Revolutionary*) or Dennis Friedland and Chris Dewey (*Joe*). Peter Bogdanovich, one of the most successful young directors and partner of Coppola in the Directors Company, is not a graduate of a film department in an American university. His entrance into film-making reminds one somehow of the film débuts of his French colleagues from the New Wave. Like Truffaut, Chabrol or Godard he learned film direction in the projection room, of the Museum of Modern Art in New York; he wrote both interesting and learned books on the art of film direction of Alfred Hitchcock, Howard Hawks, John Ford and Fritz Lang; he made his first feature film in 1968, *Targets,* almost without money and technical facilities. In 1972 his two films, a burlesque comedy *What's Up Doc* and a serious drama, *The Last Picture Show,* found themselves in the top ten big rentals in the U.S.A. and Canada.

It seems doubtful if there was ever in the history of the American cinema such an eruption of talent, of new artistic personalities, as the one now taking place, unless it was in the pioneering period, before the First World War, when no distinction was made between amateur and professional film-makers. The profession, with its exclusive circles of trained experts, only formed itself during the twenties. Today history appears to be moving back to a similar point. Professionalism is no longer a magic sign, opening a door to a treasure accessible only to a small, privileged group. The rules of the game are no longer being enforced. It is now possible to enter the Hollywood world by a side door, even under the flag of protest against the established, traditional American cinema. This is how the actress Barbara Loden (Mrs Elia Kazan in private life) did it with her film *Wanda,* which in the spring of 1971 achieved a normal release.

Barbara Loden's contempt for slick, expertly made Hollywood films is central to her own artistic beliefs. 'I hate slick pictures,' she says. 'They are too perfect to be believable.'[44] The smoother, the more polished the surface of the film, the more trite and banal is the content. Hollywood, for Barbara Loden, is a world of false values, where with most fantastic equipment and resources vessels of lead are being built. Of course, they will not float. They sink.

Barbara Loden managed to raise from the Foundation of Film Makers over $50,000, wrote the screenplay, cast herself in the principal part, and shot, wholly on location and in real interiors, a full-length psychological feature, *Wanda.* On 16 mm, of course. But when the fruit of her labours turned out to be quite successful, the film was blown up to 35 mm and passed on to distributors. *Wanda* is now being screened in the same cinemas that are also exhibiting, and will go on exhibiting, 'slick' Hollywood films, while the critics are praising Barbara Loden for her ability to pose and solve a serious problem with purely cinematic means. Film-makers are born, not manufactured.

Michael Wadleigh is a different sort of rebel against the Hollywood establishment. A student of medicine, after graduation he set up, with a couple of friends, a small production company for documentary films – Paradigm Films. For four years he directed for television and various sponsors short- and medium-length social documentaries. His film about the American Negroes fighting in Vietnam gained him a wide popularity in radical circles. The title, *No Vietnamese Ever Called Me Nigger*, sums up the political attitude of the director. Then, unexpectedly, Wadleigh made *Woodstock*, a full-length cinema verité report from a pop festival, wordy and with countless songs, but also interesting as a sociological study of the phenomenon. Acquired by Warner Brothers, applauded by all young audiences, *Woodstock* broke box office records all over the world.

The emergence of Wadleigh, Barbara Loden, Coppola and Lucas are symptoms of a radical change. But the process is by no means smooth and idyllic. The bosses are understanding and accommodating, ready to discuss anything up to a point – the point of commercial viability. There are no philanthropists among them. According to Daniel Selznick, assistant to the Universal producer, Ned Tannen: 'The studios are in business to make money, not to finance art. The conflict between the young directors and the studios is implicit in the fact that the movies are the most expensive art form in the history of man.'[45]

All the same, the shift of power that has taken place is very real and its effects already marked. As Frank Perry, a young director who made his début in 1962 with his very sensitive *David and Lisa*, puts it: 'What you're seeing now is the flowering of personal cinema in America. It's a revolution that can't be reversed.'[46]

4

In the Realm of Politics

A Fantasy Landscape and a Real One

According to Michael Laughlin, a young producer in his early thirties, in the old days when the film industry was in the hands of immigrants from Central and Eastern Europe, the screen image of America reflected their own fantasies. This was the America they had dreamt of in their youth in the old country, and when later they struggled through to become rulers of Hollywood they put the dream into films. This was their new, chosen Mother-country perfect in every detail, the Promised Land of boundless future potential, the land of freedom, of plenty.[1]

It was not only film producers who looked at the United States through rainbow-coloured spectacles. So did the millions of cinema-goers, from Alaska to Texas, from California to the Atlantic coast. They were obviously aware that in the pictures shimmering across the darkened halls there was an element of fairy-tale, some food for day-dreaming, that it was all fiction, but the dream landscape, and the dream environment, and also the screen heroes who moved in that fantasy context, were taken at least half-seriously. After all, America allowed a chance of dream-fulfilment to some, and the great majority could live decently, in peace and fair comfort. For a time, during the years of Depression, the screen ideal of America seemed to waver and some new, critical, realistic features appeared, but eventually it all came back to '*status quo ante*'. Hollywood fairy-tales were even used to fight off the looming threat of television. While the deep-rooted recipes and conventions were seen to be backed up by the public, nothing could shake the film industry's confidence that its attitudes were right and proper.

But towards the end of the fifties and in the early sixties something began to rot. Cinema attendances were falling year after year, and not all of those who did buy tickets were pleased with the publicized Hollywood product. The dream landscape, although presented in rich colour and on a wide screen, no longer made them happy. The fairy-tales about prosperity, success and joy no longer entertained. The gap between the screen image of life and the outside reality was widening all the time. Troubles multiplied and the mood of unrest was spreading. The Promised Land, the land of opportunity, the American way of life – formulas ingrained by school, church and press – were being insufficient, useless, offensively false. The image of a happy America was fading, melting away – first, the image of the outside, everyday reality; and then, consequently, its screen image, even more perfect and beautiful.

When the two 'easy riders', Wyatt, calling himself Captain America, and Billy meet in a prison cell in a small Texas town the drunkard George Hanson, a young lawyer and former civil rights activist fighting to improve the lot of the American Negro and now trying to drown his sense of the futility of life in whisky, Hanson communicates to his new comrades the following observation: 'You know, this used to be a hell of a good country. I don't know what happened to it. . . .'

What happened to America? Why is it that neither the old nor the young feel happy about life there? Why are both troubled by anxiety? American society is tormented by numerous problems it seems unable to cope with and yet it must face them, it must cope or the future cannot look bright. Indeed, it seems a distinctive feature of the times that Americans, naturally optimistic, have changed into pessimists. And it is the middle classes, making up the three-fifths of the population, the people who believed longest and most doggedly in the American way of life and unquestioningly accepted its screen image, it is they who now see the forthcoming years in dark colours. In a poll conducted by a Gallup Institute for *Newsweek* in the summer of 1969, based on a representative sample of families with annual incomes ranging between $5,000 and $15,000, 46 per cent considered that the country's situation had deteriorated in the past ten years and 58 per cent believed that in the next decade the deterioration would continue.[2] Such an open admission of scepticism about the future is without precedent in American polling practice. It vividly demonstrates the deep-seated crisis the society is going through. The old, unshaken imponderables are visibly breaking up and disintegrating.

The origins of these pessimistic attitudes were no doubt very complex, but three causes came to the fore, three nagging and constantly recurring motifs: the war in Vietnam; racial conflicts, involving the black minority; and the future of the young generation, unable to communicate with the great majority of the old generation. When one adds to this economic problems and deteriorating conditions of life in the big cities, the catalogue of worries looks pretty formidable. But inflation and rising prices can be lived with, pollution and the destruction of natural environment are not exclusive to America; only the problems of Vietnam, the black minority, and their rebellious youth are inherently American. They kept and are still keeping people awake at night, parents as well as children. Not the nuclear holocaust (only 2 per cent of the sample are worried about that), but rather until recently the threat of death in the jungles of Vietnam, and today as yesterday a death in a black ghetto, or on a college campus. The threat is ever-present, the wave of violence, of repression and counter-reprisals is rising. It is fertile soil for the growth of intolerance and hate, for the polarization of the old and the young, the black and the white, the enforcers of law and the reformers. Social tensions escalate. With the harm done apparent everywhere, a search for the guilty is on, scapegoats are wanted. Fascist attitudes germinate in the general mood of restlessness and confusion.

For millions of people who, until recently, believed in the unshakeable strength of American democracy and the American capitalist economy, for Nixon's 'silent majority', the conservatives and the traditionalists, the enemy is everyone who tries to change or subvert the established order.

Until the armistice they were, first of all, the Vietnamese and their allies at home and abroad, all opponents of keeping 'Pax Americana' in South-East Asia, then the blacks with their excessive demands, unwelcome to the whites, and lastly the young, rejecting the sacred values of country, family and church. In this respect no distinction is made between the long-haired and bare-footed hippies and the university campus revolutionaries. They ought to be taught a lesson, all those subversives of various colours and shades. Strong repressive measures are recommended.

A nurse in East Keansburg, New Jersey, was against messing about in Vietnam. She advised the American army to 'bomb them all out and come back home'. A manager of a furniture store in a place called Peru, in Indiana, said 'all students taking part in college riots ought to be locked up in concentration camps' and an even more extreme remark came from a man living in San Leandro near Berkeley, California: 'We ought to have a Hitler here, to get rid of all these troublemakers in the way the Germans did the Jews.'[3]

Can one wonder that in this climate the other side, the accused and the branded, is also not sparing with invective directed against the law and order lovers? Arlo Guthrie, the folk singer and the hero of *Alice's Restaurant* observes that 'In New York and around here they're pretty human, but on the West Coast they're really Nazis.' And he asks half ironically, half in earnest, what would happen if one day all the hippies suddenly cut their hair and put on conventional dress. 'People wouldn't know who to hate and who to like and who to arrest.'[4] *Easy Rider* describes how a conventional society, set in its ways, treat the long-haired but not necessarily rebellious youth. The bloody end that Hanson, Wyatt and Billy meet with is by no means implausible, or exaggerated. Prejudice is blind and anyone can fall a victim to it. Police records are full of very true stories about how easy it is to reach for a gun to clear the world of hostile elements. . . .

The Vietnam Issue

For many years television has been continuously reporting the events in South-East Asia. It spared no images of destruction, death and horror. This undeclared, informal war is the first armed conflict in history recorded by cameras day by day. Physically distant, raging thousands of miles away, it was also closer than any other war before it. Just switch a set on and you saw it in black and white, or increasingly, in a full range of colours. And when you were not actually watching it, you kept hearing about it, at the round-table discussions, interviews with politicians and generals and the White House press conferences.

But not in a cinema. Vietnam appeared there hardly at all, only on very rare occasions. In the traditional Hollywood belief cinema is a place of entertainment, and you do not entertain the public with unpleasant affairs. But this explanation of the scarcity of films about Vietnam seems far too simple to ring true. After all, during the Korean war at least a dozen films were made about the American forces' involvement in it under the 'official' patronage of UNO. The Korean War was never popular, inspired no great enthusiasm, but it was never hated as is the Vietnamese War, both by the 'hawks' who demand a quick and decisive victory as well as by the 'doves' who want an immediate withdrawal from Indo-China. Here lies the heart of the matter: the film establishment was afraid to touch themes that are not only unpopular but also controversial. Only 8 per cent of the sample in the Gallup poll, mentioned above, believed that the United States were winning the war, while as many as 70 per cent, whatever their opinion of the rights and wrongs of the intervention, considered that the American boys should have been at home, not in Vietnam.

Films about Vietnam were made by independent documentary producers who did not expect their work to be widely distributed, such as Emilio De Antonio, who directed and produced two compilation films, about Senator McCarthy (*Point of Order*) and the assassination of President Kennedy (*Rush to Judgement*). In 1969 his Vietnam film, *In the Year of the Pig* reached the screen. Using newsreel material shot in the theatre of war and available at various national archives, including the North Vietnamese one, and interspersing it with television interviews with recognized experts in the field (both opponents and supporters of American involvement) De Antonio created a valuable documentary work describing the events of the last few years against a full historical background. One of the clear advantages of *In the Year of the Pig* is the author's restraint in commenting directly on the situation. He lets the pictures and the others talk and yet his attitude comes through with more than sufficient force. The conflict of apparently contradictory views on the screen makes the film all the more interesting and persuasive. De Antonio himself describes it as political theatre. The French *Far from Vietnam* seems much weaker, with its wordiness and uncomfortably obtrusive staging of some sequences. *In the Year of the Pig* is superior in the restrained way it uses its highly dramatic and emotive material, in the logic of its argument, the precision and clarity of its structure. In short, it has all the advantages of a truly documentary work.

In cinematic fiction a counterpart to *In the Year of the Pig* was never really on. A start was made from a different direction, in praise of the American intervention. The film, *The Green Berets*, went into production in 1967, and not without misgivings. Probably no fictional picture of the Americans in Vietnam would ever have been made if it was not for the personal influence of John Wayne. Wayne could take the liberty and he wanted to. He wanted to, because he was passionately on the side of the 'hawks', and as one of the most consistently popular Hollywood stars he was able to do it. The 'Duke', as he is known, the legendary hero of countless Westerns, the embodiment of all manly virtues, of the toughness and the resilience of the Wild West conquerors, was possessed of a sufficient authority to break through the obligatory cinematic silence on the subject. In 1967 an independent company, Batjac Films, produced *The Green Berets*, and a year later the film appeared on the screen under the banner of Warner Brothers.

John Wayne's position is extremely simple: a continuous battle between good and evil is going on and the Vietnam War has to be seen in that context. It is really the same scheme of things as in his other films where, in the Wild West, white colonizers fight against Red Indians. 'Once you go over there,' John Wayne said in one of the interviews, 'you won't be middle of the road. Bobby Kennedy and Fulbright and all these goddam Let's-be-sweet-to-our-dear-enemies guys, all they're doing is helping the Reds and hurting their own country.'[5]

John Wayne not only played the principal part of a valiant colonel, but he also co-directed the film. Unofficially, without a credit, he was being helped by the old pro, Mervyn Le Roy. James Lee Barrett's novel was adapted for the screen by Robin Moore. The action, bristling with battle encounters and heroic incidents, centres around a figure of a sceptical journalist who, coming into contact with the work of the 'green berets', changes his position and becomes a supporter of the war.

The main location was not in Vietnam, but in Georgia, in Fort Benning, a military base lent them by the Pentagon. In the House of Representatives a democratic Congressman from New York, B. S. Rosenthal, objected to the provision of this sort of services, for which the authorities accepted in payment a laughable sum of $18,000, in proportion to the total production budget of $10 million. The producer, Mike Wayne, the son of John, argued that in addition $170,000 was spent on 'reconstruction and improvements' of the fort, and $300,000 was paid to the military extras.[6] But whatever the size of the expenditure it cannot conceal the fact of the Pentagon's willing support for the production. *The Green Berets* opened amidst heated controversies and the protest campaign organized by groups of 'doves'. In effect the protests availed them little, or even perhaps, as frequently happens, only drew attention to the work so violently criticized and condemned. In its first year of exhibition *The Green Berets* took over $8 million at the American box office. Startlingly, this success was not followed up with other Vietnam films, discounting a few B pictures, like the disgraceful, artistically as well as politically, *The Losers*, directed in 1970 by Jack Starrett. Without a collaboration of someone like Wayne Hollywood could not risk a major film about the unpopular war. And no other star personality came forward.

In place of films about the Vietnam War appeared films about the Vietnam problem. Some described the feelings and attitudes of the young men called up for military service, others treated war themes with full awareness that they would find an audience receptive to analogies and allusive hints. In both cases the authors' position was made uncompromisingly clear: they were opposed to the Vietnam War, considering it a futile, if not actually a criminal, affair.

Perhaps the most open and frank criticism of the Johnson–Nixon position is contained in *Alice's Restaurant*, directed by Arthur Penn. It is a semi-biographical work: Arlo Guthrie the folk singer, author of the popular ballad 'Slaughter in Alice's Restaurant', plays the leading character who, having left the Rocky Mountain College in Montana, moves into a hippy community inhabiting a deserted church in Stockbridge, Massachussets. Here Arlo commits a 'criminal act', depositing on Thanksgiving Day some rubbish in a street, because he finds the municipal dump closed. He is arrested and sentenced to a $50 fine. Called before the draft-board he is judged to be unfit for military service because of his recent 'criminal record'. Arno comments on their decision: 'You want to know if I'm moral enough to join the army, burn women, kids, houses and villages after being a litter bug?' The film also makes clear that Arlo Guthrie first entered the college to defer the draft, but backed out seeing what the studies are leading to. Superficially, the Vietnam problem is only peripheral in *Alice's Restaurant*, but its importance far outgrows the footage devoted to it. Leaving the cinema one retains a vivid memory of the draft scene. For the young generation – both the hippies among them and the 'normal' ones, as some would insist on calling them – the Vietnam question was literally a question of life and death.

Two comedies treat war themes in a significantly new manner: Robert Altman's *M.A.S.H.* (1970) and Mike

Nichols' *Catch 22* (1970). The aptitude and propriety of classing them as comedy may in both these cases seem doubtful. Can the action of *M.A.S.H.*, placed during the Korean War in a field hospital swamped in blood, human entrails and amputated bits of flesh, be regarded as admissible comedy material? The bloodiest-ever, vividly Technicolored reds make it even difficult to describe the humour in *M.A.S.H.* (the letters stand for Mobile Army Surgical Hospital) as 'black'. *Catch 22* also has its quota of entrails pouring out of an opened abdominal cavity (again in Technicolour), as well as futile deaths, intentionally criminal bombing raids, and images of sordid destitution in the liberated Italy. The action here is in the Italian campaign of 1944–5. And yet these are comedies, meant to provoke laughter as well as a sense of outrage and awe. And laughter predominates, even if it is caustic laughter, by no means drowning other feelings and thoughts. This is especially true about *M.A.S.H.*, and perhaps less so about the grotesque and in places nightmarish *Catch 22*.

The screenplay of *M.A.S.H.* was the work of Ring Lardner Jr, once black-listed in Hollywood as a communist or communist sympathizer. It was adapted from Richard Hooker's novel, describing strange adventures of drafted young surgeons who suddenly found themselves in the surreal world of the field hospital. Superficially, military order and bureaucracy prevail here. On the inside everyone tries to manage his life so as not to be drowned in the blood of the war victims and, indeed, to isolate himself from the absurdity of war. In the dock stand accused the entire mad Korean adventure and the inhuman stupidity of the chiefs, the leaders, the generals. The conclusion is optimistic: in the confrontation with the Pentagon bureaucracy it is the civilians who win – the doctors who know their work, who take no notice of any sacred rules but bring help and relief to the wounded and the sick. Even at football the unruly rebels beat, if not quite within the rules, the uniformed army professionals. Common sense wins out in the end. Why not apply it to the hopelessly muddled, diplomatically and militarily, Vietnam War?

Catch 22 is a more serious matter, though the film is perhaps not quite so immediately striking, less funny and a bit harder going. Joseph Heller's best-selling novel of the same title appeared in 1961. The bulky volume was adapted by scriptwriter Buck Henry, who eliminated a number of subplots and streamlined the sprawling narrative, centring it on two main characters: Captain Yossarian, the air force pilot, and Lieutenant Milo Minderbinder. The action is placed in the air force base on the island of Pianosa, off the western coast of Italy between Elba and Corsica. The war is about to end and the bombing raids serve no purpose. But the crazy personal ambitions of the commanders lead them to increase continuously the number of daily missions. There are really no sane men on the base except Captain Yossarian, dreaming and scheming all the time how to break out of this closed circle of vicious nonsense. There appears to be one way out: a flyer certified insane is discharged and returned home. Rule 22 states that anyone can submit to expert medical opinion, but there is a catch, only a demonstrably sane man can feel that war is insane and try to opt out. . . .

The film describes successive attempts by Yossarian (a brilliant performance by Alan Arkin) to throw off his hate-uniform and stop dropping bombs on the peaceful Italian villages and townships. The viewer is never certain if he is watching real events, or the screen projection of the hero's fantasies and dreams. Hence the feeling of being involved in a nightmare, in a ghastly farce, its logic ruled by pure nonsense. The feeling is heightened by the character of Minderbinder, the financial genius, who uses war as an opportunity for some extraordinary trading and currency operations. Behind the scenes Minderbinder grows into a dominating, dictator figure, and his syndicate, M & M, becomes sovereign, with powerful influence in the head-quarters of both the opposing armies. When his enterprise is threatened with bankruptcy the resourceful lieutenant organizes a bombing raid by the American air force to wipe out its own base. The surrealist fantasy reaches its conclusion with the triumphant progress through the streets of Rome of the new Caesar. Or a new Hitler?

Mike Nichols himself explains the emphasis placed on the character of Milo Minderbinder. 'Milo is not a real person, he can't be real. He exists to underline the central idea of *Catch 22*. The film even more than the book, I believe, is about the making of money out of the death of others; this theme is stronger in the film because Milo goes to mad extremes in his operations, much further than in the book. ... In reality my film is about capitalism. In other words, decisions, especially moral decisions, are made by money. Not by people who have money, but by the very idea of money.'

According to Buck Henry, the screen-writer, Heller's book seems prophetic, especially when you relate it to what is going on in Vietnam. And Mike Nichols adds his own comment: 'A headless monster, an act of aggression without a decision to attack being taken by any one individual – everything that's characteristic of the Vietnam situation is also characteristic of *Catch 22*.'[7]

The problem of responsibility for the criminal acts of war lies at the heart of the Nichols' film, and, of today's America. The conversation inside an aeroplane between Yossarian and the pilot Nately could have referred to the My Lai trial of Lieutenant Calley. Yossarian, asked to drop bombs on Ferrars, observes that there are no Germans there, no munition stores, no railway junction, no port. There are only people, ordinary, local Italians and a convent. But Nately is unconvinced: the place might have some strategic significance. Yossarian: 'What the devil are we doing here?' Nately: 'It's not our business to ask.' Yossarian: 'And whose business?'

Catches 22 forces people to ask these questions. It is to Nichols' credit that under another guise he introduced to the screen the festering wound of Vietnam. Funny war pictures challenge the viewer to reflect on the unfunny reality. The American war in Vietnam is over. The American soldiers and P.O.W.s have come back home. One of the most tragic chapters of contemporary history seems to be closed, but the years of bloodshed, of political and military blunders have left many marks on the life of the nation which will not be easily removed. And the cinema will not forget Vietnam. Quite possibly films dealing with this particular subject will now appear more frequently on the screen. Without direct involvement or commitment it may now be easier for film producers to talk about Vietnam from historical distance. Mark Robson's *Limbo*, a film about Vietnam war wives, had its premiere in New York in February 1973, after the signing of the armistice.

The Ideal of Freedom

The war in Vietnam was condemned by a great number of people. The big peace rallies drew tens, or even hundreds, of thousands. The greater part of the protesters was made up of young people – those who tomorrow, or the day after, might meet with Yossarian's fate. What are they like, these young opponents of war who burnt their draft cards and loudly demanded the total withdrawal of American forces from South-East Asia? Are they idealists, hippies, pacifists, revolutionaries? The list could be even longer. Obviously there is a difference between the way they see themselves and the older generation's view of them. But they are not a monolithic mass, uniform in character, outlook and manners. They differ greatly, agreeing however on one point: they all reject the traditional American ideals of comfortable security and world dominance. They are against the 'establishment' in all the fields of public life, in politics, in education from primary to the university level, in the church (or rather churches), in the mass media, and even in family life. One hears about them constantly, meets with them everywhere. Only the cinema ignored them for a long time, or showed them as a one-sided, distorted reflection. The film-makers' interest was peripheral, centred on gangs of juvenile delinquents, as in Roger Corman's *The Wild Angels*, but they seemed not to notice the mainstream, the mass movement, the entire youth subculture.

A paradoxical situation, when one keeps in mind that the great majority (62 per cent exactly) of the American cinema-going public is made up of young people, aged between twelve and thirty years. It seemed as if the truth about them was being withheld from them in favour of worn-out stereotypes and formulas. There were several reasons behind this Hollywood attitude. Firstly, for years producers as well as directors were people of the old generation, used to the traditional ideas about the young who 'must have their fling', and believing that whatever moved them was of no real consequence. Secondly, the old men of the cinema could not understand, or did not want to understand, the processes of social change. Thirdly, the studios were afraid that films about the young would not interest the older viewer and could lead to the further dwindling of the audiences. Who knows, the elders might feel offended by such an intrusion of the young? There was need of conclusive proof that all these views were false and that the time had come for the young to enter the American film in a double capacity: as creators and as screen heroes.

The crucial breakthrough was achieved by two films: *Easy Rider* and *Woodstock*. Shot very cheaply, they brought in multimillion dollar profits. Treated with disdain by the Hollywood 'establishment' studios they came through as winners and set a trend to be followed. Since their triumph youth became fashionable.

The idea for *Easy Rider* originated with two young actors – Peter Fonda and Dennis Hopper. Terry Southern helped them to script it. Long drawn-out negotiation seemed to lead nowhere and the project, like so many others, looked like being shelved indefinitely. Then Bert Schneider, an independent producer partnering Robert Rafelson in the Reybert Productions company appeared on the scene. All the people concerned with *Easy Rider* were of about the same age, around thirty, just under or just over. Schneider advanced the money – about $400,000. Fonda and Hopper shared the two principal acting parts and the two main jobs behind the camera: Fonda became the producer, Hopper the director. Columbia agreed to handle the distribution of the finished film. In May 1969 *Easy Rider* won over European Cannes Festival audiences, and soon after that it began its triumphant progress through the American screens. Its success in West

European capitals was nothing short of fantastic. Until the end of 1972 the film grossed in the United States and in Canada $18·5 million.

Woodstock was a similar case. In August 1969, in the little town of Bethel in the northernmost part of New York State, a festival of pop music was organized. Actually, it was announced under the more modest name of 'fair' rather than festival. In the fields surrounding the hastily constructed artists' platform countless crowds gathered. Hundreds of thousands, perhaps a million. There are no reliable statistics, and the legend has multiplied the multitude. Music and singing went on for seventy-two hours – three days and nights, with one unplanned break caused by a tremendous downpour which flooded the fields, turning the scene of the festival into a huge, muddy pool. All these extraordinary happenings were recorded by twelve busy 16 mm cameras. There was enough film shot to provide 120 hours of screen time. A picture lasting just over three hours was edited out of it. The film crew was directed by the documentary film-maker, Michael Wadleigh. At first the festival organizers demanded astronomical sums for the film rights, but when no takers came forward, the independent producer was authorized to cover the event at his own financial risk. The edited film was acquired by Warner Brothers and the *Easy Rider* success story was repeated all over again. The box office takings until January 1973 in the United States and Canada came to $14·6 million.

Both films were accepted by the young viewer as his own. And for the first time the official Hollywood cinematic powers, agreeing to handle the distribution of these works by independent and little-known creators, accepted, in practice, the desirability of showing a truer image of the young generation. *Woodstock* proved that talking about 'gangs' and 'isolated cases' is absurd. The movement was clearly a mass phenomenon. It developed its own manners and ethical standards, proclaiming the ideals of peace, freedom and love. Statements by the Woodstock festival participants leave no doubt about the sincerity of the views they hold. One could call them naïve, question their adolescent, or perhaps even childish, idealism, point out the lack of a coherent practical programme, but they obviously mean what they say. The content of the songs performed from the platform, and of the conversations between the young viewers, is the same: they appeal for honesty in human relationships, for a breakaway from the lies and compromises of conventional life, for the rejection of values and way of life offered by 'the establishment'. Representatives of a different America, of a new American society, had reached the screen.

What *Woodstock* reported in a true documentary manner, *Easy Rider* complemented using the freedom of a story-film. Not only complemented, but also expanded and deepened, making complex the feelings which, in *Woodstock*, appeared simple and, in the final account, optimistic. The young at the festival were among their own kind, at home in the huge, exclusive gathering, with the few remaining representatives of the older generation forced outside. The local farmers and small traders were glad of the opportunities to supplement their earnings, and, at the same time, aghast at what was going on. 'It's too big to be put into words' – said one of the local shopkeepers.

In *Easy Rider* there is a different situation. The heroes represent a minority, they have few allies; on the contrary, they are surrounded by enemies. What do Billy and Wyatt stand for? They want to live a free life, to see the world, they like the feeling of speed, the beauty of the land, the taste of marijuana. A hedonistic programme, lacking in high ambition, and with unclear perspectives for the future. And to be realized with money made from a sale of hard drugs. Breaking the official law of the land is of course of no account to the heroes, but their sense of solidarity might have been troubled by the fact that the treasure they dispose of will be used by the rich pusher to exploit their own friends and comrades. And another thing, perhaps the most important, the two motor-cyclists, setting off from California to New Orleans, possess all the attributes of freedom. They have money and no obligations, the means to move around, to see and to experience everything. Worlds of adventure open up to them.

Confrontations with the real world around them are painful and in the end tragic. The young ones are persecuted, chased away, and in the end physically destroyed. They cannot, or perhaps feel unable to, stop long enough to get used to any one place. Not even in the early Christian hippy commune, working the land. They are searching for something different, better, fuller. Here Peter Fonda and Dennis Hopper are right on target: young people, rejecting the 'establishment' and proclaiming the ideals of freedom, are constantly searching for a way to express these ideas in practical, day-to-day life. At the same time they are striving to discover their self-identity, and finding it even more difficult. The picture is clear and persuasive, getting the point forcefully across to viewers as young as their screen heroes. On one side there are the non-conformist young, living their own searching lives, impractical and inconsistent, but denying everything around them that has the stamp of tradition and authority. On the other side are the old, or at least the older, the ordinary bread-eaters, perhaps also dreaming of change, but fettered to the daily treadmill of work, to the humdrum business of earning their living. The more tolerant and sophisticated 'old' might have tried to set up some kind of dialogue with the young ones, but this is not how it is, especially not in the far-out provinces. There intolerance reigns supreme and all long-haired scroungers, tramps, all preachers of the new religion of total freedom, qualify for persecution.

Easy Rider exaggerates – which in art can be right and proper – those two opposing positions: the motor-cyclist wanderers in search of freedom and themselves, and the groups of rigid supporters of the conventional order, allowing no deviation from the familiar rules of the game.

The search for identity and for such forms of existence as would make practical the ideals of freedom and let one overcome the pulverizing weight of the 'establishment' is a constantly recurring theme in films about the younger generation. And the search almost as a rule takes place on the road, in travels, on the trail of these twentieth-century Don Quixotes. In *Midnight Cowboy* Joe Buck, leaving behind his small town in Texas and moving on to New York is looking in a different way for the same thing that has evaded Billy and Wyatt in *Easy Rider*. To put it bluntly, he would like to avail himself of the fruits of freedom, without dirtying his hands with work. He has had enough of it in his country town. In *Alice's Restaurant* Arlo Guthrie is searching for himself and his own way of life. For a time he seems at home in the Stockbridge hippy commune of Alice and Ray, but Arlo feels that this, too, is not the right solution. Ray's words at the wedding party, when he proposes the sale of the church serving as their refuge and the purchase of a farm in Vermont 'where everybody could have his own home . . . see each other only when they wanted to . . . and still be all together,' do not sound too encouraging. Doesn't a home of one's own mark a way back to the middle-class ways and habits, once so violently rejected? No doubt this is the question the film hero asks himself before moving on. But he finds no answer, feeling that yearning after a home and the need for seclusion amidst friends are perhaps among the basically human emotions.

Bobby, the hero of Bob Rafelson's *Five Easy Pieces*, is another one of the seekers and rovers. He differs from Billy, Wyatt, Arlo or Ray in that he feels able to work. He doesn't mind even a strenuous physical effort involved in a job like that of a holer in an oil well. But he is never satisfied and cannot find a proper place for himself. He used to be a musician, but nothing came of it. He could have stayed at home with his wealthy father, but does not want to watch the slow agony of the incurably ill old man. 'This is a guy who is out of touch with his feelings,'[8] is how the director, Bob Rafelson, describes his hero. It may sound enigmatic but it is in fact a relevant comment. Bobby, in fact, would like to understand his feelings, would like to learn what it is that he really wants, whom he loves and what sort of love he needs. Attempts to find himself prove futile, leaving a vague feeling that staying for long in one place, in the same situation, puts him in danger of a sudden distress, a catastrophe. And so he finds himself on the road again, without his jacket, without money, as a hitch-hiker in a passing lorry. 'Everything's got burned,' he says, to explain his get up. This spontaneous lie conceals the truth about the nature of this Jack London-like tramp of the seventies. He burns everything behind him.

The two positions are irreconcilable. The young seek themselves through the rejection of the old order of society. Arthur Penn, the maker of *Alice's Restaurant*, sees the conflict between the generations – because, in the final account, this is largely the conflict in question – clearly and without embellishments: 'This kind of life-style isn't viable beyond a stage, perhaps, and it's dependent on the affluence around them. But these kids belong to America. They belong no place else. It's an indictment of America that these kids can't follow their own sense of honesty and still live in our society.'[9] For the young looking for their own way, seeking their own solutions, there is no room in the country of over 200 million inhabitants. Films like *Easy Rider* and *Alice's Restaurant* make that clear. Paul Newman, the actor–director–producer in one person, sums it up: 'The old heroes used to protect society from its enemies, now it's society itself that's the enemy.'[10]

The Banner of Revolt

Not all young people choose the life of a lone nomad in search of freedom and identity. There are others who seek to take an active part in the fight to transform society. And the fight means not just participating in political discussions, but confrontations with the police or the national guard. These young revolutionaries, or 'new radicals' as they are frequently called, have become the target for the most passionate and fierce attacks by representatives of the 'establishment'. The students, next to the Black Panthers, qualify as Public Enemy No. 1.

The hate – and this is the proper name for it – expressed towards the students by conservative opinion of all shades and denominations originates primarily from the frustrated hopes once held about the content and significance of college education. In the twenties and thirties a group of American films appeared, known as 'Collegians'. They were filled with care-free boys, winning laurels on the sporting fields, drinking coca-cola, flirting innocently with pretty girls. Books were hardly ever mentioned. It was taken for granted that studies were proceeding smoothly and, after completion, a graduate would take his place at his father's side – in an office, a factory or a trading company. As in *The Graduate* of Mike Nichols college was an initial step on the way to a professional or a business career. Reserved at first for the propertied classes, after the Second World War the colleges were gradually becoming more democratic. In the course of fifteen years, from 1955 to 1970, the number of students doubled. At the beginning of the seventies there were over 9 million students at the universities and junior colleges – an army accounting for about 4·5 per cent of the entire population of the United States.

To the great surprise and indignation of the 'right-thinking' supporters of the established order, it became clear, even in the sixties, that the idealized image of student life, as painted in the 'collegians' genre, was very far from the truth. The students not only ran about with the ball and sat diligently for their exams, but also took an interest in many other things. For instance, they asked indiscreet and seditious questions about the system of higher education: was it not anachronistic, did it measure up to the proper standards of knowledge, did it meet the social needs of the latter half of the twentieth century? The Berkeley student rebellion of 1964 began with purely internal problems. Later it increased its scope, embracing the key political issues, especially Vietnam. At the turn of the seventies American colleges became the scene of violence, of riots lasting for days and weeks. There were fatalities in Ohio, in Kent State University, where the bullets of the national guard took the lives of four students.

Films about rebellious students appeared quickly. In 1970 a series of films picturing contemporary college life reached the screen. It included *Getting Straight* directed by Robert Rush, *The Strawberry Statement* directed by Stuart Hagmann, *The Revolutionary* directed by Paul Williams, and Michelangelo Antonioni's *Zabriskie Point*.

These films differed greatly in their artistic quality as well as their social attitudes, but their constant feature is the apparent lack of historical background. As Stephen Farber observes in his study, 'Movies from behind the Barricades', published in *Film Quarterly* (Winter 1970–1)[11] students quite suddenly became aware of what was going on in their country, suddenly became revolutionaries, as if the gradual process by which the college campuses had become radicalized had never existed. After all it was largely the students who, as Freedom Riders, formed the vanguard of the Civil Rights Movement, or were later active in election campaigns on behalf of such candidates as Robert Kennedy or Senator McCarthy. Without that background it is difficult to understand the shift to the left, often accelerated by political disappointments and frustrations, and leading to the setting up of SDS (Students for Democratic Society), designed to guide and co-ordinate the protest movement.

Public response to 'student' films was far from the unanimous acceptance which had greeted *Easy Rider* and *Woodstock*. The critics were rather sparing in their praise, and the students themselves voiced a number of objections. One frequent charge was that Hollywood had a purely commercial interest in the young rebels, and even perhaps – though this is hinted at rather than made explicit – that it hoped at the same time to discredit the movement by holding it up to ridicule.

It is a complex question and all generalizations tend to distort the truth. However, it does not seem right to treat the 'student' films as just another example of the cynicism of the Hollywood establishment. Their makers – with the single exception of Stanley Kramer, the old liberal – are young. Script-writers and directors have a measure of sympathy for the students, and loyally attempt to set out their point of view. It is difficult to believe in their evil intent, in a conspiracy to subvert the movement.

The fact that such suspicions are current at all seems due to the misunderstanding of the comedy convention, or rather a deliberate mixture of conventions employed by the authors – as in *Getting Straight* or *The Strawberry Statement*, the two most representative films on that theme. Both Rush and

Hagmann did not hesitate to include comedy, or even slap-stick effects. Far from glorifying their heroes, they often ridicule their weaknesses, stressing the intimate aspects of great public events. Perhaps this tends to upset the balance of the presentation. Some viewers and critics read into this manner a disrespectful, supercilious attitude to momentous matters. Simon (Bruce Davison), the hero of *The Strawberry Statement*, joins the militant students by accident rather than design. His commitment to the protest movement is not the result of a deep political awareness and a mature choice. Pure chance, and emotional responses play a decisive part. But perhaps this in the end makes the violence of the forces of order all the more frightening – as in the scenes where the charging civil guards seem like blood cousins of the Nazi praetorians from the SA or SS.

Getting Straight has many moments bordering on farce or burlesque. These elements are further emphasized in the acting style of Elliott Gould who plays Harry Bailey, a thirty-year-old ex-serviceman returning to the college to get his degree and qualify as a teacher. Bailey sets himself principally against the college bureaucracy, the cabal of thick-headed professors, and only indirectly gets involved in the protest movement. During the riots he backs out with his student girl-friend and busies himself with love-making. This, also, was resented by some critics.

The Revolutionary, made in England by a young director, Paul Williams, with American actors and for an American distributor, is dead serious about everything. It is based on a novel by Hans Konigsberger, adapted by the author. Originally, the action was placed somewhere in Europe, in the early part of the nineteenth century. The film brings the plot up to date, but places the action 'somewhere in the Free World'. This attempt to universalize the problem did not come off. To explain the student rebellion one must set it in a real place and at a given point of time. *The Revolutionary* addresses the American public, employing allusion and in-nuendo, sometimes vague and misty, occasionally, in the scenes of the scuffles with police, cruelly clear and obvious. An honest attempt, but in the final count less successful than the stylistically heterogeneous films of Rush and Hagmann, provocative and irritating, but more immediate and topical.

Much was expected from *Zabriskie Point*, Antonioni's first American film. But the hopes were not realized. The critics treated the Italian's contribution rather severely, perhaps too dismissively. The public, especially the young public, responded guardedly, without rapture, but also without explicit disapproval.

Antonioni set himself the task of getting to grips with the difficult, complex motivation of the American rebels. Assisted by some SDS activists, he undertook pretty thorough research into the mechanism of the student movements, attending meetings and discussions, observing, in the summer of 1968, with his own eyes the riots at the Chicago Democratic Convention. What he saw made a tremendous impact. Antonioni wrote about it in the Italian press in words full of pathos and a sense of drama. 'In front of my eyes there was a terrifying picture of the forces of the American "establishment", and at the same time a marvellous picture of another America, belonging to the young. . . . These young, many of them, shall learn how to defend themselves, and then – how to attack. All hope for the future of America is here.'[12]

One could expect that the same tone of political and emotional commitment would be echoed in his film. In the event, there is no revolutionary rhetoric in *Zabriskie Point*. Instead, it recalls the mood of this director's earlier, Italian works. Antonioni called it an 'interior' film, analysing the feelings of two young people,[13] frustrated, and especially in the case of the girl, rather passive people, not obviously committed to the cause. The involvement in rioting, the killing of the policeman and the climactic death of the hero – all this comes about through a chain of circumstances. Antonioni is right in his assertion that a story like this could actually happen. But for the viewers a screen story about what is inevitable rather than just plausible would have carried a greater meaning. Antonioni rejected this approach at the very outset.

Perhaps it was unreasonable to expect from a foreigner a

full analysis of a complex social phenomenon. And yet the same director managed in *Blow up* to capture the authentic mood of London, to reveal its significant features, and to present the modern English attractively. In *Zabriskie Point* California seems only a backdrop, with dressed-up props taking the place of really significant features. Intuition, believed by Antonioni to be a key element in creative drive, here proved inadequate. Numerous script-writers engaged on the project, both Italian and American, did not help. Only visually is *Zabriskie Point* faultless.

Hollywood's quick and willing response to the student movement illustrates the breakthrough that has taken place, and the newly increased courage of the producers, even if it is dictated by commercial considerations. These are optimistic features. The not unimportant negative features are the complete inability to show the mechanisms, the drives, or even just the content of the student activities. As a rule the rebels are shown as passionate, tub-thumping orators, motivated by purely emotional drives, which is at best only part of the truth. One comes out of the cinema with a feeling that the affair is not to be taken seriously, that it has no future. Of course, one sympathizes with the beaten and the persecuted, but without being persuaded that they are right in what they do, or that they have any chance of victory.

The views of Gerald Lefcourt, a lawyer, the counsel for the defence in the Black Panthers trial, are worth quoting here: 'They just won't handle a real film about revolution, one that shows the successes of the movement or even its potential for success. People talk about the *Strawberry Statement* and *Getting Straight* – those aren't revolutionary films. Who's kidding who?'[14]

The Black Minority

Already in the early sixties there was a perceptible change in the Hollywood treatment of the Negro minority. A number of traditional taboos and restrictions have lost their validity. Mixed marriages, the involvement of black citizens in the country's political life, or even in social life – these themes which twenty or thirty years ago could not be put on the screen, are quite acceptable now. The old stereotype of a 'faithful servant' has been replaced with a new stereotype, that of a 'black gentleman'. Hollywood now takes delight in presenting the successful representatives of the black minority, who differ from their white colleagues and friends only in respect of the colour of their skins. They are well dressed, apparently prosperous, and blessed with an abundance of virtues, kind-hearted and noble. And, like their poor screen relations of thirty years back, quite unreal. Of course there are in reality black individuals who are well off; the minority is not without a class structure of its own. But those who have 'made it' are by no means typical. Such films promote the attitude that perhaps it isn't worth one's while to fret over the unpleasant social problems when the way to success is now open to everybody. Superficially everything seems in order: a film supports the correct programme of assimilation and integration, but the heart of the matter is elsewhere; starting from a false premise and evading anything that calls for real action, for radical reform, modes of appeasement are propagated. There are different films about the Negro minority, but it is the appeasing pictures which until recently were the most popular, especially when the hero is played by Sidney Poitier, winner of the 1963 Academy Award for the best male performance of the year (in Ralph Nelson's *Lilies of the Field*).[15]

Accepting his Oscar Sidney Poitier commented: 'It was a long road for me,' and no doubt his road to current pre-eminence has been stony and difficult.[15] By 1968 he was not only the best black actor in Hollywood but one of *the* best actors there. He enjoys all the privileges of a star, including the right to approve the screen-play and a say in the choice of director and in the casting of a film. A couple of years ago his fee for a single film was $300,000, and now it is $700,000. This is comparable to the fees commanded by Cary Grant or Paul Newman – the heights of achievement, the heights of success.

In 1967 three films with Sidney Poitier in the principal part scored box office as well as prestige success: two were

American – Norman Jewison's *In the Heat of the Night* and Stanley Kramer's *Guess Who's coming to Dinner*, and one British – *To Sir, with Love*, directed by James Clavell. The first two captured a large booty of Oscars: *In the Heat of the Night* five, including the prize for the best picture of the year, and *Guess Who's Coming to Dinner* two more. Significantly, in both these cases the screenplay was also awarded an Oscar, emphasizing the importance attached to the Negro problem on the American screen. In its morning news bulletin (11 April 1968) Paris Radio placed this item first, ahead of international or home affairs, as politically the most significant piece of news. This is, commented the newscaster, a great triumph of liberal and progressive trends in American film opinion: two pictures preoccupied with the racial question, untouchable until very recently, come first in the Oscar stakes.

And now '*sine ira et studio*', without the bombast of the news bulletin and leaving aside the feeling of real satisfaction that the acting talent of Sidney Poitier has won through, let us delve into the deeper meaning of the new trend. In the first case Poitier plays a very able detective, adept at solving the most difficult crime riddles, displaying much quicker wits than his rather fortuitous white partner – a rough-necked sheriff from a small Mississippi town (Poitier repeated this impersonation in 1970 in *They Call Me Mr Tibbs!*) in the second he is a successful doctor with remarkable scientific achievements to his credit, an eminent specialist in tropical diseases. In the British film he is a model teacher, winning unstinted devotion from his pupils. These are, in other words, three stories of success, views of a black man who manages to get on in the white world. This is the content of the three films.

Thus a new stereotype is being forged: a fully integrated, assimilated Negro, presented, like any other popular hero, as an idealized, shiningly perfect figure. 'Mr Nice Guy dedicated to his work and living as celibately as a Tibetan monk,' is how Bill Cosby, a black television actor, describes the new type. His comment about Sidney Poitier is also worth quoting: 'Sidney's made a few movies where he walks around. Almost as a king would walk. To me this depicted a lonely man – which is what the black man was until he found himself. That character is all alone. He's lost identity.'[16] In *The New Yorker* Brendan Gill contributes yet another view of the modern black screen hero: 'A Madison Avenue sort of Christian saint, selfless and well groomed.' Such screen characters, so successfully created by Sidney Poitier, apart from embodying all the conventional features of Hollywood 'good guy' heroes, also offer a valuable alibi, hinting that 'it cannot be altogether bad, while . . .'[17]

I am not suggesting that there are no Hollywood films that do take account of racial conflicts or that they all present integration as a successfully completed operation. *In the Heat of the Night* does not gloss over the tension existing in the Mississippi settlement between the white and the black inhabitants. But the black protagonist, in the guise of a detective – a classic occupation for a popular screen hero – employs his resourceful wits to defuse the rumbling volcano. It is an optimistic conclusion. The same as in Ralph Nelson's *Tick . . .Tick . . . Tick . . .* where in some God-forsaken hole in the Deep South a black sheriff, played by that popular Negro actor Jimmy Brown, is able to deal successfully with a few white racists.

Things look different in William Wyler's *The Liberation of L. B. Jones*, adapted from a novel by Jesse Hill Ford. No conflicts there seem likely to be solved by friendly persuasion, or by the resilience and the noble sentiments of the black heroes. Wyler describes life in Somertown, a small town in Tennessee, without embellishments or optimistic conclusions. A bullying white cop kills the Negro owner of a funeral parlour. The leading white citizens try to hush up the crime with every indication of success until a black avenger in turn kills the murderer. A family of white liberals leaves Somertown in a mood of bleak pessimism about chances of any change for the better in the South. William Wyler is not sparing in his use of violence and of sexual attractions, perhaps somewhat coarsening and commercializing a theme which deserves rather greater austerity in its screen treatment. But it is to the undoubted credit of both the director and the screen-writer that they have made the conflict sharper and more desperate by the introduction of the second murder, in place of the suicide (as in the novel) of the policeman troubled by his conscience. 'This film was made to open the eyes of the racists,'[18] says William Wyler.

Racism can be opposed in a variety of ways: seriously, with humour, or even through science fiction. In *Change of Mind* the authors (screen-writers and co-directors Seeleg Lester and Richard Wesson), describe the consequences of a brain transplant, from a white skull into a black body. This black-and-white creature is played by a Negro actor, Raymond St Jacques. Melvin Van Peebles in the comedy, *Watermelon Man*, undergoes another extraordinary transformation: an intransigent white racist, passing no opportunity to demonstrate his supposedly inherent superiority over all of his black-skinned fellow men, wakes up one day to find himself black all over. Ointments and deep X-ray treatment do not help – he becomes a Negro. Stripping down in a bathroom he asks God for a rescue, assuring Him that there are no atheists under the shower . . .His prayers are not answered: once you are black, you stay black for the rest of your days.

An amusing comedy on the racial theme is *Putney Swope*, written and directed by Robert Downey. Mr Swope sits on the Board of Directors of an advertising agency. He is there as the only symbolic representative of a Negro minority, recruited for purely tactical reasons. At the Board Meetings he is present as a silent extra, free to doze through them – until the day when things take a most unexpected turn. The Chairman dies suddenly and his successor has to be found. The white members, who all harbour a private hope of winning the appointment, naturally hate each other and cannot agree on a common candidate. In the secret ballot they play safe voting for the least likely member of the Board. Predictably, Putney Swope is elected, and soon reverses the conventional racial pattern inside the agency: on the Board only one representative white man is left and all the personnel changes to black except for a white messenger. In another comedy, *The Landlord*, a New York high society playboy buys a house in Harlem, mainly to spite his proud and snobbish mother, and gets a crash course in inter-racial relationships. Here, also, the underlying dramatic principle is to reverse the conventional order; not a white but a black lady reigns over the entire affair. The Negroes feel free and at ease, while the white outsiders are nervous and inhibited, plagued by an inferiority complex. A small point, made in passing, throws some light on the uses of film in this area of racial conflicts and inter-racial contacts: a white lady, whose attitude to the Negroes comes under suspicion, replies. 'Of course we're liberal. Didn't we all go together to see *Guess Who's Coming to Dinner?*'

In the majority of cases films about the black minority are the work of white people. Apart from any commercial motives there is the manifest need to get rid of a deep-seated sense of guilt, a feeling that the time has come to compensate for the wrongs accumulated over the centuries. Their films proclaim that things have got to change now, or, less optimistically and with a certain reserve, that they ought to change.

And how do the people most directly involved – the blacks – see all this? Until recently they have had no opportunity to express their point of view on the screen, if one discounts short films or cheap small-scale independent productions of local scope. The first black director to make a film for one of the big studios was Gordon Parks, a photographer on *Life* and the author of an autobiographical novel *The Learning Tree*. His screen version of *The Learning Tree*, describing the experiences of a young Negro in one of the farming districts of Kansas in the early twenties, came out in 1969. The hiring of the first Negro director by Warner Brothers was hailed by Jack Valenti, President of the Motion Picture Association as 'one of the finest hours of Hollywood history'. In a letter addressed to Eliot Hyman, then the board chairman of the company, Jack Valenti wrote: 'You have brought new distinction and honor to the company and to the industry. I am prouder than ever to be associated with this industry of art and heart. With admiration and affection, sincerely – Jack.'[19]

Another black director is Ossie Davis, the actor and dramatist, with a number of stage and television plays to his credit. His film début, adapted from a short story by Charles Hines, carries the title *Cotton Comes to Harlem*. Its central characters are two Negro policemen: Coffin Ed Johnson (Godfrey Cambridge) and Grave Digger Jones (Raymond St Jacques). The action, located in the Negro districts of New York, concerns a search for a bale of cotton concealing a large sum of money. During the shooting, volunteer black patrols were posted – a necessary precaution, because filming on such locations can easily disturb the black population and sometimes leads to rioting. The Negroes are suspicious of film and television people, knowing that images can be distorted, words can lie. White racists try to exploit those fears for their own ends, and when they feel that the film in making may be directed against them, they try to stop the crews from entering their territory. Typically, the Mayor of Birmingham, Alabama, dealing with one such application, allowed the film-makers in but declared at the same time that he could not ensure the crew's safety or unhindered conditions of work.

The *Cotton Comes to Harlem* marked a turning point in the history of black-slanted theme films in America. The commercial success of this film far surpassed the most optimistic expectations. In the beginning of the seventies a new 'black wave' appeared in Hollywood, and a new black hero was born: no longer imitating white gentlemen but affirming victoriously his superiority over white enemies and, sometimes, white friends.

Two films made by Negro directors, with a Negro cast, can be taken to represent the birth of a black American fairy-tale, a black American dream. The second feature film of Gordon Parks, the *Life* photographer, was *Shaft*, the story of a black detective, with the talented Negro actor, Richard Roundtree, in the main part. The plot is full of thrilling and dramatic incidents, with the mighty, wise and charming private detective, Shaft, always coming out on top. The whites are either evil or, at least, clumsy and shiftless. At the very best they are allowed to appear as background characters,

assisting the black hero. It may be different in life, but on
the screen the American Negro is on top. Gordon Parks
considerably changed the book from which the film was
adapted, eliminating all scenes not acceptable to the black
community. For example, the black private eye, John Shaft,
in the novel has a white girl friend. His girl friend in the film
is black, and Shaft himself no longer kills just for the sake
of it. Parks believes that this idealization is necessary to
counteract 'all the damage done by Hollywood films for
years and years'.[20]

Similar in attitude is a film by Melvin Van Peebles, with a
mouthful of a title: *Sweet Sweetback's Baadasssss Song*. Van
Peebles can claim the entire credit for the work, as its producer, director, script-writer, composer of the background
music, and actor playing the main part. The hero, named
Sweetback, is a rebel: he fights the white cops, and although
chased by them for the entire duration of the picture, he
manages to slip out of all the tight situations, promising to
return to 'settle all accounts'. He is a romantic figure,
fighting for a just cause, but set in the vividly realistic
surroundings of modern Harlem, by no means idealized.
Sweetback himself is not a flawless diamond, but his faults
are overshadowed by his great qualities. He is strong, clever,
lucky and sexually attractive. Operating on the wrong side
of the law he cannot keep on winning, but viewers are left
with the conviction that the day of the black heroes won't
be long in coming. Melvin Van Peebles' screen character
recalls the swashbuckling heroes played by Errol Flynn.
Only in those days the fearless and peerless adventurers
were always white. Melvin Van Peebles explains in the
following words his philosophy: 'I told my story from the
black point of view. All the films about black people up to
now have been told through the eyes of the Anglo-Saxon
majority: in their rhythms and speech and pace. They've
been diluted to suit the white majority. I want white people
to approach Sweetback the way they do an Italian or
Japanese film. They have to understand *our* culture.'[21]

Films built around black heroes, and made by black
directors, enjoy a tremendous success with Negro audiences.

And it seems that the cinema-going habit is stronger among them than among white Americans. *Shaft* and *Sweetback* were commercially successful and, as usual, the big studios, sensing in the black stories a new vein of profit, are getting ready to follow up. Sequels have already followed, such as *Shaft's Big Score*, and it is not without significance that *Shaft* was distributed by the once rigidly conservative and almost racist Metro-Goldwyn-Mayer. Another sequel: *Come Back, Charleston Blue*, using the same principal actors in the same roles as in *Cotton Comes to Harlem*. The board of directors, responsible for the shareholders' interests, have taken a realistic assessment of the market conditions. Population movement within the big cities has meant that the better-off, mostly white citizens have settled in the suburbs, far from the large cinemas, which were built in the twenties and the thirties in the city centres. During the sixties 3·4 million blacks moved into the central cities and 2·5 million whites moved out. Glamorous movie palaces, prosperous twenty years ago, suddenly faced bankruptcy.[22] Those cinemas can now pay their way only if they are supported by the new influx of city-dwellers, that is by the Negro proletariat and Negro middle class. And black audiences are not likely to take to a gentleman hero like Sidney Poitier in *Guess Who's Coming to Dinner*.

Black gentlemen, appearing as equal partners to white gentlemen, do not impress this public. On the contrary, they irritate. The public wants heroes endowed with hard knuckles, tough enough to overcome the white cops and other white oppressors. In the spring of 1971, in the centre of Detroit, four out of five first-run cinemas were running Negro films! In September 1972 no less than fifty films of 'the black wave' were either produced or in process of being prepared for production. The list of titles in which the adjective 'black' appears is both long and impressive. To quote some of them: *Blackfather, Black Christ, Black Gunn, Black Girl, Black Majesty, Black Rodeo, Black Bart, Black Vampire, Black Fantasy* and, a new version of an old horror story, *Blacula*.

Joe Shaft, Mr Tibbs and Sweetback are always the winners. Looking at them and their exploits one is tempted to forget

E

about the conditions of life of the black minority. It is true: race riots ceased to be a part of everyday reality for Americans in the seventies, but this is not so far in the past. One read about them in the papers, watched them on television, and in many towns and cities the inhabitants have directly felt their destructive force. In the summer of 1967 disturbances occurred in over a hundred places, including 31 towns (25 in the North and six in the South) and 130 people died, including 46 killed in Detroit and 25 in Newark, New Jersey. The injured numbered over 3,600. Material losses, according to the still provisional estimates, amounted to $714 million. That was the harvest of one hot, long summer – the wave of unrest that swept the United States in July and August 1967.

In April 1968 in Houston, Texas, Martin Luther King, the preacher and spiritual leader of millions of black Americans, was assassinated. The man who, with all the moral force at his command, preached non-violence, who believed in protest by peaceful means, died from a white racist's bullet. And again, during one week in spring, a new wave of violence swept the country. For the first time it reached the capital, Washington D.C. Negroes were protesting against intolerance and discrimination, demanding not only formal, but actual, equality for 20 million dark-skinned citizens – the second-class citizens.

These events were not featured on the screen. (The student films show greater courage in this respect, but the risk of political repercussions is much less apparent there.) The studios prefer to keep away from these explosive issues, and when they do touch them at all they seek safety in well-tried stories, in re-makes and adaptations. Paradoxically, after the tragedies of Detroit, Newark and, in the earlier years, Los Angeles, Irish antecedents are used to provide dramatic structures for the race disturbances and riots of today. As his first come-back American film after long years of enforced exile, Jules Dassin presented a new version of John Ford's ageless *The Informer*: the writer Robert Alan Arthur based his directional début on Carol Reed's British *Odd Man Out*. What is it – a smart, evasive move, or paucity of imagination?

In his film *Uptight*, Jules Dassin refers clearly to the assassination of Martin Luther King. The action is placed in the black ghetto of Cleveland, Ohio. An extremist group, modelled, no doubt on the Black Panthers, decides to mount a terrorist action in response to the murder of a black political leader – a supporter of non-violence and of integration. Tank Williams, the central character (played by Julian Mayfield who collaborated on the screenplay) argues against this decision. However, the film does not develop then into the expected dramatic confrontation of the two positions, but, true to its origins, turns into the study of the moral disintegration of the man whose bitterness leads him to treason, with drunkenness as the only excuse. The character's ambiguity (is he just a drunkard, or a defeated supporter of non-violence?) weakens the ideological force of the work.

The Lost Man introduces to the screen for the first time a different Sidney Poitier. He plays a terrorist who holds up the factory coffers to get money for the black children of political prisoners. The action follows fairly closely the British prototype: the hero trying to escape his pursuers encounters in his wanderings both friends and enemies and, in the end, encircled, he chooses death. In the dialogue political arguments are exchanged, with Sidney Poitier stressing that non-violence, as expounded by Martin Luther King, cannot mean passive submission to the violence practised by the other side. In other words, circumstances can lead to, and justify, armed resistance.

The American cinema circles around the theme of the confrontation between the white majority and the black minority, only touching on its violent, physical aspects. One of the rare exceptions to this rule of non-intervention is a film made by an independent director, producer–writer Oscar Williams, with the financial help of the American Film Institute. *The Final Countdown* was shown for the first time in Chicago in April 1972. The author's thesis is that the only way to solve racial conflicts is to rebel against the white-dominated society. It is unnecessary to add that the white masters, as depicted on the screen, use brutal force to suppress any kind of rebellion.

It is easier for outsiders, free from the internal Hollywood restrictions, to put across the point of view and the aims of the Negro radicals, opponents of integration and the apostles of full sovereignty for the black Americans. Such a film is the feature documentary *Eldridge Cleaver* made with assistance from the Algerian Film Bureau, by an expatriate American, William Klein, a photographer and artist domiciled in France. In 1965 his interesting documentary about Cassius Clay won a prize at the Tours shorts festival; he has also contributed one episode to *Far from Vietnam* and directed a surrealist burlesque, *Mr Freedom*, about the exploits of an American strip cartoon-like hero, always pulling for the right side.

Eldridge Cleaver, one of the leaders of the Black Panthers, lives in exile in Algiers. Klein recorded several long camera interviews with him: at home, in the parks and the streets of the city, intercutting this with documentary images from Vietnam and the States, particularly the Berkeley riots. Cleaver comes across as an interesting personality, articulate, coherent and full of fire. He speaks persuasively and with great passion. Anger and bitterness do not confuse the logic and clarity of his frankly propagandist arguments.

Klein's film was imported into America by V. Rugoff, the owner of a chain of cinemas specializing in European pictures of a good artistic standard. At the New York opening tickets were available at the usual price of $3, but later were reduced to just $1. There was no advertising in the national press but Rugoff put on a special show for black journalists, for Greenwich Village and the radical student press. In this way a new system of distributing and publicizing political films of revolutionary content was introduced. A narrow door was opened, a beginning was made.

There is No Retreat

A film representative of the new trend, of the politically conscious Hollywood, is *Medium Cool*, the directorial début of the renowned cameraman, Haskell Wexler. The title refers to a phrase first coined by Marshall McLuhan. According to the author of *Understanding Media* a 'cool medium', leaving a wide margin to be filled by the viewer's own effort of imagination, forces him in effect into intense involvement. In this way the 'cool medium' of television plays on the sensibilities of its mass audience. Choosing a title for his film Wexler no doubt remembered McLuhan's definitions. *Medium Cool* has yet another significance, suggesting the impersonal, ruthless and almost inhumanly objective attitude of the television image-makers to the reality around them. Technicians and creative workers are so thoroughly adjusted to the drama of life that they retain a cool and apparently indifferent attitude to whatever happens. The film opens with television pictures of a car crash. John, the T V reporter (Robert Forster), shows no concern for the victims (they might have been still alive and not beyond help) but is calmly filming the smashed-up remnants of the car. Only when he has finished does he call an ambulance. In the film's last scene John is himself killed in a car accident, and a driver passing by just takes a photograph (the photographer is in fact Haskell Wexler in person – *Medium Cool's* script-writer, director and cameraman).

Wexler is not a novice in the profession. He has spent over thirty of his fifty plus years behind a camera. He has worked on documentaries of short and medium length, on independent feature films, and on outstanding Hollywood hits like Mike Nichols' *Who's Afraid of Virginia Woolf*. This was the film that won Wexler an Oscar. Accepting the statue so greatly valued by the establishment, he made a speech of literally one sentence, rather unusual in celebrations of this sort: 'I hope we can use our art for love and peace.'[23]

Wexler is, as they say, a committed film-maker. He is aware of the changes American society is going through and he wants to be involved in them. 'Because,' he says, 'the world today is in a state dangerously similar to the time of the rise of nazism in Germany the artist has a definite social responsibility.'[24] A sense of social responsibility is one thing, the opportunity to act on it is quite another. In Hollywood it is not easy to take wings in the direction you want, especially when one is a cameraman, making a contribution to someone else's creative vision, and at best collaborating harmoniously with the director. It became clear for Wexler that to express himself he must be in sole charge of the creative process. To be an author of a cinematic work involves, in practice, both script-writing and direction. This is how *Medium Cool* came about. The project was financed privately by the director's family, produced wholly independently and only after completion taken up for distribution by Paramount.

'I have very strong opinions about us and the world and I don't know how the hell to put them all in one basket,' stated Wexler.[25] He tried to solve those self-confessed problems by combining the conventions of '*cinéma vérité*' with the structure of a story film. *Medium Cool* is at the same time a documentary description, almost a television report, of certain true events, and a story of one man's transition from a neutral observer into a sympathizer of the protest movement. His own television company unwittingly pushes him in that direction when John learns of the practice of handing over actuality films to the FBI for viewing, and protests about it. He gets the sack for his pains and launches himself as an independent reporter, operating on his own. He covers the Chicago Democratic convention and the break-up, by the police and the National Guard, of the anti-Vietnam demonstration. One can speculate that if it wasn't for his death in a car crash, John's further political education would have taken him from the position of a sympathizer to that of an active participant in the protest movement.

Medium Cool reflects faithfully, like a mirror, almost all of the agonizing problems modern America is tormented with. The Vietnam War is ever present in private as well as in public life. A visit to a black ghetto shows the racial antagonisms deepening and becoming even more explosive. Students, who make up the majority of the demonstrating anti-war crowds, are attacked with armoured cars and tear-gas bombs. 'It's the establishment we were trying to hit at and question,' says Haskell Wexler.[26]

Medium Cool is a beacon of a film. It has proved that it is feasible and therefore desirable to make films directly involved with social reality and attacking the established order. Wexler has demonstrated that outside Hollywood, but for Hollywood distribution, one is free to produce full-blooded dramas about contemporary issues. Audiences, paying at the box office to see *Medium Cool*, (the film has recouped its costs and is bringing in profits) have indicated their acceptance of the experiment. There is a clear demand for such films, the public expects them.

Obviously, the approval is not unanimous. The establishment opposes such work, seeing in it a distant but quite real threat. During the American cinema season in Sorrento, in October 1970, Mr Frank Shakespeare, chief of the United States Information Agency, gave vent to his feelings, suggesting that the work screened belonged to 'the category of films dedicated to social aberrations which do not reflect the true America'.[27] (The films shown at Sorrento included *The Liberation of L. B. Jones*, *Soldier Blue*, *Medium Cool*, *Putney Swope*, *The Revolutionary* and *Alice's Restaurant*.) Not surprisingly this assertion provoked a wave of protests from film-makers present at the festival. The official opposition counts for little: the process once set in motion, cannot be reversed. Temporary halts and reversals might happen, but there can be no return to the rosy landscape of dream America.

5

Violence and Sex

'Violence is the American speciality, like a cherry cake,'[1] says Rapp Brown, the black revolutionary. Brutality, outrage, violence, brute force whatever name you give it the fact remains that a prominent feature of contemporary American life is a ready recourse to physical force to settle any disagreement, argument or controversy. Times are restless, marked by blood-letting and pain. Violence is lurking everywhere: in the city streets, in the universities – the shrines of knowledge, and in the superficially calm, sleepy, provincial settlements. Political assassinations are no longer regrettable, exceptional aberrations but, increasingly, a constant threat, an inherent feature of the game of politics. It is not film and television that teaches violence, but the violent reality spills over on to the large and small screens. Sometimes it appears uninvited, but more often its presence is fully approved of by the producers and the creative film-makers. If one wants to make films about the United States today, about the problems and the feelings of a contemporary American, one cannot fail to see the growing part violence plays in the everyday life of the nation.

It may be argued that this is nothing new, that this has been a permanent state of the society. There is some truth in the assertion that Americans have always been a violent people. One knows from the pages of history that well before the black ghetto riots and the Vietnam atrocities there was the conquest of the West, extermination of the Indian tribes, violent dealings in Mexico and Cuba, gangland warfare in the thirties, etc. Indeed, over the two hundred years of its independent existence, America has been swept by successive waves of violence. But the waves have never before swelled to such gigantic proportions and have never been accompanied by such a universal feeling of utter helplessness. How can it be otherwise when the authorities and the governing classes, defending the established order, resort to the same forceful methods employed by the subversives? The entire structure of the social order rests on repression, and repression breeds dissent and mutiny.

Edwin Schurr, an American sociologist, points out that the law in the United States serves to preserve and consolidate the existing divisions, being primarily used as an instrument of repression: by the whites against the blacks, the rich against the poor, the old against the young.[2] Violence is indeed 'the American speciality', served both by establishment and the anti-establishment groups. The right of free availability of fire-arms holds out against all attacks, helping to keep 'the American speciality' on the menu.

The American screen has been flooded, in the course of its history, by displays of violence but there has always been in operation a system of outside and internal censorship, official and unofficial, acting as a brake against the excesses of brutality, though it would be an error to overestimate those restraints. In the thirties the activities of the various Leagues of Decency were a reflex phenomenon, a secondary aspect of changing social relationships. The wave of gangster films subsided as the social consequences of the Depression were overcome. The situation is quite different in the early seventies. Firstly, violence has become a staple diet to such an extent that apparently even the moralists and the moralizers have largely become adjusted to it. Secondly, and this is surely more important, the political situation is still deteriorating: conflicts, far from dying out, are springing forth from newly developing hot-beds. Reality spurs the film-makers to increase the intensity of violence in all the traditional screen genres: in Westerns, thrillers, war films, science fiction, etc. At a time of furious social antagonisms the trade mark of the American cinema is violence.

The Wild West: The Legend and the Reality

Generally speaking, popular Westerns can be classified under three different headings. There are film-makers who celebrate, without reserve or qualifications, the legend of the conquest of the West and in effect contribute to the consolidation, the petrifaction of the myth. In the forefront of this tradition were, amongst directors, the late John Ford and Howard Hawks, with John Wayne the actor – the immortal living symbol of the valiant frontiersman. A different position is articulated by film-makers who, without denying the legend, stress at the same time that it is on the wane. Films within this second stream contain lyrical and nostalgic, even melancholy accents of regret that the epoch fit for heroes is now at an end. The third attitude opposes the myth and tries to debunk it through a realistic view of the West and its history.

Classic Westerns (as they are called), increasingly scarce, belong almost exclusively to the first stream. Apart from Ford and Hawks and also Hathaway, of the younger generation Andrew McLaglen (son of the unforgettable Victor McLaglen the actor) tries to follow the old masters. A classic Western lauds strong men setting themselves against threatening nature and no less predatory criminals, or the primitive, bloodthirsty redskins. According to Burt Kennedy, the director of *The War Wagon*, in such a film 'you're selling big open space and ritual'.[3] The ritual is celebrated according to the ageless liturgy obligatory for all knights of the prairie. The high priest is, of course, the cowboy hero, a marvellous horseman and a fast gun, but also, more importantly, the supreme judge, meting out punishment and dispensing justice. *The War Wagon* marked the 162nd film appearance of John Wayne, who describes the character he plays as 'The big tough boy on the side of right – that's me.'[4] Clare Huffaker who wrote the screenplay gives a similar definition: 'Strong, silent, with a certain sense of humour, and an innate feeling of justice.'[5] The stress on justice, on being always on the side of 'right', entitling him to pass judgement on others, is significant. On the side of justice one is allowed, indeed, obliged, to swing a few hard punches and even to shoot it out; and justice is a matter of instinct.

In this eulogy on tough, strong men holding sway over the Wild West there are some clearly contemporary, not at all legendary, references. The Western myth, for all its classical shape, can carry specific, transient political messages. It feeds the ideology of 'vigilance committees' – volunteer militia, arming to guard their rights and possessions, allegedly menaced by black and 'red' enemies. In *True Grit*, directed by the veteran Henry Hathaway, the indestructible John Wayne plays an ageing, one-eyed sheriff from some God-forsaken hole, setting off in pursuit of an escaping murderer. Initially it all happens *'lege artis'* – in accordance with the rules of the civilized society. But Rooster Cogburn, alias John Wayne, shows scant respect for the proper legal procedures. Holding a finger on the trigger of his gun he declares: 'You don't hand summons to a low-down rat.' A bullet settles the matter quickly and in the correct manner. To generalize: noble individuals need no recourse to the state and its legal system; they manage well enough by themselves, and what they do is, anyway, a blow struck for the preservation of public order, to protect other decent folk and their country.

In lyrical Westerns the heroes depart and the era of 'open spaces' comes to an end. David Miller's *Lonely are the Brave*, from a screenplay by Dalton Trumbo, is a story of a noble horseman who refuses to come to terms with reality. The cowboy, as interpreted by Kirk Douglas, would like to roam freely on his faithful steed over the endless prairies, but the prairies are no longer there. Everything is now fenced in and signposted as Private. The last cowboy meets a symbolic end on the freeway, struck down with his horse by a heavy lorry loaded with . . . lavatory pans. In this truly moving story the conventional power relationships are reversed. Here the cowboy-hero is powerless, and the entire legal apparatus, with its courts, its prisons and its police, is ranged against him. The new forces of law possess helicopters and modern fire-arms, but they do not scorn physical beatings or even the use of torture. In the industrial and technological era there is no room for the noble cowboy – the twentieth-century anachronism.

But were they really so noble and romantic, those knights errant of the Far West? Representatives of the third stream give a negative answer to this. The time has come to debunk the myth, to show the truth about the conquest of the West. From the late fifties, throughout the sixties and early seventies, the number of realistic Westerns has constantly grown. They afford excellent opportunities – from different motives but no less enticingly than a classic or a lyrical Western – to flood the screen with violence and savagery. In the foreground of this debunking trend were Westerns produced in Italy, and hence known as 'spaghetti Westerns'. Sergio Leone is the most successful exponent of the trend.

Sergio Leone, who early on in his career had been using the screen name of Bob Robertson, was not the originator of the Western *'all'Italiana'*. Eduardo Manzano had been making them already in the early sixties. But Leone invented a new formula which brought him success not only in his native Italy, but also in the United States. His first hit was *A Fistful of Dollars* with Clint Eastwood, imported from American television to play the part of an unheroic cowboy. The plot of this Italian Western, shot, incidentally, in Spain, was very similar to that of the Japanese film, Kurosawa's *Yojimbo*. The following two films, *A Few Dollars More* and *The Good, the Bad, and the Ugly*, smashed all the Italian box office records, which persuaded United Artists to acquire them for American distribution. It wasn't a bad acquisition: *The Good, the Bad, and the Ugly* was placed twenty-fifth in the box office records of 1969, ahead of many authentic Westerns made in the U.S.A. Building on this success Sergio Leone went to America to direct a long, three-hour spectacle, *Once Upon a Time in the West* with a star-studded cast including Henry Fonda, Jason Robards, Charles Bronson and Claudia Cardinale. The cost of the production was shared between the Italian partnership, Rafran–San Marco and the American Paramount. 'This is not a Western *all'Italiana*,' said Sergio Leone. 'I want it to be remembered as an American Western by an Italian film director.'[6]

What is the secret of Sergio Leone's success? In his own belief it is a rediscovery of the original sources of inspiration. 'I am showing the Old West as it really was,' he says. 'Cinema takes violence from life. Not the other way round. Americans treat Westerns with too much rhetoric.'[7] Plots of Sergio Leone's films are invariably woven around the theme of greed, grabbing of money, '*per fas*', but mostly '*per nefas*'. There is not a lot of love but plenty of fighting. The director insists that his heroes, in their actions, faithfully reflect the era dominated by violence and lawlessness. Only in the last of the series, *Once Upon a Time in the West* is there a perceptible turn towards the more traditional structures, the conflict of good and evil, which *Variety* acknowledged ironically, hailing the appearance of . . . Giovanni Ford.[8]

Through their warm reception the films of Sergio Leone and his numerous imitators (well over 200 'Eastern Westerns' were made in Spain and Italy in the years 1964–70) have set a trend for brutally naturalistic stories of the Wild West. Thus *Hang 'em High*, an American production directed by Ted Post, was dismissed by *Variety* as 'a poor imitation of a poor, Italian-made imitation of an American Western'.[9] Significantly, this poor imitation of an imitation climbed quite high on the box office list of 1968, having been placed twenty-first out of 730 films screened.

Violence is the cheapest box office attraction to put into a Western, but occasionally it does serve some higher ideals. Certainly *The Wild Bunch*, directed by Sam Peckinpah, should not, in this respect, be classed together with Sergio Leone's blockbusters. Peckinpah tells a story about a gang of outlaws who plan to hold up a munition train on its way to Mexico and sell the valuable cargo to Pancho Villa's revolutionary army. The action takes place in 1913. The film contains violent scenes of the utmost brutality (the blowing up of a bridge and annihilation of the gang). At a press show before the official opening many American critics reacted sharply to this violence. Sam Peckinpah, who not only directed but also collaborated on the screenplay, retorted that his

film was meant to act as a catharsis. 'No, I don't like violence,' he said. 'In fact when I look at the film myself I find it
unbearable. I don't think I'll be able to see it again for five
years.[10] This possibly sincere but certainly pretentious-
sounding statement failed to convince the press. To extol
violence in order to turn a viewer against it? Is that the best
way?

At the press conference one questioner came straight to
the point: 'If you want to make a statement against violence
and war, why make a Western? Why not make a film about
Vietnam?' The director's delphic answer was: 'The Western
is a universal frame within which it is possible to comment on
today.'[11] The circle has been completed. John Wayne
upholding the heroic traditions of the Western, endeavours
to justify, in *The Green Berets*, the American intervention in
Indo-China; the violently realistic Western, *The Wild Bunch*,
is to serve, according to the author, as a biting comment on
the American involvement in South-East Asia. No doubt a
perceptive minority can read those statements, but the overwhelming majority finds nothing in those Westerns beyond
the glorification of violence.

Films about Indian genocide did go one step beyond that
point. Here there were layers upon layers of deeply ingrained
tradition and legend to break through, to get at the naked
truth about the total extermination of the Indian tribes and
nations. These films endeavoured to call the people's attention to the continued existence of the red-skinned minority,
the sad remnants of the former master race of the American
continent. The Indian films of Ralph Nelson (*Soldier Blue*)
and Arthur Penn (*Little Big Man*) were animated by such
impulses.

Ralph Nelson set out to describe a particularly savage
incident during the exterminatory operations: the attack by
the American military forces on the Cheyenne settlement in
Sand Creek, in what is today Colorado, on 29 October 1864.
Several hundred people were murdered, mostly women and
children. After raping the squaws, the soldiers cut off their
breasts to use as skin bags for pipe tobacco. The men were
scalped. Ralph Nelson shows all this without evasions or

euphemisms. The final sequence is an anthology of barbaric atrocities, dripping with blood and resounding with the agonizing moans of the victims.

'In fifty years in pictures', says the director of *Soldier Blue*, 'the war was always glorified. I tried to show how brutal it was. The Cavalry always won, but by conquest, and the Cavalry played a savage role.'[12] The Federal Government of the United States, as Ralph Nelson has reminded us, had signed over 400 peace treaties with the Indians, guaranteeing their security, and subsequently all those treaties were trampled upon and broken.

Soldier Blue is not a faultless film, and the romantic plot that serves as the main narrative thread is neither deeply felt, nor original. One also has doubts about the accumulation of atrocities in the final massacre sequence. Quantity does not always add up to quality. On the contrary, the rivers of tomato ketchup blood create a gradually diminishing impact. And yet *Soldier Blue* is not easily forgotten, perhaps because it inescapably fosters some urgently contemporary thoughts. 'There is more than a chance analogy between my story and the facts of Vietnam,'[13] says the director pertinently.

Like Ralph Nelson, Arthur Penn in *Little Big Man* came out against the legend of the savage Redskins who had had to be put down to protect the peaceful and good-natured white settlers. Children's books read in the schools, picture strips, big screen and television stories – all in concert sing the praises of the same heroes. One of them is the legendary general George A. Custer, the fearless scourge of the Redskins.

Penn has made his film from a screenplay by Calder Willingham, adapted from Thomas Berger's novel. The action is placed in the late 1870s, when General Custer was 'dealing with' the Indians, letting go uninhibitedly with a series of slaughters and massacres. The director is not sparing with them either, showing on the screen three of the exterminatory operations. The hero of the film is one Jack Crabb (played by Dustin Hoffman), a white man brought up by the Indians, existing in a limbo between two worlds, between two different cultures and civilizations. As an old man, a centenarian, Crabb describes to us those times, with the battle of the Little Big Horn as the climax of the story.

Arthur Penn purposely takes up an extreme position. His Indians call themselves 'human beings'; the white conquerors are ruthless and murderous. There are no extenuating circumstances, no exceptions: everything white is base, degenerate, and criminal. *Little Big Man* purports to provide evidence that the Americans (the white ones, of course) always have been racist, and no one should have been surprised at their contemporary behaviour – at home, towards the black minority, or in Vietnam.

This proposition, as with all attempts to generalize from the most extreme instances, appears not entirely convincing, all the more so because it was presented in the form of a popular ballad where humorous interludes and the somewhat facetious figure of the hero seemed to conflict with the 'message'. One understands Penn's motives, respects his moral impetuosity, his anger and sense of outrage, but his choice of the convention is rather surprising. The film is chatty, discursive, with echoes of a picaresque novel *á la* Henry Fielding. Admittedly entertaining it adds up to a fairy-tale with a different moral than in the classic Western. In the end the representation of all the white-skinned Americans as a murderous gang seems as simple-minded as the racist view of the savage and primitive Redskins. But the very fact that such a film could be made, was widely distributed and proved fairly popular, demonstrates the American public's readiness to accept debunking of the once sacred myths.

The Criminals and the Upholders of Law

What better genre to show off the entire spectrum of violence than the gangster thriller? Since 1960 crime has increased at a rate nine times greater than that of the population. These figures alone seem sufficient to explain the interest creative people show in crime and criminology. Crime and criminals are favourite subjects of film-makers, whatever their talents or ambitions, of those who habitually view such phenomena from a sociological perspective as well as those who seek to unravel all complex issues with the help of the psychological insights. In America there is no screen genre more closely concerned with contemporary realities, with the urgent issues of the day, than the crime thriller, even when it moves back in time to explore the past – the Depression years in the thirties.

Within the last ten years the American gangster thriller has developed certain new dramatic structures, which had first appeared – though only sporadically – in the post-war 'black series'. These new forms have not only dramatic, but also ethical and philosophical, significance. No longer is there the obligatory, clear-cut juxtaposition – in the spirit of Conan Doyle – of the criminal and the upholder of law, in practice usually a policeman, or a private detective. Nowadays the inclusion of a screen character in the criminal, or the law-upholding group no longer carries the force of a moral judgement. Frequently the law-breakers' actions are shown as justified, while the law-enforcers are condemned. This is by no means the expression of a moral indifference or a wholly amoral outlook, but a mark of needling doubts and hesitations about the sufficiency of accepted standards. The world is full of likeable and even noble sinners without real guilt and with loathsome defenders of the public, only superficially concerned with justice.

In order to judge a criminal one must inquire into his motives and the circumstances of the crime. In the sixties the whole series of actual, recorded crimes, were carefully and faithfully reconstructed on the screen. These were always the sensational cases which had captured the front pages of the newspapers for weeks, months or even years. Such feature films, through the soundness of their factual basis and the comprehensiveness of their inquiries into the human environment or the psychological make-up of the characters, became genuinely valuable documents of their time.

This new documentary trend in the crime thriller was initiated in 1963 by Burt Topper, with his artistically rather weak *The Strangler*, based on the actual murder of eight hospital nurses. But the genre has achieved its current standing with such films as Richard Brooks' *In Cold Blood*, Richard Fleischer's *The Boston Strangler* and Arthur Penn's *Bonnie and Clyde*. In each of these films, whatever the part played by the makers' artistic imagination, one can find a description of actual events, and an analysis of their causes and consequences.

In *In Cold Blood* the subject of the initially literary work (by Truman Capote) and eventually the screen vivisection (scripted and directed by Richard Brooks) is the killing of four people of the farming Clutter family in Holmcomb, Kansas, the crime committed on 15 September 1959 by Perry Smith and Richard Hickock. The literary original (an inquiry shaped as a documentary novel) has been treated by Brooks with great respect but in the adaptation the field of interest became narrowed. This was, however, made necessary by the inevitable limitations on the footage. Truman Capote describes at some length the personalities of the four murdered people and the course of the investigation; Richard Brooks leaves out those sub-plots and concentrates on the two murderers. The rigidly documentary tone of the adaptation is stressed through the use of natural locations (for example, the Clutters own homestead in Holmcomb) almost throughout the film.

It might have seemed that the two descriptions, the literary and the cinematic, should have come up with identical conclusions. But in fact, despite the equal insistence on documentary realism, there are perceptible differences in attitude. Truman Capote takes up the position of a ruthlessly objective observer, recording for his readers all the facts and only the facts: the police and the court records, the accused's own stories, various pertinent evidence by other interested parties. He leaves the reader to draw his own conclusions unaided. Brooks goes about it rather differently. Employing editing to relate the present to the past, the real world to the world of memories and imaginings, the director tries to explain how his characters feel and think. Brooks rejects neutrality, proposing instead that the viewers identify with Smith and Hickock. Cinematic fiction ousts a literary report. The second difference is perhaps less clear-cut and is offered here hypothetically. The two authors both analyse the factors that have led to the crime. They both stress the psychopathological features in the make-up of the two young criminals, but Brooks more emphatically – perhaps through the autonomous expressive force of the film's audio-visual texture – points to the influence of the economically and culturally backward environment in which Smith and Hickock grew up. Throughout the film there is an implicit feeling that justice is different for the rich and for the poor. In the final sequence the author's (Brooks' not Capote's) conviction comes across that a death sentence solves nothing, leading just to another murder committed 'in cold blood'. In effect the inhumanly savage execution makes a greater impact than the murder at the opening of the film.

The Boston Strangler was based on a book by Gerold Frank, which in turn was a literary record of the murderous deeds by Alberto de Salvo, who in the years 1962–4 had strangled thirteen women in Boston. Richard Fleischer reconstructed in the authentic scenery of the city both the crimes (eleven of the thirteen murders, to be precise) and the successive stages of the investigation. He is on the whole content to set out the facts as recorded and his rare attempts to delve into the psychology of the murderer are rather superficial and unconvincing. There is one significant and, objectively, quite unnecessary departure from the truth: the murderer's invalid little daughter – a very real cause of his increasingly disturbed state and of the growing incompatibility with his wife – never appears on the screen. Thus *The Boston Strangler* does not try to explain why it all happened, but simply to communicate the climate of terror, with the invisible horror lurking in Boston while the strangler is prowling through the city with apparent impunity. The conclusion does not go beyond the observation that the police are helpless when dealing with a criminal from outside the familiar circle of the 'professionals'. But that rather obvious truth was already noted by Fritz Lang in his *M*, in 1931.

Undoubtedly the most ambitious film of this crime series

was *Bonnie and Clyde* directed by Arthur Penn from an original screenplay by Robert Benton and David Newman. Bonnie Parker and Clyde Barrow died on 23 May 1934 in a police ambush, cut down by ninety-four pistol and machine-gun bullets. It happened at a spot with the poetic and idyllic name of Arcadia, in the state of Louisiana. Thus ended the epic story of the famous gang led by the youthful bosses, 25-year-old Clyde and Bonnie, with eighteen killings and a countless number of hold-ups to their credit.

This was by no means their first screen appearance. In 1937 Fritz Lang presented their story in the romantic and histori-cally none-too-accurate *You only Live Once*. In 1949 Nicholas Ray returned to the same subject in *They Live by Night*. In 1958 there appeared *The Bonnie Parker Story*, a cheap 'B' picture directed by William Witney with Dorothy Provine in the title part. All these films, variable in their artistic ambition and achievement, offered a similar view of their heroes as victims of unjust persecution.

In 1967 the script-writers and the director of *Bonnie and Clyde*, joined by Warren Beatty – the animator of the project, who took the producer's chair as well as playing the part of Clyde – approached this story in a different manner. Firstly, they took great care to make their reconstruction of the thirties (the Depression, the years of unemployment and want) as authentic as possible. The film was intended as almost a documentary biography of historically true charac-ters. But at the same time this trip into the past was meant to open a perspective on contemporary issues. *Bonnie and Clyde* aims a sharp blow against the establishment. The heroes, it is true, are psychologically unbalanced, even neurotic, but it all seems of secondary importance. The foreground view is of the fearless rebels against the established social order, against middle-class morality and the American system of government. There is an implicit suggestion that little has changed in the last thirty or forty years, that in modern America you can still find the same deserted, poor and forgotten province, exploited by remote and powerful bankers or the smaller local tyrants.

Bonnie and Clyde proved immensely popular, especially

with younger audiences. They responded readily to the non-conformist attitudes projected by the film. Its philosophy was extremely simple: the world is vile and badly run and the likeable heroes are quite right to set themselves against it. The fact that they also kill is of secondary importance. Anyway, they move around in the vindicatory halo of folk-heroes, avengers and benefactors in the Robin Hood tradition. They rob the rich to lavish gifts on the poor (but mostly on themselves). The ruthless annihilation of the gang leaders further swells the audience's emotional involvement in their fate. As in *In Cold Blood* the final scene has the greatest impact. The earlier murders are overshadowed, fade into oblivion.

One finds it difficult to accept such an attitude. The film-makers suggest, as John Simon has rightly observed, that 'the outlaw is a far finer fellow than the inane solid citizen'.[14] It may seem smart but it is certainly superficial. The victims of Bonnie and Clyde – bank clerks, minor craftsmen and local policemen – may be inane, but they are also poor, bullied and ill-treated by the wicked world. No less than their murderers they are the real casualties of the crisis. It is a serious error to show those opponents of the gang as the representatives of the establishment. Can it be right to take arms against them? Does not this story of the likeable murderers fail to pin-point those who are really responsible for the deprivations of the American society?

Bonnie and Clyde are ever-smiling, frivolous, somewhat childish, certainly charming. They kill also somewhat frivolously and without meaning to. It is difficult not to like them, not to regret their death so early in life. From here it is only a step to apotheosis and, moving on, to identification. In December 1967 *Time* printed a letter, posted in Peoria, Illinois, written by one Lynda Bender, a student: 'The reason it was so silent,' she says, 'so horribly silent in the theater at the end of the film was because we *liked* Bonnie Parker and Clyde Barrow, we identified with them and wanted to be like them, and their deaths made us realize that newspapers headlines are not so far removed from our quiet dorm rooms.'[15] A significant letter, full of admiration for the heroes and full of ambiguity. Does Miss Lynda Bender mean to go out into the streets with her boyfriend and get some shooting practice?

Bonnie and Clyde has set a trend, if not in life, at least in the cinema. Usually it is coupled with a return to the Depression years. The central character of Roger Corman's *Bloody Mama*, scripted by Robert Thom and Don Peters, is Kate Barker, who in the thirties ravaged the state of Arkansas with her four sons spreading death left and right, until she herself died, hit, literally, by a hail of bullets. Why this viciousness, this thirst for blood? Kate Barker, beautifully played by Shelley Winters, answers: 'It's a free country, but unless you're rich you ain't free. I aim to be freer than the rest of the people.' A clear-cut programme, put into practice through a hasty liquidation of 'the rest of the people', to get them out of the way. Violence is dished out unsparingly, the screen is swamped with blood. *A Bullet for Pretty Boy*, directed by Larry Buchanan, takes us to Oklahoma, again at the time of the Depression, where a gang operates under the leadership of Floyd and Betty – almost a carbon copy of *Bonnie and Clyde*.

Noel Black's *Pretty Poison* is a variation on the theme of Arthur Penn's film. This time the action is contemporary and the place is Winslow, a small, sleepy town in Massachusetts. A youth is released from a detention centre and directed to a place of employment. A probation officer warns him: 'You're going out into a very real and very tough world. It's got no place for fantasies.' This piece of good advice is scorned and the youth gives vent to 'fantasies' – like the idea to poison the town's water-supply. Soon he finds a suitable partner in an apparently sweet and innocent girl who promptly teaches him how to kill people in cold blood (her mother is one of the victims). In the end the boy becomes fed up with this way of life, and the girl-partner helps him to change it by sending him, in her place, to the electric chair. Once again the criminal heroes are rebels against the grey reality of life, living out their fantasies by disposing of other people's lives. Is this how one achieves the full meaning of freedom?

And what has happened to the traditional heroes of the crime thriller, the upholders of law and order? They still do exist and act, but how changed they now seem, how unlike the resourceful James Cagney as an F.B.I. man in *Four Men*, or William Powell as the philosophic amateur detective in *The Thin Man* series. Then, fortified by an unshaken belief in the justness of their cause, backed up by the authorities, they were always bound to win. Now, in the sixties and seventies, they are alone, fighting an individual battle. The establishment which they are trying to protect gives them no help, or helps them insufficiently. Even worse, they are further handicapped in their work by the cancer of corruption affecting those at the top; by their dishonesty and amorality. The detective Madigan (Richard Widmark) in Don Siegel's film of the same title, Lieutenant Dave Bullitt (Steve McQueen) in Peter Yates' *Bullitt*, or Lieutenant Joe Leland (Frank Sinatra) in *The Detective*, directed by Gordon Douglas, all find themselves in this position. Private investigators, operating on their own and responsible to no one else, like Lew Harper (Paul Newman) in Jack Smight's *The Moving Target* or Tony Rome (Frank Sinatra) in Gordon Douglas' *Lady in Concrete*, do not differ greatly from their opposite numbers in the police.

The police films are not, of course, lacking in violence, in fights and murders. How could it be otherwise? The ability to fight and to shoot are among the professional skills of the heroes, and the fact that the film-makers grasp this opportunity to introduce images that shock is, after all, no more than an inherent part of the modern cinematic manner. Thus in *Bullitt* the impact of a shot fired at a man seated on a bed is so powerful that the victim is literally rammed into the wall. Shooting and killing is of course bound to be there, but how is it rationalized? The conventions of the police thriller demand that you shoot to protect the law. In *The Detective* the screen-writer Abby Mann and the director Gordon Douglas afford us a glimpse of the reasons for the establishment's use of terror. One of the New York police officers speaks about it openly, employing a most picturesque and expressive metaphor: 'They (the people) don't like living in garbage cans and our job is sitting on the lids of those garbage cans.'

Can these tired, weary and sometimes ageing (Henry Fonda, Frank Sinatra, Paul Newman) policemen and private detectives, themselves of doubtful moral character, acting often without the conviction that justice is on their side, counterbalance the attractions of the romantic criminal rebels? Are they really the positive heroes, and can the others, like Bonnie and Clyde, be numbered among the 'baddies'? It is surely a rhetorical question – the answer is obvious. At this juncture it would be unfair to omit mentioning some attempts to revive on the screen the image of a policeman as a positive hero. Like the good old times of James Cagney and William Powell, Gene Hackman, the tough cop of *The French Connection*, William Friedkin's film, is a hard-working, very brave and absolutely honest man. He is not appreciated by his superiors, sometimes misunderstood, but nevertheless relentlessly persists in his endeavours to liquidate a dangerous gang of narcotics smugglers.

In *The New Centurions* of Richard Fleischer, George C. Scott as Sergeant Kilvinski of the Los Angeles police force is, without any reservation, an ideal hero, almost a grown-up boy scout, unable to do anything wrong. The character of Kilvinski was created by a retired policeman, Joseph Wambaugh who, becoming a writer, wrote a popular novel which turned out to be a United States best-seller, later adapted by Stirling Silliphant for the screen. Scott, playing an old and experienced policeman, teaches his young assistant, Roy Fehler (Stacy Keach) how to protect society against all kinds of evils. The relationship between the two heroes somehow reminds one of the television pattern of the immortal Dr Gillespie and Dr Kildare. Penelope Gilliat in *The New Yorker* described *The New Centurions* as 'a sort of Agnew production in praise of the police.'[16]

On which side is justice? This eternal question, asked so many times by so many film-makers, in films about policemen, private eyes and romantic criminals, received rather an original and unexpected answer in the new box office champion of all times, Francis Ford Coppola's *The Godfather*.

The amazing success of this film is due to many factors. Undoubtedly, the professional and, at the same time, imaginative direction, was one, if not the most important of them. Then the magnificent acting of Marlon Brando, impersonating the head of the powerful Mafia family, Don Vito Corleone, was very important. To this must be added the acting of the carefully chosen interpreters of the secondary roles: Al Pacino as the heir to the Mafia kingdom, Michael Corleone; James Caan as the impetuous Sonny and, later in the picture, Richard Castellano as Clemenza, Richard Conte as Barzini, and Al Lettieri as Sollozzo – all officers in the underground Corleone Army. Then, finally, there is the fascinating story of the Mafia and the Mafiosi, keeping the spectators breathless during the three hours of projection. And what is the moral lesson brought home by the spectator as he leaves the cinema in which he viewed the exploits of the members of the Corleone family? Firstly, he finds the heroes likeable; he admires them, and their actions do not strike him as abhorrent. Yes, the heroes are cruel and ruthless, but they have some justification for the bloody deeds they commit. The official establishment, the State and its organs, didn't give them protection, so they took justice in their own hands. The spectator is inclined to forget that what he sees on the screen is organized, ruthless crime. The official system of justice and protection of human rights is non-existent. We see corrupted policemen and we hear about corrupted judges, senators and politicians. The conclusion is surprising and, at the same time, frightening: those poor Italians were forced by America's social iniquities to create the Mafia in order to protect themselves and to enable them to live like ordinary, law-abiding citizens. The Corleone family doesn't want to have anything to do with drugs – isn't it an additional proof of the inherent honesty of the Mafiosi? How right is Penelope Houston in saying that 'The Godfather is a return to conservatism: a celebration of corporate America, a law and order movie in the twisted context that wins reader acceptance.'[17]

The trend to violence did not spare other action films. In the spy thriller James Bond (Sean Connery) and his enemies put on a fair exhibition of torture, sadism and brutal fighting. These British pictures about Her Majesty's secret agent inevitably originated a trend. An entire legion of imitation Bonds sprang up. Twentieth Century-Fox have a rival counter-espionage agent in Derek Flint (James Coburn), in Columbia it is Matt Helm (Dean Martin), in Metro-Goldwyn-Mayer it is Napoleon Solo (Robert Vaughan). The last one rules, or at least did rule, the television screens, but he does occasionally favour cinema programmes with his presence. In the early seventies the spy vogue was clearly subsiding.

The master of suspense, Alfred Hitchcock, is careful not to overdo the shock effects, but he never hesitates to use them when required. In *Torn Curtain* his intention was to debunk the spy thriller, and to counter the fashionable frivolity which other film-makers were bringing to screen killings. Perhaps 50 per cent of this programme was put into effect: the audience tends to take the spy affair quite seriously, but the murder scene, as intended, becomes a realistic nightmare. It is not easy to put it out of one's mind. In *Topaz* the Cuban goings-on lead to the screen being splattered with blood-coloured paint.

In *Frenzy* the violent scenes of strangling are used in a masterly way. They shock, but they do not last a fraction of a second too long.

The war film affords ample opportunities for violence. In the old days, before the war in Vietnam, the public could be entertained with the heroics of soldiers in *The Guns of Navarone*. But modern realities have destroyed the effectiveness of the old formulas. The Second World War may still hold some cinematic interest, but not in its heroic aspects, not as material for romantic epics. A typical example is *The Dirty Dozen*, directed by Robert Aldrich from a screenplay by Nunnally Johnson, adapted from E. M. Nathanson's novel. In the American army a punitive company has been formed, made up of the cream of the criminal underworld: the murderers, the gangsters, the sex manics. These 'heroes', properly trained, are to make a daring sally behind the German front lines. Their mission is to enter a certain French castle and kill some German officers stationed there. The mission is successful, but apart from the commanding officer only one of the dozen comes back alive. To reward him, his prison sentence is set aside, and his comrades are post-humously rehabilitated. Robert Aldrich leaves it to the viewer to pronounce on the ethics of the project, to decide who is a criminal here, where the punishment and the rewards are due. Only one thing is stated clearly: high-rank-ing American officers are thick-headed, narrow-minded and show no respect for human life. A similar situation, if somewhat less extreme, is described by director Andrew McLaglen in *The Devil's Brigade*. Here, also, we meet a punitive company, trained for a special mission at the front.

The end of 1971 brought a new explosion of cinematic violence. Brutality, rape, sadistic set-pieces and gushing torrents of tomato-red blood, were all hall-marks of some outstanding and, in a sense, representative films. *A Clockwork Orange*, Stanley Kubrick's fantasy of violence set in the immediate future, was voted by the New York critics the best film of the year. Anthony Burgess' excellent English novel, adapted for the screen by Kubrick himself, is a vision of city life, harassed by roaming gangs of violent youths. Kubrick does not spare the tender feelings of his audience, presenting on the screen a full range of savagery, including murder, beatings up and rapes. These explosions of violence, almost unbearable in their intensity, are accompanied by perversely soothing musical accompaniments. Watching scenes of horror one listens to popular, sentimental hits or to familiar operatic arias. Stanley Kubrick believes that 'violence itself isn't necessarily abhorrent', and that 'everyone is fascinated by violence'. 'Our interest in violence,' says Kubrick, 'in part reflects the fact that on the subconscious level we are very little different from our primitive ancestors.'[18] Perhaps, then, *A Clockwork Orange* is meant to be a warning, a call to society to retrace its steps while there is still time? Yes and no. Yes, because reality, as perceived by the director, for all the wit and satirical edge of the presentation, is night-marish and hopeless. No, because of the sympathetic treat-ment of the violent hero, who expresses his vitality through rape and murder, thus making his protest against the grey conformity and the mechanization of life. This is the Kubrick case for the social need of violence.

Kubrick made *A Clockwork Orange* in England, where Sam Peckinpah also directed his *Straw Dogs*, finding a different justification for a concentrated dose of violence. The central character of *Straw Dogs* is an expatriate American intellectual who leaves his country for a peaceful retreat in Cornwall. But he fails to find the expected favourable conditions for work and a rewarding family life. A physical weakling, he is held in contempt and laughed at by the villagers and scorned by his own, sexually frustrated, wife. Soon he becomes the victim of a savage attack. Almost as a joke several rowdies rape his wife. But they also wake a lion hitherto asleep in the breast of the wretched intellectual. He picks up the gauntlet and deals effectively with the gang. Initially he takes up his stand in defence of the sanctity of his home and family life, but soon finds wrathful pleasure in meting out justice with his own hand. The violence goes on for many long minutes: bullets fly and people fall dying, blood squirting out of open arteries.

'I want to rub their noses in the violence of it,' – says Peckinpah, referring to his audience. And he goes on to explain: 'I regard all men as violent, including myself. I'm not cynical . . . When you see the degree of violence in men, you realize that we're still just a few steps up from apes in the evolutionary scale.'[19] An argument analogous to that of Kubrick, except that Peckinpah is quite unjustly abusing the apes. Those innocent animals are not remotely capable of dreaming up the savageries practised by man.

Stanley Kubrick and Sam Peckinpah are two American directors of high standing. The fact that they have shot their films in England is incidental, due to production and financial expediency. But the setting of both these stories in the British Isles may have some significance. Is there an attempt to ease the American sense of guilt through finding an accomplice? The films seem to say that violence is not indigenous to home, that the wave is sweeping the entire Western world. Or perhaps it is the other way round: 'Violence made in the U.S.A.' is a part of a cultural export, of the new 'culture' exemplified by Charles Manson and his followers. In *Straw Dogs* David Summer (Dustin Hoffman), a mathematician, flees overseas in search of peace, to find, in Cornwall, another Texas.

The Offensive of Sex

In the early sixties outside the official, Hollywood production system there were semi-professional or purely amateur, private workshops and small studios producing and distributing 16 mm films popularly known as 'nudies'. Undressed girls were showing off their busts there, the action being usually placed in nudist camps. Sometimes it moved from the Californian beaches indoors, allowing the film-makers to show a couple, or several couples in socially intimate situations. But judged from the modern viewpoint it all seems rather innocent and, as the moralists would say, only slightly pornographic.

After ten years the situation has changed radically. Under the new label of 'permissiveness' everything has been thrown open, everything is considered a fit subject for discussion and writing, and therefore for presentation on the screen. Films about the secrets of sex – which, anyway, once filmed and exhibited are no longer secret – have become quite an important branch of the cinema, with a sizeable corner of the market. They are no longer known as 'nudies', but 'skin flicks', from the acreage of human skin they expose in all its glorious detail. Nudity is a matter of fact and is in itself of little importance. 'Action' is what counts – what the naked heroes do. Films are made with sound and in colour, but still mostly on 16 mm. Most of the 'mini cinemas' specializing in 'skin flicks' use 16 mm projectors, but some find it more profitable to ask for 35 mm copies.

At the beginning of 1970 there were over 700 cinemas given over exclusively to sex films, and at certain times, with the appearance of some especially enticing hits, this number was increased to a thousand or even above. In 1969 200 feature-length films of that description were distributed – the work of around a hundred production companies, although the term 'production company' is rather misleading. Apart from several bigger fish this easily marketable product was provided by individual private entrepreneurs. The financial risk involved is not great, although the competition is such that the cinemas share with the distributors (who are usually the producers as well) 75 per cent to 25 per cent of the profits. It is still possible to squeeze out of an average 'skin movie' around $75,000, while the production costs do not exceed $50,000. After all, the actors, or the technicians, do not have to be paid the union rates. So far the system operates on the fringes of Hollywood, with Los Angeles and San Francisco as the main centres of production.

In the seventies the porno movies invaded the cinemas in all American cities. The film *Deep Throat*, produced by Vanguard Productions and directed by Jerry Gerard, is called, because of its great commercial success, the '*Ben Hur*' of porno pictures. This dramatic story of a young woman, unable to find at first satisfaction in sexual intercourse, presents during seventy minutes of projection, fifteen overt sexual acts. *Deep Throat* cost $25,000 to make and, from June 1972 to January 1973, grossed over $3·2 million! Another successful porno film is *Bijou*, directed by Wakefield Poole and showing, amongst various homosexual attractions, a male orgy in the concluding scenes of the film. Cost of the film – about $16,000: estimated gross nation-wide circa – $400,000.

It is difficult to pin-point exactly the moment and the immediate causes of the start of the sex offensive in the American cinema. There were a number of contributory factors: the remarkable success of the Swedish *I Am Curious, Yellow*, directed by Vilgot Sjöman, the abolition of censorship in Denmark, and the import, both legal and illegal, of Danish sexual attractions. Finally – and most importantly – there was the general trend of public opinion, increasingly liberal towards the treatment of themes that were once considered strictly taboo. One can add that the activities of the local censors, appeals to higher courts, controversy in the press – all this has created a climate of interest and provided most effective publicity for those free, unfettered films.

In 1967 in Kansas 'The Adult Film Association of America' was set up. It grouped producers, distributors and exhibitors of 'Adult' films. This conveniently euphemistic description was applied to all sex films made outside Hollywood. Well over one hundred members expect the association to foster and protect the interests of all those who want to offer to cinema audiences pictures tackling serious problems in a courageous and serious way. They have in mind, of course, sexual problems. In its book of rules and regulations the A.F.A.A. cuts itself off resolutely from the producers of pornographic films. There is no room for them in the organization.

The word 'pornography' is a pivot around which all the discussions revolve; various actions are initiated for and against the word. There are many who declare their opposition to the sex offensive under the banner of the crusade against pornography. But there appears to be an equal number of those who demand freedom from sexual taboos, whether in literature or on the screen, rejecting all accusations of offensiveness and immorality levelled against individuals or institutions. Pornography is a concept extremely difficult to define and prone to subjective interpretations.

The formula for acceptable sex films is simple. The 'flesh' of the film, the presentation of 'sex in action', has to be contained within an outer packaging, either 'scientific' or 'documentary'. A scientific approach is usually assured by the presence of an 'expert' commentator. A doctor is seen in his study, surrounded by books and diagrams, talking about how much the knowledge of sexual techniques – or in the old-fashioned phrase, the secrets of the bedroom – can enrich and embellish human life. And immediately, to illustrate the lecture, a couple appear, demonstrating various copulative postures. In the documentary approach it is important to decide the place, the time and the environment. For instance, what goes on in Denmark after the abolition of censorship; or what are the sexual manners of African Negro tribes, and does anything of these traditions survive in the black communities of the United States? There can also be a third kind of packaging, the psychological, but it gives little help in any censorship troubles. This approach stipulates that the partners be torn by doubts, and have to overcome their complexes before making it in bed. The audiences, impatient to get to the point, on the whole dislike those additional complications, and the guardians of public morality do not care for the psychological motivations.

Among the producers of skin flicks, three outstanding specialists merit a mention: Matt Cimber, Alex de Renzy and Russ Meyer. Matt Cimber, now in his middle thirties, had been for a long time Jayne Mansfield's agent and her husband – the third one – at the time of the popular sex-symbol actress's death in a car accident in August 1967. Cimber believes in the scientific approach. 'I don't make sexy movies', he says, 'I make movies about sex.'[20] They are, in his opinion, extremely clinical and boring. These are some of Cimber's screen credits: *Man and Wife*, *Married Satisfaction*, *ABC of Marriage*, *Black is Beautiful*, *Sex and Astrology*. In *Man and Wife* two pairs of actors worked in shifts. The action was photographed in eighteen hours of shooting time. The total cost was $86,000, and the gross receipts from a hundred cinemas that have screened the film reached $2½ million. Ample evidence that scientific tracts about the techniques of sex pay more than well. In 1972 Matt Cimber switched to a more elaborate and costly production. His *Sex in the Comics* cost $150,000 to make and grossed between $2 to $3 million.

Alex De Renzy operates in San Francisco. Cimber's contemporary, he started as a cameraman in a small company making commercials. Getting bored with the job, he changed to skin movies, producing them in an almost conveyor-belt fashion. De Renzy shoots a lot of short films, paying little attention to the script and the packaging. His preoccupation is with speed and volume of production. He owns a premiere cinema, where the programme changes every Thursday. As in the old, prehistoric days, before 1914, the 90-minute programme is made up of five or six films. De Renzy made a fortune on such porno hits as *Pornography in Denmark* and *Sexual Encounter Group* and now spends a lot of time travelling around the world. In 1972 he directed a docu-

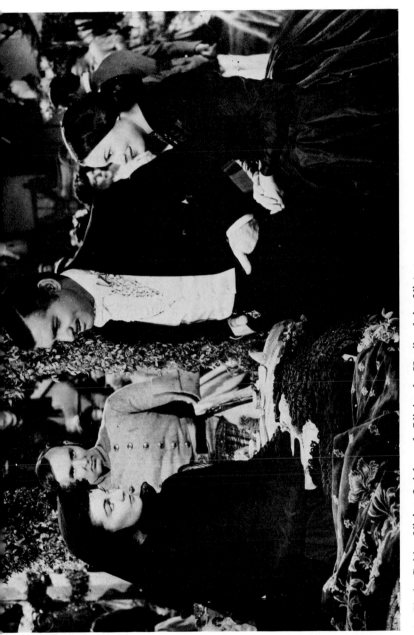

1. Clark Gable, Vivien Leigh and Olivia de Haviland in Victor Fleming's *Gone with the Wind*

2. Elizabeth Taylor as Cleopatra, directed by Joseph Mankiewicz

3. John Huston as Noah in the super-spectacle production, *The Bible*, which he also directed

4. Anthony Perkins and Tuesday Weld in Noel Black's *Pretty Poison*

5. Frank Sinatra and Lloyd Bochner in Gordon Douglas's *The Detective*

6. Tony Curtis as Albert de Salvo in Richard Fleischer's
The Boston Strangler

7. Robert Blake as Perry in Richard Brooks's adaptation of the Truman
Capote novel, *In Cold Blood*

8. Warren Beatty as Clyde Barrow and Faye Dunaway as Bonnie Parker in Arthur Penn's *Bonnie and Clyde*

9. Shelley Winters as Kate Barker with her four sons in Roger Corman's *Bloody Mama*

10. Barbra Streisand in Gene Kelly's *Hello, Dolly*

11. Barbra Streisand as Fanny Brice in William Wyler's *Funny Girl*

12. Julian Mayfield a
the exiled black militan
in Jules Dassin's *Uptigh*

13. William Wyler's *The
Liberation of L. B. Jones*

14. The lyrical Western: David Miller's *Lonely are the Brave* with Kirk Douglas

15. Debunking the myth: Sam Peckinpah's *The Wild Bunch*

16. Henry Fonda in Sergio Leone's *Once Upon a Time in the West*

35. Andy Warhol's *Lonesome Cowboys* and (below) *Trash*

36. The futuristic fantasies by Stanley Kubrick: *2001: A Space Odyssey* and *A Clockwork Orange* with Malcolm McDowell

37. Dustin Hoffman in Arthur Penn's *Little Big Man* and with Susan George in Sam Peckinpah's *Straw Dogs*

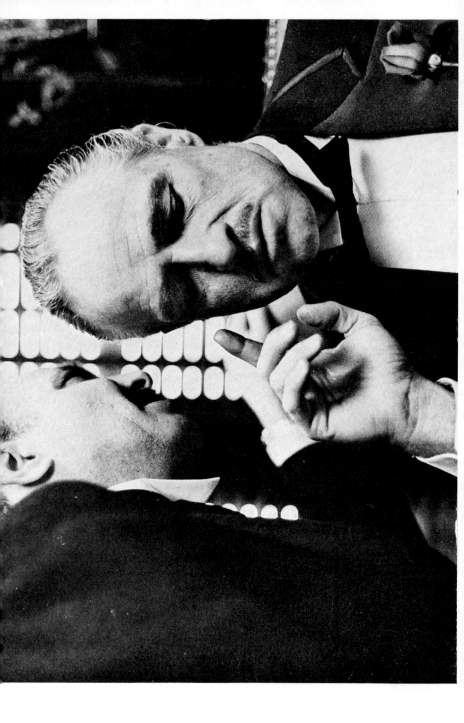

mentary, non-porno film *Weed*, about the use, cultivation, smuggling and sale of marijuana.

The uncrowned king of the formerly 'nudies' and now 'skin flicks' is Russ Meyer, born in 1922. He had his first great success as far back as 1959, with *The Immoral Mr Tess*, in which he had invested the sum of $24,000. Profits from this film exceeded a million! *The Vixen* in 1968 cost three times more ($72,000), but paid back six times more than *Mr Tess* ($6 million!). Some critics, including a few on serious newspapers and magazines, liked this story of a nymphomaniac who, while her husband (a pilot flying his own passenger plane) is away, has fun of whatever sort, and with whoever was available – age, sex, kinship and colour of skin notwithstanding. The star of the film, Erica Gavin, endowed with a bust of dazzling proportions, goes through countless varieties of strip-tease. Good fun and good production values was the reviewers' verdict about Russ Meyer's show piece. But his attempt to mix eroticism with politics was widely ridiculed. The heroine, finding herself in a plane hijacked by a sinister communist assisted by a black deserter, manages to convert the Negro to the American way of life. The plane lands in the United States, instead of Cuba, and the girl hands the hijacker over to the police. Judith Crist of the *New York Post* explains that the sub-plot with the hijacked plane and the Negro was to serve as sociological packaging, paving *The Vixen's* way to the cinemas.[21]

Russ Meyer can boast of many successes, but surely his greatest triumph was to break through the barrier separating official Hollywood from its unofficial sex-and-pornography fringe. Richard Zanuck entrusted him with the direction of a feature film for Twentieth Century-Fox. Some inside gossip has it that Meyer's film, *Beyond the Valley of the Dolls*, though at the time not yet released, was responsible for the Chief of Production getting the sack late in 1970. Gentlemen on the New York board felt that the employment of the master of erotica stained the good name of the studio. The film industry should keep away from pornography, was the judgement of the highest studio authorities. From pornography? Russ Meyer would no doubt feel offended. During his entire career he has tried not to overstep the mark, to show good taste and avoid accusations of open indecency. He says as much in an interview printed in *Time*: 'I am worried about *I Am Curious, Yellow*. That film has put me at a cross-road. I have never shown genitalia in any of my films. Once you have to show that to get people into the theater, how many people are going to do it with taste? I have always been against censorship in any form, but I have also maintained that you should leave something to the imagination.'[22]

There is, of course, no central Federal State censorship system extending over the entire territory of the United States. But there is a great number of local censorship bodies: the state, municipal, and even, in some cases, district ones. If all the authorities entitled to it chose to claim their rights, we would have to deal with a host of over 50,000 censoring institutions. There is also the custom-house watching over the import of films. In December 1967 custom officials seized the prints of *I Am Curious, Yellow*, regarding it as obscene. A year later the Federal Court of Appeal reversed this decision and allowed the film to reach the screens. Even then the local authorities refused to let it be shown in the state of Maryland.

The film industry tried to cut through this veritable jungle of censorship by introducing a system of rating for all films released. The system came into operation in November 1968 and was overhauled in January 1970. There are four categories, marked with one or more letters: 'G' (general) means a programme for unrestricted exhibition; 'GP' (formerly 'M') means children are allowed but the company of parents or guardians is recommended; 'R' means children up to the age of seventeen (formerly 16) must be accompanied by a parent, or another adult; 'X' is for adults only, above the age of seventeen. Members of the Motion Pictures Association of America, producers, distributors and exhibitors, are asked to keep to those regulations. It is the desire of every producer of 'skin flicks' to get an 'X' for his film. This is regarded as an accolade of sorts, a sign of admission to the Hollywood family. But to get an 'X' the film must be cleared of all suspicion that it is pornographic. Otherwise the official committee acting for the film industry will refuse to consider the application, and cinemas will screen the unrated picture at their own risk. It means that in practice the market narrows to several hundred mini-cinemas with, obviously, an adverse impact on the receipts. Russ Meyer's *The Vixen*, having obtained an 'X', gained access to the large cinemas, hence its box office success. Thus it all comes down, as I have already said, to the problem of defining pornography in a clear and workable manner. And this, not unexpectedly, has proved far from easy.

The principal issue is how to reconcile the First Amendment to the constitution of the United States, guaranteeing freedom of thought, speech and the printed word with the direct interference of censorship, or laws restricting those freedoms. In 1957 the Supreme Court of the United States pronounced on this issue (in two cases: Roth against the United States, and Alberts against the State of California), stating that the First Amendment cannot be used to shield the distribution of pornography. Giving grounds for the decision Judge Brennan cited three distinct factors characteristic of a pornographic work: (1) its dominating tone is directed at provoking a prurient interest in the recipient; (2) the work offends against accepted public standards; (3) it is lacking in any compensating social values.[23] Judge Brennan's judgement, clarified later by the President of the Supreme Court, Warren, remains to this day '*magna charta libertatum*' in the realm of pornography. It is quoted whole or in part in all the court cases and arguments, with the greatest controversies revolving around possible definitions of 'accepted standards' and 'social values'.

In 1969 the Supreme Court gave judgement in the case of 'Stanley against the State of Georgia', creating a precedent of great significance. The case concerned the seizure of pornographic books and films that were in private possession. The Supreme Court ruled that 'anyone had a right to keep any sexual films or published albums, whether or not they were obscene, for private use in his home'. Some lawyers argue that if one has a right to possess those materials, it follows logically that one also has a right to acquire and to produce them. And, to continue, if an adult is allowed to use them at home, and no one can forbid him to invite friends and acquaintances to a projection, why are other adults denied their right to see similar films in a cinema? In other words, is the state competent to control the private inclinations and the uses of leisure of adult citizens when their activities cause no social harm? In this fight to legalize pornography children and under-age teenagers are firmly excluded. Here the overwhelming majority believes in the retention of all restrictions and prohibitions.

Ambiguities in court judgements and wide divergences in interpretation of at least two elements of the 1957 Roth against the United States decision (accepted public standards and the social values), and the increasing impact of the sex offensive, persuaded President Johnson to set up The National Commission on Obscenity and Pornography. Congress sanctioned the Commission in 1967, and the President nominated eighteen members under the chairmanship of William B. Lockhart, dean of the law faculty at the University of Minnesota. This body, made up of the representatives of the world of learning, the churches of various denominations and social organizations, considered the matter for over two years, spending around two million dollars on research and inquiry. The study resulted in a published document of over 1,000 pages, two-fifths of which (400 pages) was taken up by the minority report, opposing the conclusions of the majority.[24] Twelve members of the Commission supported the conclusions, six others opposed them. It may be interesting to add that all the members except one were appointed by Lyndon Johnson. The new President, Richard Nixon, had only one nominee of his own – a Cincinnati lawyer, Charles H. Keating, who promptly became the leader of the opposition, heading the dissenting group of six.

The majority confirmed the position expressed in the Supreme Court ruling in the case 'Stanley against the State of Georgia'. The Commission declared that 'adults should

be able to see and hear and read what they choose, though
nothing should be forced upon them and those of tender
feelings should not be assaulted against their will'.[25] This
'assault on tender feelings', constituting an offence against
public morality, takes place when unsolicited pornographic
materials are sent by post – as advertisement and exhortation
– or when pornography is obtrusively exhibited in public.
The Commission also recommended an intensified programme of sex education for the young, fostering a healthy
attitude to sex and rendering them independent of secret and
illegal sources of information. In conclusion the Commission
stated that an interest in pornography is for an adult a
private matter and there is no need for the state to intervene.
The state on the other hand has a duty to see that the pornography trade does not offend the feeling of people of different
habits, or arouse prurient interests in the under-aged.

This verdict was not accepted by the minority of six, and
did not please the new administration. Both President Nixon
and Vice-President Agnew made public their disagreements
with the conclusions of Professor Blockhart and his colleagues. Spiro T. Agnew lost no time in turning from the
Commission's report to an election call for a change in the
make-up of Congress. 'Voters should elect a Congress,' he
insisted, 'that will see to it that the wave of permissiveness,
the wave of pornography and the wave of moral pollution
never becomes the wave of the future of the country.'[26] And
the Commission's minority leader, Charles Keating, declared in a Hollywood speech in January 1971 that 'pornography is a greater menace to U.S. society than war'.[27]

It is patently obvious that the Presidential Commission
changed nothing and made no contribution to the solving
of many arguments and controversies which have been going
on for years. It might have been different – though even that
seems doubtful – if there was no change of government, if
the Johnson administration was still at the helm. Now the
conservatives, and the silent majority enjoy the sympathy
of the White House, suspicious of liberal goings on. Once
again, as in the thirties, the churches of various persuasions
went into action, led by the Roman Catholics. The Morality

in Media Association was founded by a New York Jesuit, Father Morton A. Hill. The Association operates on a three-year budget of $2 million and has set up branches in many cities. It attacks vehemently all the alleged manifestations of pornography in cinema, television, press and radio. The state parliaments are being lobbied and mobilized: in the spring of 1971 proposals of acts introducing or tightening the system of censorship were drafted in twenty-three states. The Supreme Court, considering the appeal of Grove Press, handling the distribution of *I Am Curious, Yellow*, against the Maryland State ban on the film, gave a Solomon's judgement: four votes to repeal the ban and four to retain it. The ninth judge, William O. Douglas, who favoured the setting aside of the ban, was prevented from making use of his vote because a piece signed by him had once been printed in a book published by Grove Press. According to established practice, in the absence of a clear-cut ruling, the local censorship decision remains in force. And it established a precedent for the other states which have followed the example of Maryland. The Morality in Media Association counts on the new members of the U.S. Supreme Court nominated by President Nixon. The four Nixonian Supreme Judges, together with one conservative judge nominated by Kennedy, now have a majority in the body of nine. If the Supreme Court in one of the cases brought before it decides to abandon or lessen the qualification of the 'social redeeming value' of a film considered to be obscene, then the fight against pornography would be easier and more effective.

Until the beginning of 1973 the Supreme Court didn't do anything to please the anti-pornographers. On the contrary, they instructed the lawyers to study and argue the central question, that is, 'whether a display of any sexually oriented films in a commercial theatre when surrounded by notice to the public of their nature and by reasonable protection against the exposure of the films to juveniles, is constitutionally permissible'. The wording 'sexually oriented films' strikes one as having a far more liberal and non-committed connotation than 'obscene' or 'pornographic'. The two conditions, on the other hand, 'notice to the public' and 'reasonable protection, may be interpreted in different ways.[28]

In June 1973, however, the Supreme Court tightened the law on obscenity, giving the States and the Federal Government broad new powers in obscenity cases. It 'rejected arguments that a national rather than local standard should govern and refused to make exemptions for obscene films, magazines and books on grounds that they are aimed at "consenting adults". The court discarded an obscenity definition which gave constitutional protection to forms of expression unless they were "utterly without redeeming social value". In its place Chief Justice Warren Burger announced that the test will be whether the work, "taken as a whole, does not have serious literary, artistic, political or scientific value".'[29] Previously it had been difficult to prove that any material was quite without any redeeming features but Chief Justice Berger said that prosecutors and censors no longer had to carry that burden.

One thing is certain: all the courts underline and stress that the seizure of films considered to be obscene by police squads is illegal without a previous judicial decision. This anti-censorship stand of American justice renders futile all police raids, arrests and confiscations. Police action initiated by New York Mayor, John Lindsay, to clean Broadway of smut was, on the whole, a complete failure.

This is one side of the coin. And the reverse? 'Skin flicks' are still being produced, ever more daring and leaving less to the viewers' imagination. In San Francisco, after several weeks of untroubled exhibition, the police finally seized the print of *The Animal Lover* – a Danish film, in which the heroine selects domestic fauna as partners for love-play. *Air Hostesses*, an erotic film in 3D (necessitating the use of two-coloured glasses) ran not in a mini-cinema, but in a huge 4,500 seater Music Hall Theatre in Boston. And a significant new development in the kingdom of sex: Eve Meyer, Russ Meyer's divorced wife, herself in the business of producing nudist and strip-tease pictures, sold her past, current and future films to Cassettes Optrionics Inc. A praiseworthy foresight: the future belongs to TV cassettes!

The Counter-offensive: Love Story

In 1969, when all the producers, both in Hollywood proper and on the fringes, could see salvation only in sex, something really unusual happened. Against all expectations, a romantic film – the supremely romantic *Romeo and Juliet* by Shakespeare – proved popular with the public. The story was as old as the world, was not at all concerned with permissiveness, and had archaic dialogue lifted straight from the play. It had an Italian, therefore an unknown director, no stars (youthful debutants instead of familiar names), in short, all the conceivable warning signs. By all known portents, Franco Zeffirelli's screen version of *Romeo and Juliet* should have been a financial disaster but, unbelievably, it turned out to be a box office winner. In the 1969 list of records it took fifth place, taking $14½ million. This was twice as much as Sjoman's *I Am Curious, Yellow* which, with $7,290,000, was placed twelfth. For several months, rain or shine, outside the New York cinema, the Paris Theatre, long queues were forming, made up mostly of young girls. *Variety* asserted – God knows on what grounds – that each teenage girl in the United States saw *Romeo and Juliet* at least twice.[30]

Taken together with the extraordinary success of the rejuvenated screen Shakespeare, the triumph of Arthur Hiller's *Love Story* (from Erich Segal's screenplay), should have occasioned no shock and bewilderment. Shakespeare's name on the credits is a handicap rather than an asset. As a rule a contemporary story has a head start over classical adaptations. In the twenty weeks after its release the romantic *Love Story* yielded as much as *Romeo and Juliet* in over a year. But the reasons for the success are in both cases identical. The multi-million audiences responded readily to the archetypal story of love and death. The public likes to have its emotions touched, to be moved to tears. There is nothing strange or improper in it, and one is entitled to fume and protest against it only when these emotions are lavished on something cheap and trivial. This was, in fact, a frequent objection to the success of *Love Story*. The film-makers were accused of playing a confidence trick on the unsuspecting public, asking it to respond wholeheartedly to an artificial, sentimental, sugary fairy-tale. The majority of critics, both in America and in Europe, condemned *Love Story*, trying, unsuccessfully, to turn the viewers against the film. If anything, the critical disapproval helped to create even greater interest in this cinematic as well as literary best-seller.

The phenomenon of *Love Story* merits closer attention: '*Sine ira et studio*', without wooing the *élite* critics, or succumbing to the tastes of the millions who read the book and went to the cinema with uncritical enthusiasm. Erich Segal, who wrote the script and later transformed it into a novel, is not an ordinary literary hack. He is a man of learning and of intellectual refinement. He graduated from Harvard and won a chair in Classical Philology at Yale. He is a translator of Terence and Plautus and the author of a study of Euripides. Screen-writing was his hobby, but even before *Love Story* he won some acclaim for his scripting contribution to *Yellow Submarine*.

What induced Segal to tackle, in a romantic and sentimental vein, the life of American students – not the politicized, militant young, but the conventional ones, those who keep out of the streets? Observations from the Professor's chair, or '*esprit de contradiction*' – taking perverse pleasure in seeing the young in an unfashionable light? Another supposition, perhaps closer to the truth, is that Segal has turned for inspiration to one of the oldest story structures in existence, meaning to produce an updated, modern version of it. The son of a powerful American banker family and the daughter of modest Italian immigrants fall in love. One can easily recognize the pattern of Romeo and Juliet: the young are in love, but the parents (in this case only the rich parents) are opposed to the marriage. Defying fate, Oliver Barrett IV and Jenny Cavilleri marry, and after years of poverty, fortune smiles on them. But Jenny is incurably ill (with leukaemia, though this is never made explicit) and dies at twenty-five. Oliver is left to lament her and to tell the viewers the story of great happiness interrupted by untimely death.

In an interview given to the Paris *L'Express*[31] Erich Segal revealed that it was one of his former students who suggested to him the idea for *Love Story*, describing the death of his friend's wife. It was a marriage of twenty-year-old graduates, contracted on leaving the college. Initially the wife was the only bread-winner, but in time the husband also managed to find employment. At twenty-five the wife suddenly died, and the youth – not quite a man yet, not fully mature and self-reliant – felt forsaken, without a purpose in life. That was the origin of the story.

Of course, the former student's tale about an unhappy friend could not have been the only influence. Perhaps Erich Segal is familiar with Edgar Allen Poe's dissertation, *The Philosophy of Composition*, published in 1846, where we can read that the death of a beautiful young woman is the most poetic of subjects. The famous poem, *The Raven*, is based on the same principle as *Love Story* – recollections of the departed one. This is also true of *Annabel Lee* ('And this maiden she lived with no other thought than to love and be loved by me.'). A class difference between the lovers is a conflict familiar from thousands of novels, plays and films.

It is absurd to criticize Segal for the way he has constructed the plot of his book and the film. But the adverse critics have other grievances as well. They point out that the image of student life, as reflected here, is untrue, lacking, as it does in Segal's work, any political background. It is true that even the most exclusive Ivy League colleges have been affected by the political ferment. But it would be wrong to suppose that all students belong to S.D.S. Some are passionately concerned with ice hockey rather than politics. Oliver, the fourth in line of the banking Barrett family, was one of them. Obviously, those other young people could be shown as part of the background, but was it absolutely necessary to put everything into one cinematic pot? Secondly, there are no black characters in *Love Story*, no really bad people. Everybody is shown as basically noble, even the father, the hard-headed banker and opponent of the marriage. In a realistically-conceived film such sugar coating would have been unbearable, but in a deliberately romantic story – is it really a mortal sin?

Love Story is certainly not a masterpiece, and it does not really aspire to the accolade of the work of art. It is a competently made, competently written and competently acted cinematic pot-boiler. Certainly of a better standard than a score of other sentimental or, at the other extreme, violent stories. Blasting *Love Story* with the heaviest ammunition purely because the public likes it seems a sterile occupation. The critical complaint that Segal and Hiller did not make a different film is clearly pointless. Crowding into the cinema the public does not necessarily testify to its lack of judgement, as some reviewers would have us believe. There is nothing here that offends the accepted canons of good taste, and the one scene which rightly has raised greatest doubts in the book is not in the film. It comes when Oliver meets his father after Jenny's death. In the literary version the young man, sobbing his heart out, falls into parental arms; on the screen he says simply that help is no longer needed and departs in the opposite direction. A considerably more dignified, less tearfully sentimental, ending.

Finally, there is the matter of the social and artistic consequences of the success of *Love Story*. Fears have been expressed that this rosy image of American youth, classless, unpolitical and streamlined, might initiate a trend and push off the screen the courageous, anti-establishment films. Nixon and Spiro Agnew like the film, a fact that some left-wing critics find ominous and significant. But the risk is unlikely to prove serious. No doubt Hollywood, which has always tried to repeat and imitate its own successes, will put into production other *Love Stories*, but the formula has little chance of establishing a dominant trend.

All the same, the lesson was not lost, as the tremendous success of Robert Mulligan's *Summer of '42* aptly demonstrates. The film, made from Herman Raucher's auto-biographical screenplay seems like a rejuvenated screen version of Raymond Radiguet's novel *Le Diable au Corps* (made into a film in 1946 by Claude Autant-Lara with Gerard Philipe and Micheline Presle). A fifteen-year-old boy, spending the 1942 summer holiday on a small island at the coast of New England, meets his first love and his first sexual experience. His partner is a war widow. The critics have almost unanimously – though less aggressively than in the case of *Love Story* – dismissed the film, accusing it of sentimental nostalgia and melodramatics. But the public disagreed once again. From April 1971 till January 1973 *Summer of '42* took $18·5 million, running ahead of the sex hit *Air Hostesses* ($6 million) and Mike Nichols' intellectual sex treatise *Carnal Knowledge*.

6

Underground Cinema

The Underground Structure

Underground cinema! It is a romantic term, suggesting at once a bohemian way of life – a private sort of life with nothing and no one to intercede between an artist and his muse. The time has come to find an organized framework for all the various, spontaneous activities. On 28 September 1960 thirty independent film-makers met in New York and, on the initiative of Jonas Mekas, decided to set up the New American Cinema Group, to be known as N.A.C. The group declared in its manifesto that, firstly, film is 'indivisibly a personal expression',[1] and secondly, more ominously and uncompromisingly: 'We don't want false, polished, slick films, we prefer them rough, unpolished but alive, we don't want rosy films – we want them the colour of blood.'[2]

This was the opening of a new stage in the development of underground cinema. The rousing words of the manifesto were followed, two years later, in April 1962, with the setting up of the Film Makers' Cooperative. Every independent producer or director (in underground practice those two functions were usually indivisible) could take his film to the Cooperative which would then do its best to push the work through the non-commercial distribution channels: film clubs, museums and art galleries, schools and colleges. An admission ticket to the Cooperative was a film – of whatever length, on whatever gauge, made by whatever technique. There was no other condition of entry, no artistic or commercial standards were applied. The Cooperative collected 25 per cent of all income, leaving 75 per cent to the author who could in this way earn anything from a few dollars to several thousand dollars. An *avant garde* film, moving through non-commercial channels, was becoming a marketable product.

The third stage in the development of underground cinema began in the spring of 1962 when the Cooperative gave birth to the Film Makers' Distribution Center, a separate body set up to distribute independent films to cinemas. For this service the cut from the earnings rose to 50 per cent, but of course income from commercial distribution is proportionately greater. Around thirty cinemas are in permanent trade relationship with the Center, but in the case of Andy Warhol's *Chelsea Girls* over a hundred theatres have contracted the film, and the author stands to earn about $1 million. One swallow may not make a summer but it is a sign that the underground film has arrived as a commercially attractive proposition. The number of film-makers served by the Cooperative and the Center has risen from 30 to 480. In September 1966 at the other end of the United States a sister organization, The Canyon Cinema Cooperative was set up by seventeen film-makers active in and around San Francisco. Jonas Mekas estimates that there are in the country, working more or less continuously, at least 300 film makers with ideological and organic ties with N.A.C.

Today underground films are also distributed through channels not directly connected with the New York and San Francisco co-operatives. Films by independent artists proved of interest to companies supplying the art house market, mostly with European products. Brandon Films, Contemporary Films, McGraw Hill, Janus Film Library and Grove Press Film Division (which took over Amos Vogel's film library, Cinema 16), all now handle some underground work.

We can note, without fear of error or exaggeration, that outside the official Hollywood cinema another American cinema has appeared and is already developing certain institutionalized features, becoming an 'establishment' of sorts. The independent American cinema, out of pure habit still known as 'underground', is now complete, with directors and distributors of its own, cinemas and other projection halls, financial backers, frequently of philanthropic character (the Ford or Guggenheim Foundation), and finally a group of critics committed to it, including (apart from the universal Jonas Mekas) Susan Sontag, Andrew Sarris, P. Adams Sitney, Sheldon Renan and Ken Kelman. Its press mouthpiece is the *Village Voice* (published in New York's Greenwich Village) and a monthly (if irregularly appearing) journal, *Film Culture*.

Underground cinema has acquired not only its own critics and press, but also its theoreticians, annals and books. Sheldon Renan's *An Introduction to the American Underground Film*[3] is a concise encyclopaedia packed with information about the film-makers and their work. The book is enthusiastic and uncritical. One could conclude from it that everything made in the underground is, if not outstanding, at least extremely interesting. Parker Tyler, a prominent New York film critic who, in the forties, was close to the surrealist movement, in his book *Underground Cinema: A Critical History*,[4] carries out a perceptive analysis of the origins, development and future perspectives of the underground. It is a level-headed work, by no means rapturously enthusiastic. Tyler suggests that underground film-makers are anti-everything (anti-establishment, anti-art, anti-history), childishly peevish and madly in love with themselves. Tyler asserts that the mistake of many young film-makers is to assume that any form of anti-art is in itself significant and interesting, providing it expresses the author's feelings. The critic makes a pertinent comment that having feelings (who doesn't?) is not enough. One must also have cinematic ideas about those feelings. In conclusion Parker Tyler calls for artistic discipline in underground cinema because, as he says, 'the film medium, to achieve its destiny, must not only be pure, free of all commercial taints; it must also have scope of vision and an implacable aesthetic character'.[5]

Further evidence of the underground cinema's rise to importance is an anthology of *Film Culture* articles – a fat, 400-page volume with numerous illustrations, published in 1970.[6] It was edited, with his own comments, by P. Adams Sitney who, after Jonas Mekas and Andrew Sarris, is taking over the mantle of the 'official' theoretician of the New

American Cinema. Late in 1970 Sitney and Mekas opened a small cinema with only ninety seats, but each one partitioned off on both sides. Sinking into black cushions in these comfortable modern 'confessionals' viewers can see only the screen. Nothing can disturb their enjoyment of the *avant garde* masterpieces, carefully selected from a film library known as Anthology Film Archives.

In 1963 underground cinema shows were held at midnight in the Bleeker Theatre on the outskirts of Greenwich Village. These were famous occasions, with each of the projected films being argued about long and heatedly over cups of black coffee during the intervals. After a time the cinema owners asked the pioneers of the new cinema to move on to another place. Their manners and way of life were not approved of. 'They said we were disorganized, unsophisticated and anarchistic. It's true, we are,'[7] commented Jonas Mekas. Less than ten years later the 'anarchists' have their own, exclusive cinema, cloister-like in mood and style. Fighting furiously against the Hollywood establishment, these knights of the new cinema have themselves become, without being aware of it, the 'underground establishment'.

Predecessors

In America a cinematic *avant garde* is not a recent phenomenon. Today's leaders of the New American Cinema have their antecedents, though they are loath to admit it. The difference is that formerly the independent film-makers worked in isolation, individually, making up an almost imperceptible fringe of conventional production; now they operate as a group, heterogeneous, it's true, but quite consistent and coherent in their public actions.

Sheldon Renan calls the N.A.C. predecessors the second film *avant garde*,[8] reserving the honourable title of the first *avant garde* for the French film-makers of the twenties, like Léger, Clair and Chomette. The second *avant garde* appeared towards the end of the thirties and blossomed out in the middle forties. Its unchallenged leader was the dancer and poetess, Maya Deren, who, in 1943, in collaboration with

Alexander Hammid (the Czech documentary film-maker Alexander Hackenschmid), made her definitive, surrealist *Meshes of the Afternoon*. Among the other experimental film-makers (it was fashionable at the time to call their work 'experimental films') were Kenneth Anger, Curtis Harrington, James Broughton and Gregory Markopoulos on the Western Coast, and Willard Maas, Marie Menken, Ian Hugo and Hans Richter, a German immigrant in New York. All of them were to a greater or lesser extent involved in the surrealist movement.

N.A.C. predecessors ought also to include, quite apart from the second *avant garde*, representatives of the independent documentary movement, active in New York in the fifties and early sixties. Sidney Myers, Morris Engel, Lionel Rogosin, Shirley Clarke and John Cassavetes deserve to be noticed in this context. They can all be called documentary film-makers only in respect of the creative method they employed, but for diverse cinematic projects. Cassavetes in *Shadows*, or the earlier Morris Engel in *The Little Fugitive*, using non-professional actors, scorning make-up and studio interiors, were making fiction films, but with the texture and the general climate of a documentary work. The group was also known as the New York School.

John Cassavetes, after the world-wide success of his *Shadows*, has tried his luck in Hollywood, collaborating, as an independent director, with the big, commercial studios. But two films born of this marriage, *Too Late Blues* and *A Child is Waiting*, have not been successful. Then came a long acting interlude – to earn a living and save money for the next project. In 1968, after three years of shooting and editing, his *Faces* was unveiled – a description of thirty-six hours in the married life of a sexually frustrated middle-class couple, fourteen years after their wedding. The method is similar to that of *Shadows* – a lot of improvisation, intentionally (or perhaps of necessity?) imperfect technique, but what a different result! The revelation of a dozen years ago, fresh, real and passionately committed, has now aged into a dull, long and seemingly even longer lecture about characters who look for sexual fulfilment in a strange bed and a strange home.

In Europe, and especially at the Venice Film Festival, the film created some interest and won considerable praise from the critics. It was even awarded a prize. Perhaps it is true to life in the way it reflects the greyness, intellectual emptiness and degradation of its heroes, but that doesn't seem sufficient. At any rate it is clear that the New York School no longer exists, and its former leader is wandering alone on the fringes of the commercial cinema.

Various trends and creative personalities were grouped together in the experimental workshop of Hans Richter – the author of several German *avant garde* films in the twenties, who ran a sort of film school. With help from his European friends (among them were Fernand Léger, Marcel Duchamp and Max Ernst) and his American pupils, he made two films: *Dreams that Money can Buy* and *8 times 8* (Jean Cocteau helped with this second film). In Richter's school workshop young hopefuls were gathering, eager to learn and to experiment with film, among them Jonas Mekas and Shirley Clarke, now the leading representatives of the independent American cinemas, and Gideon Bachmann, a critic, now working in Europe.

A tireless popularizer of the experimental film in those heroic days was Amos Vogel, the founder and director of Cinema 16 – a distribution centre for *avant garde* shorts. Thanks to him they were getting around to film clubs and universities, fostering interest in film as art. On the independent radio network, Pacifica Radio, Gideon Bachmann propagated the work of his *avant garde* friends.

Jonas Mekas, Pioneer and Prophet

The name of Jonas Mekas, a leading figure in the New American Cinema, has already been mentioned here a number of times. Undoubtedly, the rise of the third *avant garde* owes everything to his energy and ingenuity. Without Mekas film-makers who prided themselves on their independence would never have come together as a group. They would still be working scattered, as before, and many would never have come to the public notice.

Who is the dynamic Mr Mekas? A fairly recent immigrant, born and raised in Lithuania, he first landed in New York in 1950. It has been said (myths grow and take shape speedily) that in his childhood he had been a shepherd in a remote peasant community. However it may be, such biographical details are of little significance, since Mekas' creative or critical works are free of any pastoral accents. He had spent most of his youth in camps – first under the Nazis, and after the war in the 'displaced persons' centres run in Germany by the American administration. His cinematic interests originated in the second stage of his camp existence. He read a lot and pondered on the subject. He is, in fact, an extremely well-read man, solidly based in European culture.

On his third day in America the 28-year-old European immigrant began making short documentary films. He had been learning his craft in Hans Richter's workshop and there had become 'infected' with *avant garde* attitudes. In 1955 he started editing a critical magazine, *Film Culture*. In 1961 he made, with borrowed money, a feature film with actors, *Guns of the Trees*. It was a complete artistic manifesto, and the film's New York opening can be taken as the birth date of the N.A.C. (New American Cinema).[9]

Three years later Mekas made *The Brig*, surprising his admirers with this concentrated charge of sadism. The director's intention was to record simply on film and sound-track a stage production of the Living Theatre. A crucial feature of this cinematic record was the spontaneity of the entire operation. Jonas Mekas and his associates were all unfamiliar with the play, and were filming it on one evening during a single performance. They brought to the job the attitude not of an omniscient director who knows how to select significant bits to knit them into a familiar pattern, but of an unprepared, unsuspecting viewer who experiences the action as it develops. The accusing character of Kenneth Brown's play, showing the brutality of the military gaol guards on board an American man-of-war, came across on the screen with even greater force. In 1964 *The Brig* won the prize for the best documentary film at the Venice Film

Festival. The decision provoked some comment as the original play is a work of fiction, but Mekas' achievement was to provide a cinematic documentary record, without any change or interference, of theatrical event.

Jonas Mekas' artistic programme took time to crystallize. Before he made *Guns of the Trees* he had been not so much a prophet as a gentle patron, encouraging artistic projects of all kinds. He even used to admonish some of his colleagues in *Film Culture* for their lack of discipline and their surrender to extreme trends.

Soon he was affected by a radical change of attitude. Mekas seems to have developed a sense of mission and started preaching his gospel truths, not only on film and art, but also his personal philosophy and even, implicitly, a political philosophy. He became an apostle, foreseeing the salvation of America through the new cinema. Images registered on a celluloid strip are suggested as a universal remedy for all the ailments of the late twentieth-century reality.

A short resumé of Mekas' thesis must inevitably oversimplify it. Firstly, modern man needs the new cinema as an instrument of cognition and expression. Modern man is seeking to open new ways for humanity; the new cinema offers him command over a modern language, more penetrating and more dynamic in its syntax, grammar and rhythm, suitable for today's developed sensibilities. This language can express the full range of feeling and reflect continuously changing reality.

Secondly, modern man, searching for a way and pushing towards it, is responsible for his doings not to society but to himself. His aim is self-fulfilment, not social achievement.

Thirdly, the world is affected by madness: on one hand society is bent on the destruction of individuals and individuality, on the other society is itself menaced with nuclear annihilation. Therefore the artist's duty is to oppose at every step the institutional and legal framework of the established order.

Fourthly, the only call which can unite individualists is the call to recapture the lost Paradise. 'We have no time to wait till to-morrow,' says Jonas Mekas. 'Paradise now! That's our motto.'[10] But he is not certain which way to go to reach that destination. Traditional theories of popular movements are treated with reserve. Ideology grows spontaneously, in the heat of action, declares the prophet.

What does this programme really amount to? Its only distinct feature is the total negation of the *status quo*. The future, the strategy and tactics, the immediate and the ultimate targets – all these are left to the artist's individual choice. The operating principle, characteristic of the American New Left, is to respect all calls, from whatever quarter, no matter how confused or anarchistic, to overthrow the established order. They may not know what the 'Paradise now' is going to be like but they want it ushered in – quickly.

The next obvious question to pose is: What makes film the privileged weapon in the fight to transform the world? According to Mekas this is the medium uniquely suited to the psychology of modern man. It is superior to literature which can only describe reality. Film can not only show action, but actually provoke it. A passive medium, like the written word, can never in this respect compare with the sound film.

All this is ambiguous, open to argument, or, to put it brutally, muddled. The idea of 'Paradise now' is undoubtedly beautiful in its innocence, but this is as far as one can go. Everything else comes down to the proclamation of anarchy in the name of opposition to the American establishment, and heady freedom for the artist responsible only to himself and moving in whichever direction his fancy takes him. These gospel truths are propagated with really apostolic fervour, in the spirit of the Holy Crusade and papal infallibility. Jonas Mekas is unshaken in his belief that N.A.C. filmmakers are the pioneers of a new kind of art and a new kind of world. Only they, and no one else. One can deride and ridicule them but, in the strength of their conviction, they really are the apostles, spreading the gospel of the twenty-first century.

The Diversity of the Underground Cinema

Do the hundreds of film-makers organized in the N.A.C. accept unquestioningly the pronouncements of Jonas Mekas? Certainly not. His creed is treated not as a system of dogmas, but as a convenient screen for enterprises of all kinds. American *avant garde* artists readily adopt and stress the Mekas principle of absolute freedom and they are flattered by his claim that they are changing the world but they all want to change it in their own way. This makes for a diversity of directions and artistic positions within the third *avant garde*. The task of detailing all the divisions and categories is almost impossible. The most one can do is sketch the principal directions.

There are three distinct streams. The first one keeps close to the fine and plastic arts, makes frequent use of animation, employs various techniques (collage is the recent favourite) and gravitates towards abstraction. The second is the poetic film, built on the shock principle, but employing metaphor and symbolism. Its antecedents are early Bunuel films, *Un Chien Andalou* and *L'Age d'Or*. The third is a record of reality, frequently treating the camera as an objective registering mechanism and limiting as far as possible the director's intervention. These are the basic streams, but they are rarely found in pure form. There are many cross-currents and deviations, mixtures and borrowings. There are some film-makers who work consistently in one field, within one genre; others – and there are more of them – wander all over the stylistic range, trying and tasting something different each time, sometimes mixing or contrasting various strands and manners within the same work.

The *avant garde* is not only stylistically diverse, but scattered geographically. The biggest centre is, of course, in New York, the cradle of N.A.C., but a large and dynamic group of film-makers is concentrated around the San Francisco bay (in Berkeley, for example), and there are isolated artists active in Boston, Los Angeles, Chicago and Colorado. The North Californian *avant garde* has developed a distinct artistic character of its own, and we shall refer to it separately.

Kinoplastics

'Kinoplastics' was the term coined by Jonas Mekas back in 1955,[11] at the outset of his career, for the representatives of the first stream. Kinoplastics' principal interest is in questions of form, in the purely aesthetic effect of their films. It is their principal, but not their exclusive, interest. Perhaps the most representative author in this group, Stan Van Der Beek, often attempts in his films a sharply satirical image of our times, as in *Science Friction*, or *Summit*. Robert Breer composes his films of still images. His *Image by Images I* was made up with 240 different still frames. In *Room* Carmen D'Avino's filmed fragments of torn wallpapers and dilapidated walls created an incredibly rich tapestry of strange patterns. The director says that cinema is for him an extension of painting and unrelated to drama. His interest in film developed as a consequence of his painterly attitude to reality.

The most refined of the 'collage' artists is Ed Emswhiller who couples his interest in dance and painting with a passion for the cinema. With help from the Ford Foundation he was able to make *Relativity* – a feature-length film about man's place in the universe, a visual poem full of sexual symbols and metaphors, and, as always with Emswhiller, consistently balletic in its rhythm.

Emswhiller has gone through a significant evolution in his artistic career. He describes it himself in one of his articles: 'In my early work I was interested in making almost pure, visual abstractions with practically no allegorical implications. Then I passed through a phase of what I call minimal reference, in which the film content and style focused closely on one emotional state or one portrait subject. More recently, with *Relativity* and my current work in progress, *Image, Flesh and Voice*, I've developed a more complex structure with broader implications.'[12] This progress from pure abstraction to a rather muddled allegory is not an artistic gain. When somewhere about the middle of the picture it becomes clear that *Relativity* is not an erotic dance of lines and shapes but a story of a man lost between microcosm and macrocosm, a feeling of impatience takes hold of the viewer. He was prepared to be 'involved at the cineasthetic sensual and emotional level', as the author himself had at one time postulated, and now he is suddenly asked, facing the picture, to recover his rational faculties, to become analytical and literary. It seems that the film artist, Ed Emswhiller, succumbed, like many of his underground colleagues, to the temptation of assuming the mantle of a prophet and a missionary, spreading the word about ultimate truths. Of course, one could disregard the doubtful philosophy and just watch the images. The London *Daily Telegraph* critic gave a typically British, pragmatic description of *Relativity*: 'An excuse, if one were needed, to introduce a well developed girl in the nude on whose body, first immobile, then dancing in slow motion, the camera dwells with understandable appreciation.'[13]

Kinoplastics started from a similar premise: they had been painters, impatient with the limitations imposed by the brush and the palette. They took hold of a camera to create their compositions from other elements. Perhaps with the exception of Emswhiller, fascinated by choreography, the other artists of this group are not interested in recording natural movement. They create their own, controlled effects of movement through animation, or, like Breer, renounce all movement within frame.

Recently, in this fortress of the 'traditional' *avant garde*, a slight wind of change has been felt. Van Der Beek has launched his idea of an extended film, or rather extended cinema. It breaks with the conventional principle of projection, that is with the motionless screen facing rows of permanently fixed seats. In the spectacle *Move Movies*, described as choreography of the projectors, two of these machines cast images on the screen while five smaller projectors, in the hands of the director's assistants, were in constant movement inside the hall, planting images on the bodies of the audience. In another experiment a film and a slide projector were synchronized with two sound tracks, making up a dense audio-visual mixture. Both Van Der Beek and Robert Breer collaborate closely with the theatre 'happening' people, like Claes Oldenburg, introducing film as an extension of stage effects.

Standing apart in the family of kinoplastics is Tony Conrad, the maker of *The Flicker*. He uses non-representative signs differently and for a different purpose than his colleagues. At twenty-eight he is the youngest of the group, and was educated as a mathematician, not an artist. He came to cinema by way of music, having been for some years concerned with modern experiments in that field. Conrad's notions sound extremely simple: he is trying to achieve a certain effect through the constant bombardment of viewers with light signals. *The Flicker* is composed exclusively of black and white frames, of various intensity of 'whiteness' and 'blackness', making up a succession of time patterns. There are forty-seven patterns in all, and the frequency of light changes varies from twenty-four to four a second. The effect is not so much artistic as physiological. Under the unrelenting visual message eyes start seeing visions, the coloured ones. Conrad asserts that *The Flicker* causes a similar sensation as that of exerting a firm pressure on eyeballs through closed eye-lids.[14] There were cases, according to the author, of some viewers being unable to take the bombardment and succumbing to a kind of nervous breakdown. Others compare the effect of *The Flicker* to that of hallucinatory drugs. Conrad's work is a clear and rather extreme example of extending the functional range of the film.

The 'flickers', who relish the trick of repeating the same images as in the early Kinetoscope, include, apart from Tony Conrad, George Landow (*Bardo Follies* and *Tibetan Book of the Dead*), and Paul Sharits, whose *Ray – Gun – Virus* consists of bombarding the audience with explosions of colour on the screen. This is how the author explains his creative method and the purpose of his work: 'The projector is an audio-visual pistol; the screen looks at the audience; the retina is a target. Goal: the temporary assassination of the viewers' normative consciousness. The film's final "image" is a faint blue (attained by *not* striving for it) and the viewer is left to his own reconstruction of self, left with a screen upon which his retina may project its own patterns.'[15]

As usual with the artists' declarations printed in the columns of *Film Culture* Sharits' credo bristles with involved intellectual jargon. To put it simply, the purpose of the film is to tire the eyes of the audience with a stream of aggressive images to a point where, after closing the lids, a coloured pattern will still appear recorded on the retina. The dosage might be so powerful and the effect so intense that the patterns could appear on the white surface of the empty screen.

The Poets

One could exclude all the kineplastics and the New American Cinema, certainly losing some of its variety, would lose nothing of its surrounding climate of outrage and feverish controversy. If today people are divided into a sizeable minority of ardently committed followers of the N.A.C., and the fiercely hostile majority of its opponents, it is the doing of film-makers such as Kenneth Anger, Jack Smith, Gregory Markopoulos and Stan Brakhage. They draw most of the invective and are the subject of the greatest adulation.

Kenneth Anger is one of the senior representatives of the movement. His *Fireworks* appeared twenty-five years ago. in 1947. Anger, an apologist for homosexuality, is fascinated by the occult and black magic. His master is Jean Cocteau, but he lacks the master's refinement, delicacy and allusiveness. Kenneth Anger is brutally direct and violent. Before entering a new era the world is to be swept by destruction and death. In *Scorpio Rising*, his definitive statement, we meet the fore-runners of the coming world of the strong – the motorcycle riders, with an affection of fetishist intensity for their machines, a fondness for Nazi insignia, and living in a permanent stage of homosexual stimulation. Kenneth Anger, believing single-mindedly in astrological prophesies, proclaims that in 1962 the Aquarian Age began, and after two thousand years of Christian domination Lucifer's turn has come.[16]

Between the making of *Scorpio Rising* (1964) and the opening of the ten-minute short, *Invocation of My Demon Brother* (1969), Kenneth Anger has had to live through a difficult time. This related to the disappearance, in mysterious circumstances, of the only copy of his *Lucifer Rising*, probably taken in 1966 from the Haight Theater cinema in San Francisco. A mixture of his depressive state and self-advertising, peculiar to underground cinema, found an outlet in 1967 in the form of a full-page obituary, published in *Village Voice*: 'In Memoriam – Kenneth Anger – film-maker (1947-67)'.

The lament for his departed talent has proved premature. *Invocation of My Demon Brother* was welcomed enthusiastically by the *underground* people. Although limited to ten minutes of screen time, the work received from Jonas Mekas and P. Adams Sitney the accolade of high artistic achievement. The *Film Culture* award for the year 1969 put the 'official' seal on the accomplishment of this artist who tries to marry film-making with magic. The motivation for the *Film Culture* award helps one to understand the prominence of Kenneth Anger's place in underground cinema. In this drawn-out document, reading like a litany to an underground saint, we come across such phrases as: 'For his unique fusion of magic, symbolism, myth, mystery and vision with the most modern sensibilities, techniques and rhythms of being ... for giving to our eye and our senses some of the most sensuous and mysterious images cinema has created; for being the Keeper of the Art of Cinema as well as the Keeper of the Eternal Magick Direction.'[17]

The description of what goes on in *Invocation* conveys nothing of the quality of this film. On the screen appear Lucifer, Mag, Brother and Sister Rainbow, Acolyte, etc. One has no idea about the meaning of all this unless one is familiar with the confusing multiplicity of magic signs and references, or with the master's, Aleister's Crawley's, book *Magic*. But is it essential to understand all the symbols and myths, the entire ritual? Jonas Mekas insists that this is quite immaterial. What is important is the energy released by the images, the movement, the symbols and the situations.[18] Undoubtedly such a critical attitude is quite legitimate as regards painting, music or poetry, and there is no reason not to approach the poetry of the screen in the same way. One's doubts refer not to the refusal to clarify the content, but to the ardent faith of the enthusiasts in the extraordinary artistic force of the film, the belief that the experiment represents the summit of imaginative achievement. But it is well known that it is impossible to argue with the proselytes of a new faith. The only choice is to accept their credo or to reject it. For Mekas *Invocation* will always be the source of a mysterious energy, such as is emanated only by great works of art.

Jack Smith lacks the philosophical pretensions of Kenneth Anger, and does not issue ideological manifestoes to support his work. In *Flaming Creatures* he shows simply and in detail a private party, developing into a free, general sex-play. The term 'orgy' seems absolutely inappropriate, suggesting, as it does, unbridled and violent debauchery. In Smith's film devotees of heterosexual or homosexual love (the last ones are more numerous and seem more sympathetically treated by the author) behave peacefully, or, as Susan Sontag has observed, gayly and rather childishly: '*Flaming Creatures* was banned by the New York State censorship and even proved an embarrassment to the organisers of the experimental film festival in Knokke le Zoute.'[19]

Another poet and veteran of the movement, with a fondness for cinematic metaphors and symbols, is Gregory Markopoulos, the maker of Greek myths about homosexual love. In the late forties his film trilogy appeared: *Psyche*, *Lysis* and *Charmides*. Homosexual themes appear also in his other works, including the most ambitious of them, *Illiac Passion*. Recently Markopoulos has left behind *avant garde* fiction and turned to making 'portraits' – pointing a static camera at a living subject and shooting interminably long takes. In this way *Galaxie*, a ninety-minute-long collection of 'portraits' came into being. This is how the *Chicago*

Tribune reviewer dismissed the Markopoulos opus at the Chicago festival: 'The worst offender was an hour and a half number entitled *Galaxie*, which interminably dragged out these artsy portraits of thirty-three people – each sequence separated by the clanking of an anvil, which might have served better coming down on the film-maker's head.'[20]

The group of cinema poets includes the 'Colorado loner', Stanley Brakhage, the author of a philosophical parable in five parts *Dog Star Man*.

The action is deceptively simple: a lumberjack (played by Brakhage) climbs up a hill and starts chopping down a tree. But this situation serves as an excuse to set off on a variety of digressions about the meaning of existence. Recently Brakhage, like Markopoulos, turned to making 'portraits'. But his only model is his little daughter, and the films are known as *Songs*, and marked with successive numbers. All the editing is done inside the camera.

Finally, a peculiar pair of poets – the brothers Mike and George Kuchar. Sometimes they make their films together, sometimes independently. They are not interested in philosophy or revolution, but are steeped up to their necks in the persiflage of Hollywood mythology. The twins, born in 1942 in the Bronx suburb of New York, have literally spent their entire childhood in the cinema. Seven hours daily day by day in the local cinema, which was often offering three hits in the same programme for 25 cents. The cheap 'Republic' Westerns, the gangster thrillers from Warner Brothers, RKO and M-G-M musicals, formed the spiritual nourishment the twins lived on between eight and thirteen years of age.[21] When they could handle a film camera themselves they started both to parody and mythicize the Hollywood world. They made satirical fantasies about fairy-tale lands populated with Hollywood heroes.

The Observers

Trends, fashions and production cycles are familiar phenomena in the underground cinema, just as in Hollywood. In the early sixties kinoplastics were in high fashion; later, during the scandals surrounding Jack Smith's *Flaming Creatures*, the film poets gained the ascendance; today attention is drawn principally to the 'observers' who record on celluloid what they see, or, increasingly, what they can spy and peep at. The master and leader of this N.A.C. stream is Andy Warhol. He began as a young painter propagating the precepts of pop-art. He sold his canvases of a Coca-Cola bottle or a tomato-soup tin for thousands of dollars and invested the money in film-making. Some of the films he shoots and directs himself, others are made with his money and under his general supervision. Occasionally he accepts an invitation from a colleague to appear as an actor (for example, in Markopoulos' *Illiac Passion*).

Andy Warhol has over fifty films to his credit, from short exercises of no more than a couple of minutes screen time, to the six-hour-long *Sleep*, the chief and only attraction of which is a sleeping man, occasionally snoring and grunting or turning over in his bed. For six hours the viewer, if he has the patience and the resistance, can watch the gentleman resting – to put it poetically – in the land of Nod. But the film has little to do with poetry; it is an extremely boring description of a perfectly ordinary event. The sleeping person, oblivious to the watchful camera, is a continuous presence on the screen. The director is interested in the movement of time, not the physical movement. Another film based on the same principle is *Empire State Building* – the New York sky-scraper photographed at various times of the day, in a changing light. The experiments of Claude Monet transferred to a different medium. One can see a certain logic in this, or even a glimmer of poetry (light in the windows, flashing on or disappearing), but the final effect is, as in *Sleep*, of desperate boredom.

Sleep and *Empire State Building* date from 1963 and 1964. In 1965 Andy Warhol enlarges his interests, making excursions into fiction, usually from screen ideas by Ronald Taval. These were short sound films, centred on sexual themes, with homosexuality prominently displayed. Warhol's leading male star is Mario Montez, a native of Puerto Rico, performing usually in drag and made up to look like a Spanish beauty.

In his next period (1966–8) the director began experimenting with a split screen. Towards the end of 1966 *Chelsea Girls* appeared. With this, underground cinema saw the light of day, or at least tasted the advantages of commercial distribution. His method and artistic principles remain the same as at the time of his début. He considered himself, as a film director, to be a bystander only, an observer, watching and registering what is going on on the screen. He does not interfere by giving instructions to actors: they improvise, trying to behave as naturally as if their actions were taking place in real life. He does not edit his films, but presents them 'straight' or 'raw'.

Chelsea Girls consist of two separate films, projected simultaneously on the left and right side of the screen for three and a half hours. The action takes place in the rooms of the Chelsea Hotel in lower Manhattan. A viewer witnesses the wooing and masochistic love-play of two lesbians, watches a homosexual couple in bed, and a junkie self-injecting a dose of heroin. Three of the sequences were shot in colour, the others in black-and-white. Normally the sound track accompanies only the images on one side of the screen, and the definition on the same side is perceptibly sharper, but this can vary. Andy Warhol leaves freedom of self-expression to technicians and projectionists; they decide in what order and in what inter-relationship the parts of the film are to be screened.

The film's success was due in some measure to the novelty of the split-screen method, but the decisive influence was a curiosity about the human environment shown on the screen. Respectable citizens were intrigued by this key-hole view of the forbidden world. In *Chelsea Girls* there also appear, apart from the authentic inhabitants of the hotel, professional underground actors, including the inevitable Mario Montez. There are conflicting versions about where and how the action was shot. According to one version (followed by Sheldon Renan in his book) the work is an anthology of short sequences actually filmed, at various times, in the Chelsea Hotel[21]; according to Susan Pike in *Film Culture*[22] different New York locations were used, between 23 Western Street and 47 Eastern Street, and even some scenes photographed in Cambridge, Massachusetts were included. This is not an entirely sterile argument because the degree of authenticity of what goes on on the screen is at issue. Although it seems that the term 'exhibitionism' would be more apt than 'authenticity'. Whether these human shreds who share with us their experiences and thoughts are the permanent occupants of this junkie retreat, or non-resident clients of similar establishments, Andy Warhol transforms a very private dimension of their lives into a public spectacle. In whose interest and to what purpose? Undoubtedly to foster a climate of scandal and perhaps to make money this way; also, to throw some light on the unmentionable recesses of the American reality. A reviewer of the conservative *Los Angeles Times* has dealt with *Chelsea Girls* briefly and explicitly: 'There is a place for this sort of thing, and it is definitely underground. Like in a sewer.'[23]

At the beginning of the seventies Andy Warhol became an underground cinema producer almost in the Hollywood manner. His company, Factory Films Inc., is working at full speed, and a sizeable group of assistants, collaborators and ordinary yes-men has gathered around the master. The underground stars have made their appearance, the outstanding ones known to their followers as super stars. In most cases Andy Warhol supervises the productions from a certain distance, lending his name to them, but the real moving spirit of the enterprise is Paul Morrisey, acting in the multiple capacities of a director, co-producer, editor and a general impresario.

Developments in the structure and style of the Warhol productions move them, in almost all aspects, closer to the conventional, commercial cinema. Firstly, the films are no longer mood exercises or fragmentary studies but contain distinct, if rudimentary, narrative passages. The plots of *Lonesome Cowboys*, *Flesh*, *Trash*, *Blue Movie* and *Women in Revolt* can be described and summarized in several sentences or so – a task quite impossible in the early Warhol films.

Secondly, films from the Warhol factory lean heavily on acting personalities, as in the best days of Hollywood. They are, of course, stars of a particular kind, somewhat different from their Californian colleagues, more closely related to the semi-professional protagonists of the off-Broadway theatre. Warhol seems to favour homosexual types, both active and passive, but most of all transvestites. Apart from Mario Montez, trying to recapture on the screen the feminine charms of the beautiful Maria Montez who died in 1951, Holly Woodlawn in *Trash* makes a successful appearance in 'drag', even in erotic scenes. And when too much physiological detail makes simulation impossible the authentically feminine 'superstar' Viva takes over. In *Blue Movie* the copulation scene (with all the refinements) lasts for ten minutes – the first 'performance' of this sort especially designed for cinema audiences, *avant garde* or not.

Andy Warhol, in accordance with the prevailing fashion, adopts the principle of absolute sexual freedom. In his films there is a lot of male and female nudity and a variety of heterosexual and homosexual relationships. No doubt this attracts the public who care little about the erudite and obscure *Film Culture* manifestoes. Andy Warhol believes that eroticism is ever-present. 'This is the way life is and you can't change it,'[24] he says. He is very far from romanticizing sex. On the contrary, he often shows it brutally, in a repulsive rather than an attractive way. In *Trash*, directed by Paul Morrisey, the mystery of drug-taking is debunked for the first time. The central character of the film, a junky, is shown as a shred of humanity, a permanently vague look in his eyes and lice in his hair (seen in close up).

What then, if anything, has remained of the youthful spirit of the *avant garde* experimentation? The freedom to make the kind of films you want, without any restrictions, to shoot them in the most direct and immediate manner, quickly, cheaply, and untroubled by demands for technical perfection. What Andy Warhol preached in 1966 – 'Enough of films well made and uninteresting. The time of badly made but interesting films has come,'[25] is still in force, although Paul Morrisey, not always with the full approval of the master, tries to introduce elements of craftsmanship into editing and photography. On the whole, however, the cult of the primitive

G

still flourishes, rationalized by smooth phraseology. On *Chelsea Girls* Andy Warhol has pronounced: 'The lighting is bad, the camerawork is bad, the sound is bad, but the people are beautiful.'[26] It is impossible to disagree with the first two statements, but the third is a matter of taste.

Andy Warhol has become an institution. It seems less important now what sort of films he makes, or lends his name to, than the fact that they come out with his factory trade-mark. No longer do they have to wait for their chance in college halls, or to be screened secretly with a certain embarrassment. On the contrary, they are accompanied by a noisy and aggressive publicity. The New York Garrick Theatre cinema even changed its name on the occasion of the *Lonesome Cowboys* opening to the Andy Warhol Garrick Theater. *Trash* ran successfully in the exclusive Don Rugoff's Cinema II Theatre, not in Greenwich Village, but in Manhattan. Warhol's cinematic successes strengthen his position as a painter. In 1971 the Whitney Museum put on a retrospective exhibition of his art. A canvas showing a tin can of soup of the popular Campbell brand was sold for the sum of $62,000. Who could have expected it when, in 1962, Andy Warhol made his début as a budding artist in a Stable Gallery exhibition! The film *L'Amour*, shot in Paris and shown for the first time at the Locarno film festival in August 1972, marks another stage in the process of relinquishing *avant garde* extremes. Andy Warhol gives his own version of the immortal Hollywoodian theme of *An American in Paris*. This time it is a story of two American girls and a rich American who is living with a French boy. At the end the rich American throws out his boyfriend and marries one of the American girls. Sex no longer dominates the screen, and homosexuality is only hinted at and not shown. On the whole, this Andy Warhol Factory production does not differ very much from the commercial films made in Hollywood or elsewhere. Once the great man of the underground, nowadays Andy Warhol is an independent film producer–director, interested in the commercial possibilities of exhibiting his products. And what about sex? In the February 1973 issue of *Vogue* magazine, one could read the following statement made by Andy Warhol: 'I think sex is the biggest nothing of all time.'[27]

In San Francisco and Its Environs

In San Francisco, the unofficial capital of the 'hippies' and 'flower children', a favourable climate existed for the growth of a cinematic *avant garde*. A start had already been made at the time of the beatniks, the forerunners of the hippy movement. Here too, as in New York, the themes include sexual obsessions and affirmation of the drug culture, but, perhaps under the influence of the California landscape and the general (social as well as geographical) climate, the black and grey colours do not dominate to anything like the same extent. Life is not permeated by a sense of desperation. The protests seem more direct and specific, the outlook more optimistic and joyful, occasional images and sound are poetic and graceful. Perhaps the San Francisco *avant garde* is also less of a show-off, not as snobbish and conceited as the New York groups.

The most prominent exponent of the West Coast *avant garde* is no longer there. Ron Rice died in 1964 in Acapulco, in his late twenties. He left *The Flower Thief*, a lyrical tale about a city tramp, a maladjusted man, half crazy and half saint, a mixture of Charlie Chaplin's tramp and Myshkin from Dostoevsky's *Idiot*. He is played by Taylor Mead, a poet and talented amateur actor, with a rich vein of comedy. Much weaker was Rice's New York film, *Chumlum*, an oriental fable set in an enormous, palatial brothel, where couples make love not in beds but in hammocks.

Ron Rice left unfinished *Queen Saba Meets the Atom Man*, begun in 1962. The material was supplemented and edited in 1967 by Howard Everngam. This is how Alberto Moravia, the Italian novelist, describes the film in the weekly *L'Espresso*: 'The beat hero is a nihilist, let us say, of Anglo-Saxon species, clowning, ironic, full of humour (a little bit Keaton, a little bit Chaplin, a little bit Tati), but the negress, in contrast, is all affirmation of life, from her head to her feet. Completely naked, she moves about the apartment on elephantine hips; she uses the electric razor, makes a phone call, plays with a cat, and then, after a grotesque ball, both of them, in an embrace, collapse amid the mish-mash of the pad. The film describes, poetically, a way of living. The film is a protest that is violent, childish and sincere – a protest against an industrial world based on the cycle of production and consumption.'[28]

Since Rice's death the leading figure in the San Francisco group has been Bruce Baillie, an aggressive, dynamic film-maker, and, surprisingly, clearly moving towards social interests and commitments. Baillie is a sort of a West Coast Mekas. He has been organizing film shows and an underground paper, the *Canyon Cinema News*. In 1961 he made *Mr Hayashi*, a film about a poor Japanese workman wandering through Berkeley in search of a job. An interesting item in the context of the N.A.C. is *A Mass* (1963–4), a film about the gradual dying out of the Dakota Sioux, and an allegory about the disappearance of human features in the technological age. Gregorian chants serve as a musical illustration. *A Mass* opens and closes with an image of a man dying on the corner of a busy street.

In *Don Kichote* Baillie attempts a condensed visual cross-section of the United States, complete with political, social, artistic and moral intimations. A weakness of this film, as of the other less ambitious work by Bruce Baillie, is an over-employment of camera and laboratory tricks. Unusual angles, the use of distortion, wide-angle lens, double exposures, are the hallmark of this director's style. He appears to be endlessly fascinated by the potential richness of the techniques available to him and, experimenting with them, cannot resist exaggerating the cinematic quality of his work. One feels exhausted rather than overjoyed by the audio-visual richness of the film and intricacy of the editing. This surfeit of cinematic effects is rather characteristic of many, if not the majority, of the N.A.C. film-makers.

Finally, Robert Nelson, a young San Francisco painter who won a well-deserved acclaim for his burlesque *Oh, Dem Watermelons*. The origin of the film is similar to that of René Clair's *Entr'acte*: it was made to fill an interlude in a stage production of *A Minstrel Show*, and featured the same cast. However, the real protagonists were not people but big, black and juicy watermelons, appearing in different situations and triggering off a variety of gags. Watermelons are desired, they are thirst-quenching, tasty, but also, treated without respect, are dumped as garbage, rolling about among the street litter. In this playful and amusing film a sad refrain keeps recurring, all the more rankling for those who are able to read the metaphor: the black watermelons are the black people . . .

Common Denominators

Kenneth Anger, Jack Smith, Andy Warhol, Stan Van Der Beek, Stan Brakhage, Bruce Baillie, and five or ten others are the luminaries of the American *avant garde* cinema. Behind them there is a legion of lesser known or 'unknown' lights. In the catalogues of the Film Makers Cooperative one finds a long list of names and a longer one of film titles. Hundreds of film-makers, hundreds, or perhaps even thousands, of titles representing the New American Cinema. The fact is significant, at least quantitatively. Perhaps not quite to the extent imagined by the underground followers, but not to be passed over unnoticed.

Let us, then, having described the dominant streams of the third *avant garde*, try to find in their gaudy variety certain common features characteristic of the entire new American cinema. To begin with the obvious, it is the author's cinema in its purest form. Sheldon Renan, already quoted here, has rightly called it an explosion of personal statements in a variety of forms, styles and directions.[29] An underground film is completely the creation of a single person who, in the majority of cases performs the four-fold function of producer, director, cameraman and editor. In the exceptional case of Andy Warhol it is the producer who stamps his individuality on films leaving his 'factory'.

This authors' cinema is also violently and uncompromisingly anti-Hollywood. Aspiring to save America, leading her people back to Paradise, once lost and now to be retrieved, the *avant garde* film-makers mean to free the millions from the slavery of Hollywood, from the myths and way of life propagated by the powerful linked systems of the official cinema and television.

P. Adam Sitney argues that anti-Hollywood attitudes originate from a specific set of economic circumstances.[30] When Jonas Mekas and his colleagues were ushering in the N.A.C. many of them would probably have preferred to work on 35 mm rather than 16 mm, and with the assistance of qualified technicians, but they could not afford it. And Hollywood at the turn of the sixties was bureaucratic and set in its tracks, ill-disposed to any change. This was, says P. Adam Sitney, a lucky break for the young revolutionaries of the cinema. They have not been absorbed by the established film industry. In Europe, where the commercial cinema is more flexible, there is little room for the underground. In France the New Wave was born within the established cinema industry, and in England the 'angry young men' could force their way into the fortress.

Film authors avail themselves of absolute freedom of expression – this is another unified feature of underground cinema. They make films the way they want to make them. They are not always able to present them to large audiences, but among friends and acquaintances, at club shows and college halls, everything gets by. Carl Linder, one of the minor figures of the underground, the maker of *Devil is Dead* and *Skin*, preaches solemnly that 'sex is the greatest metaphor of our times' and that 'through sex one can express everything, even things that have nothing to do with sex'.[31] It appears that many *avant garde* artists firmly believe in the Linder gospel. Jonas Mekas, at the time when he was still an outside observer of underground cinema, wrote in *Film Culture* that 'the homosexual conspiracy is one of the most shocking and the most persistent features of the poetics of the American cinema'.[32] The words, written in 1955, seem even more true today.

According to Parker Tyler, freedom of expression is in certain ways akin to voyeurism, and affords some of the 'Peeping Tom's' pleasures.[33] The philosophical premises on which the activities of the underground film-makers rest may be sound, but the practical effects of their acts are open to argument and doubt. Their original point was that the established cinema is constrained and paralysed by various bans and taboos. It shows – without showing. The advantage of the cinema is, as Béla Balázs wrote back in the twenties, that it extends the human capacity for seeing, enabling one to see wider, sharper, more penetratingly. To reclaim this cinematic potency, or even the very belief in the powers of the cinema, it is necessary to penetrate into forbidden corners of experience. Now all private worlds, all manifestations of humanity, however cruel and shocking, or labelled by the guardian and censorship bodies as immoral, ought to be thrown open to the inquisitive cameras and microphones.

In practice the film-makers' daring explorations take them mainly into the private worlds of sexual behaviour, hence the key-hole attitudes and 'Peeping Tom' comparisons. The enclosed worlds of political behaviour prove for the majority of artists much less attractive, and any references to burning issues like race, the Vietnam War, or student militancy, have been either sweepingly general or marginal. The affairs of the world appear as incidental to the search for solutions to individual problems, usually leading to drug-taking and sexual licence.

When underground artists do reflect on the world they live in, and try to express its complexity and absurdity – which they regard as self-evident – they tend to employ an over-simple and easy method, a montage of contrasting images, double exposures, sounds thrown together in a discordant cacophony. Chaos on the screen is meant to convey that chaos is ruling the world.

A more recent common denominator is the emergence of 'psychedelic cinema'. This recently coined adjective 'psyche-delic' denotes a state of hypersensitiveness that is euphoristic and fosters creative impulses, usually induced by drugs: marijuana, LSD or mescaline. The formula is simple: the creative artist should take a course of drug 'treatment' before setting out to make films. Strictly speaking the method is not new. It had been used many times (one example is

Stanislaw Ignacy Witkiewicz, known as 'Witkacy', a Polish writer and artist who used to sign his canvases with the chemical recipe of the drug used). But now psychedelic cinema is hailed as the revelation of the only true art.

One aspect of creative freedom, as mentioned earlier, is a general scorn for technical perfection. *Avant garde* films are purposely made in a slap-dash, careless way, with total disregard for conventional rules. It may be that in the majority of cases this attitude can be traced back to a lack of skill in operating a camera, an editing table or even a splicer. But what is creative interpretation for? Even illiteracy can be made into a virtue. The same Jonas Mekas who in 1955 castigated the independents for their lack of artistic discipline, by 1967 reached a different conclusion: 'Even the mistakes,' he declared, 'out-of-focus shots, shaky shots, overexposed and underexposed shots, are part of the new cinema vocabulary, being part of the psychological and visual reality of modern man.'[34]

And the final common denominator: American underground film-makers are not over-concerned about the public accessibility of their films, still less about their intelligibility. They use a camera to release creative energy, and it is not their business to provide a key to the meaning of the work produced. One of the directors has compared the viewer's encounter with his film to the reading of a poem off an electric board installed on top of a building to provide up-to-the-minute news items.[35] Another has declared that a viewer watching his film for the first time cannot possibly perceive the nature of what is on the screen.[36] Inaccessibility and obscureness are extolled as high virtues.

Perspectives for Tomorrow

One may be excused for surmising, on the strength of the above discussion, that the American underground cinema is largely an artistic fraud. There are arguments to support this, but with two important reservations: among the mass of mystification and incompetence there are several, or more, genuine talents. They are perhaps erratic, confused, affected, but true artists nevertheless. Among their number one can certainly include Bruce Baillie, Stan Brakhage, Andy Warhol and even Jonas Mekas of *Guns of the Trees*. Of course in such an enormous and populous country the emergence of twenty, at the most, probably less, genuinely creative artists seems an insufficient reason to proclaim a 'Second Coming' in the realm of film. Thus the first reservation does not entirely refute the accusations of 'fraud'.

The second reservation seems conclusive. It has to do with the pressure of sheer quantity. Jonas Mekas estimates that in private hands in the United States there are no fewer than 7 million film cameras, 8 mm and 16 mm. A huge army of amateurs is busy making films. At one time young people used to express their artistic longings in painting or attempted to write poetry, now they find it more attractive to transfer their poetic feelings on to celluloid. Cheap magnetic tape and recorders allow them to accompany their short, or not so short, films with sound. This dissemination of film-making is of the utmost significance. Jonas Mekas speculates that cinema from a public institution is going to change into a household implement, and an entirely new network of communications is going to emerge, independent of the established system. Science fiction? It may be closer than most people imagine. Probably this household cinema will have nothing, or little, in common with the current forms of the American underground cinema, but one of its main features will no doubt persist: it is bound to be primarily a personal cinema, free of all the constraints imposed by the Hollywood establishment. Jonas Mekas believes that this cinema of the future will emerge as an important political force.[37] The Film Makers' Cooperative intends to distribute 200 ciné cameras to young Negroes, to provide them with stock and pay lab costs, only asking in return that they make the kind of films they really want, may have some influence on the political development of 'household' cinema. The only question is: will the young Negroes accept the gift?

American underground cinema has a strong following in the colleges. When the young, training at a couple of hundred film courses, come to test their flimsy skills in school exercises, they show no influence of *Cleopatra* or *A Sound of Music*, but of films made by Mekas, Warhol or Brakhage. These not only mean much more to the young people but are less demanding when one's control over the material is not too sure. Festivals of experimental cinema, subsidies from art foundations, support from the press are some of the factors strengthening this activity. The N.A.C. has managed to build up a solid basis from which to develop.

If it does survive, will the new cinema continue unchanged? One hopes that it is going to change, that it can cure itself of its deadly sins so prominent at present. Perhaps the film-makers of the third *avant garde* will no longer believe themselves to be so significant, that before them there has been nothing to speak of, and after them only the rediscovered Paradise. Perhaps the pseudo-scientific and pseudo-philosophical prattle is going to disappear from the columns of *Film Culture*, with all those interminable declarations about discovering America again and again, by anybody who has first laid his hands on a camera and then on a typewriter But if this self-admiration continues the output of the New American Cinema is unlikely to improve.

One doubts whether the salvation, or rather the renaissance of the underground cinema can come about through the two aesthetic theories propagated at the beginning of the seventies. The exponent of one, that of structural film, is P. Adams Sitney. A structural film, carefully planned and composed, may appear to be an antidote for a 'spontaneous' statement, where anything goes into the same cinematic sack in the hope that something personal, expressive of a state of mind or a shift in feeling, will come out. Sitney observes that some directors are now seeking a strict, formal discipline, trying to design their films in precise detail, to achieve in the structure of their work a sense of permanency rather than a spontaneous, transient movement.[38] It suggests a development similar to Cézanne's rebellion against the amorphous fluidity of the impressionists as represented by Renoir, Pissaro or Sisley.

However, when one takes a closer look at the characteristics of structural film, as understood and elucidated by

Sitney, it becomes clear that far from opening extensive new perspectives it threatens to stifle inspiration in a strait-jacket of dogmatism. To this apostle of structuralism form is absolutely decisive, with content entering into it only as an afterthought – as an additional ingredient, injected in minute quantities into an already going project. There are three features characteristic of structural film: a static camera (the viewer is faced with a fixed frame), the flickering effect (bombarding the viewer with flashing images), and repetition of an image, as in the kinetoscope. The limited and restrictive nature of those formal devices, may, indeed, force the film-maker to submit to a discipline, but at the same time they are leading him into a blind alley. Sitney's theories, taken literally, would reduce the entire range of cinematic means of expression to the formula of Fernand Léger's *Ballet Mechanique*. Certainly this film with its repeated refrain of a woman climbing a flight of stairs was an interesting work, with an impressive clarity of structure, but the acceptance of *Ballet Mechanique* never implied the rejection of Clair's *Entr'acte*, or Bunnel's *Un Chien Andalou*.

The other theory, known as 'expanded cinema', is by no means dogmatic, but utopian and unreal. Its chief exponent is Gene Youngblood, and if one follows his line of reasoning to its logical conclusion, it would lead to the total liquidation of cinema as we know it, and the petering out of all organized production. Youngblood preaches the unification of all mass media, the development of which is to result in films without a frame and without a conventional system of projection. Gene Youngblood's book *Expanded Cinema*[39] was published in 1970, but the idea is not all that new. During the 1966 New York Film Festival a symposium to consider the possibilities of expanded cinema was organized, and a special, com-memorative issue of *Film Culture* was subtitled 'Expanded Arts'.[40] A published programme of the Mekas '*Cinematheque*' festival announced that 'the programs will explore the uses of multiple screens, multiple projectors, multiple images, interrelated screen forms and images, film-dance, moving slides, kinetic sculptures, hand-held projectors, balloon screens, video tapes and video-projectors, light and sound experiments'. This list is sufficient in itself to explain the principles of expanded cinema – the vision of a viewer and a listener receptive and responsive to a surrounding, simultaneous, continuous and variable audio-visual environment.

Experiments of that kind have been practised for some time at the big international exhibitions (Brussels, New York, Montreal, Tokyo). Their impact is considerable, if not long-lasting, and the costs sky-high. But how can expanded cinema be practised by artists who find it hard to raise money for 8 mm film stock? At the most they play an expanded cinema game with their friends, linking up projectors, or devising their film-making as a part of a larger 'happening'.

Amos Vogel, once a forerunner and pioneer of the independent cinema, published in the *Evergreen Review* an article titled 'Thirteen Misconceptions', reprinted in 1967 in an anthology called *The New American Cinema*.[41] It is a sharp, often pitiless criticism of underground cinema attitudes. Here is the concluding paragraph of that piece: 'Blind adulation and hermeticism are the enemies of growth and lead to the repetition of what has already been achieved; the rise of epigons and mediocrities; the progressive narrowing of vision and the cumulative deterioration of taste. What the American *avant garde* is confronted with is sectarianism parading as freedom, flattery as criticism, sterile ecleticism as artistic philosophy, anti-intellectualism and know-nothingness as liberation. Dogmas, myths and popes are inevitable stages in human pre-history; a higher stage will be reached when they are superseded by men of free will.' We are awaiting for this new and higher stage.

7

A Leap into the Unknown

Reciprocal Services

The marriage of cinema and television was not a love match but one of convenience. Television could not manage without feature films, and the cinema industry found the small screen a worth-while market. Thus after years of cut-throat competition came the era of fruitful partnership. Particularly since 1966 when the television success of *The Bridge on the River Kwai* demonstrated that old films, designed for the cinema screens, could recapture their youth through direct electronic transmission to millions of American homes. Martin Ransohoff of Filmways Inc. declared in 1969 that every good film can recover from television sales at least half of its production costs.[1] This estimate appears over-optimistic, and ought to be treated with caution. Huge sums paid for expensive spectacles like *Cleopatra* are the exception. On average the three big television companies, ABC, CBS and NBC pay around half a million dollars for a film; another half million can be earned through the syndicated companies from a second transmission in various local stations. Altogether, around one million dollars, a considerable sum, certainly, but only in comparatively few cases reaching 50 per cent of the total production budget. But which company can afford to scorn 25 per cent, 15 per cent or even 10 per cent?

Another area of co-operation is production for direct television demand. In the early sixties 'live' television programmes started losing ground in favour of items pre-recorded on film or magnetic tape. In 1955 live television accounted for 84 per cent of the total; fifteen years later, in 1970, for only 5 per cent. This technological transformation of live pre-recorded television in the late fifties saved Hollywood from certain liquidation. The old film capital has changed into a giant factory producing canned material for the small screen. Day after day big, average, small and very small programmes were being registered on film stock and magnetic tape to satisfy a hungry demand from large companies and independent stations, feeding on an unending stream of new dramas, comedies, Westerns, slapstick and variety shows. Hollywood has lost the romantic glamour of the pre-television era of the super-stars, but it has gained a powerful new drive, pumping life into the studios threatened not so long ago with extinction.

Several factors contributed to this transformation. Hollywood has everything needed to ensure a continuous supply of the product television has become dependent on since the almost total disappearance of the live show. Attempts to set up other centres of production, principally in New York, but also in Chicago and San Francisco, proved economically non-viable. These great cities lack the resources, such as fully equipped shooting stages and a suitably large and highly qualified pool of technicians and creative artists. Significantly, even one-minute commercials, not long ago produced almost exclusively in New York, have, since 1966 moved to Hollywood. The West Coast concentration of acting talent has caused even the pre-recording of variety shows, at one time a Broadway speciality, to be done increasingly in California.

Nevertheless, the entire range of television production, although a profitable operation, remained for Hollywood a secondary line of activity. The big studios still concentrated their efforts on the production of 'real' films, designed for theatre exhibition. Tradition, habit and the gambling instinct all played a part here. One could make millions out of one big screen hit. *The Sound of Music, Doctor Zhivago*, intermittent re-issues of *Gone with the Wind*, helped to preserve the myth of a flourishing, indestructibly cinematic and not television-dominated Hollywood. And television serials brought their own considerable problems: popular one season they could suddenly lose their rating in the next.

It was then necessary to suspend production and to search hastily for new scripts, new producers and directors. Life would have been easier if it had been possible to standardize production – making the same pictures for both the cinema and the small screen. But that had seemed a dream solution: hard economic practice was ruled by the principle of diversification, demanding that a variety of clients must be served, seeking a wide range of audio-visual entertainments.

However, in the late sixties a pronounced shift in the programmes of the 'big three' could be discerned, a shift which, strangely enough, moved towards the 'dream' solution, and away from the 'practical' one. The feature film, designed for cinema exhibition, was taking up the privileged position on the small screen. The 1968–9 television season was written about as 'the great film season'. Of course, feature films had been shown earlier on the small screen. There were many of them, but with two significant qualifications. Firstly, there was a great prevalence of old films, and the few more recent were not of the top rank. The supply was dominated by the early thirties hits, supplemented, whenever possible, by foreign imports, dubbed into English. Secondly, features were screened in the off-peak viewing hours: before noon, early afternoon and late evening. On CBS and affiliated networks, three different programme slots were available for the cinema: the early show (before 12 noon), the late show (after 10 in the evening) and the late, late show (after midnight).

Of course, even at this early stage some interesting films were finding their way into television programmes, but they were not advertised. A film fan had a job to find interesting items in the maze of television programming. Printed programmes as a rule omitted names of directors, year of production and sometimes even skipped the cast list. This information was only provided by the valuable *TV Key Movie Guide*, edited by the *Los Angeles Times* critic, Steven H. Scheuer, and appearing since 1958. The *Guide* changed its name in 1969 and is now published under the title *Movies on TV*. It contains descriptions and ratings – from one to four stars – of 7,000 feature films.

The first break through the practice of relegating feature films to off-peak viewing times was made in September 1961 by the National Broadcasting Corporation. The rating figures, issued by the A. Nielsen Corporation – a powerful instrument for measuring public response – showed a sinister fall in the number of viewers watching the NBC Saturday evening programme. Millions of sets were being switched to the channels served by the rival ABC and CBS networks. As a desperate measure – or perhaps through a brilliant fore-sight – the NBC directors decided to replace their Saturday programme, at 8 p.m. with a screening of a conventional Hollywood movie. Jean Negulesco's *How to Marry a Millionaire*, a comedy with Marilyn Monroe and Betty Grable was shown. The eight-year-old picture with two sexy blondes returned NBC to the place of honour at the top of the Saturday night ratings according to A. C. Nielsen. With a great clattering of knobs millions were switching back to the channel showing a Hollywood attraction.

It took time to absorb the lesson of the 1961 NBC experi-ment. Television had established its own traditions and habits of a dozen years or more, and it was loath to abandon them. But when the omniscient Nielson signalled that people in increasing numbers were watching feature films, the screening time was moved to the peak hours, between 8 and 10 p.m. in the evening, normally reserved for the most popular serials and variety shows featuring popular stars. Statistical inquiries demonstrated that viewing trends were moving away from specifically television attractions, and towards good films. ABC and CBS began with two evening programmes every week, Tonight at the Movies, starting at 8 p.m. NBC, the third of the big three, soon followed their example, also reserving two evening slots for Hollywood. What is more, at the opening of the 1968 season it embarrassed the rival networks by introducing, tactlessly, a third weekly cinema evening, threatening to upset the balance. ABC and CBS were forced into a hasty re-arrangement of their programme schedules to counterbalance the NBC film show with suffici-ently attractive items. The 1972–3 season shows a further growth in the proportion of movies in the weekly schedule of the three networks. Films now occupy almost a half of the prime time. The ABC shows them four times a week, CBS three times and the NBC five times.

The promotion of feature films to the forefront of TV attractions runs parallel with the narrowing of the gap between the cinema release and the television screening of a film. In 1968–9 the big three transmitted jointly 141 films, of which no less than 94 had been produced in the preceding five years. Only two of the films dated from the forties and fifteen from the fifties. Of the pictures shown 75 per cent had been photographed in colour.

The 'Great Cinema Season' of 1968–9, when one could watch a cinema hit every evening has not been repeated to the same extent in succeeding years (1969–70, 1970–1 and 1971–2). The dosage proved too big and too strong. Nielsen, the television oracle, once again provided the evidence that not one of the feature films broke into the top thirty programmes with the highest audience ratings. In 1969–70 the number of films shown was reduced to 120, with an increased percentage of repeats (some of the films were screened on TV for the fourth time). The downward trend continued in the 1970–1 season: only seventy-six feature films were shown at peak viewing times. The reduction proved a shrewd move: the feature film television audiences were reported to be on the increase again. At the same time Kenyon and Eckhardt, a firm of publicity consultants, conducting a survey of viewing patterns in the autumn months of the 1970–71 season, came up with significant findings. According to the firm's report, a sizeable part of the audience habitually switch their sets on only when a feature film is about to start, as a clear-cut choice on the parts of viewers who want to use their TV screen as a home cinema.[2]

The 1972–3 season again brought films to the forefront. Of thirty-five films shown in the hours of evening, more than half (nineteen), got the highest ratings, leaving behind TV serials and other shows especially prepared for TV screens. However, the present revival of interest in films doesn't completely cut out some anxieties about the future.

Prophets of doom appeared a couple of years ago, seeing

the future in decidedly gloomy colours. Prominent among them is Mike Dann, one of the CBS directors, who, in an interview given in January 1970, revealed that the reserves of feature films at the disposal of television are running out and supply would fall considerably short of demand.[3] The number of repeats of films shown in previous seasons is steadily growing. This is particularly so in the case of very attractive and previously successful films, which are reappearing on TV screens quite often. To quote examples, *Vertigo* and *The Man Who Knew Too Much*, both Hitchcock films, were shown in the 1972–3 season – for the sixth time! The only difference is that another network presents them: CBS at present, NBC and ABC in the past.

What about recent and current productions? There are problems here, arising out of the reigning Hollywood trend towards full sexual permissiveness. Television is and shall remain a family entertainment, shared, in cosy surroundings, by a cross-section of all generations. This is not a natural public for screen dissertations on homosexuality, sodomy or group marriage. True, standards do change and the taboos of a few years ago are now violated without raising anybody's blood pressure, but permissiveness has its limits which are not likely to be overstepped. Also, television is particularly exposed to a counter-attack by the countless guardians of public morality.

What are the television companies to do, what card should they play? Should they gamble on a liberal one, or play safe with the conservative? As a rule, at least in the majority of cases, the three big contractors show great caution in these trading operations. Excessively daring films are excluded, and as they are increasingly numerous, the stock of available product is contracting.

There are yet other problems. Analysis of successful and unsuccessful films on television in 1969–70 suggests that different qualities make for success in cinema release than in the 'home cinema'. Three famous box office hits – *Tom Jones*, *Georgy Girl* and *A Man and A Woman* (a Lelouch film dubbed into English) – were received without enthusiasm by TV audiences. The Nielsen rating failed to come up to expectations. One could surmise that a different sort of public crowded into cinemas to see those films a few years ago from the one that sits down today in front of television screens. Who knows, perhaps for this family audience even *Tom Jones* and *Georgy Girl* are too permissive, or too sophisticated? Walt Disney Productions would probably meet with the approval of this public, but so far the Disney studio, the only one in Hollywood, is loath to part with its stock of feature-length films. They appear only in segments in Disneyland TV programmes.

How might the deadlock be broken? It can be tackled in several different ways. The simplest one, though in its ethical and artistic aspects the most questionable, is the preparation of specially edited television versions of cinema films. Apparently Universal have set up a separate department to adapt its films to the more delicate television market. In 1971 three pictures were operated on in this way: Hubert Cornfield's *Night of the Following Day*, Joseph Losey's *Secret Ceremony* and Peter Hall's *Three into Two Won't Go*.[4]) In all three cases strong erotic scenes were removed altogether or cut, and the plot was supplemented by new scenes, sometimes reversing the basic precepts of the work. A happy end was also introduced, where possible. Joseph Losey and Peter Hall reacted to it by asking that their names be removed from the credits: Hubert Cornfield contented himself with making his displeasure public in the press. The studio put Josef Lejtes (a pre-war Polish film-maker) in charge of these operations. He apparently sees his activity as a kind of creative debate with the authors.

This barbarous method of emasculating films to fit them to the demands of television does not appear to have much of a future. Few productions are suitable for this sort of purifying and edifying treatment. And forewarned film-makers are likely to insist on the inclusion of a respective clause in their contracts, preventing such tampering with their works. Precedents of authors rising in defence of the integrity of their work multiply: there are protests against the cutting of films, and even against the frequency of commercial breaks on television. This is indeed a plague, especially during the late, late show. There is, though, a way to overcome the difficulty of making permissive films acceptable for television screening. Twentieth Century-Fox couldn't sell *M.A.S.H.* to any of the three networks. All of them refused the film on the grounds that it was too grim, too bold, in short – no good for family audiences. But this unanimous decision has not prevented one of the three, CBS, from buying a video version of *M.A.S.H.* from the film company and showing it, without any prejudice, as a TV serial.

A more promising way of meeting programme needs and replenishing dwindling stocks is for the TV companies to start their own production of full-length television films. Basically, they should differ from cinema films only in that they are backed and sponsored by the television companies and open not in the cinema but on the small screen. In the 1969–70 season the number of such films rose sharply, reaching over 60 per cent of the films shown in cinemas. ABC premiered as many as twenty-three of them, CBS six and NBC ten.

This new production line of feature films for television was started in 1965 by the partnership of Universal studios and the National Broadcasting Corporation network. The productions were shown in the programme called 'World Premiere', of course at the peak viewing time, between 8 and 10 p.m. in the evening. Up to the end of 1968 forty of such features were produced, and in 1969 fifteen more.

Television feature films are unpopular with critics, and rarely rise above artistic mediocrity. They are a throw-back to the typical old Hollywood 'B' picture, professional, competently directed, well cast and decently played, but dramatically weak, banal and predictable. And yet the viewers appear not to share those critical objections. Several times 'World Premiere' came out top of the rating figures. But if on the television side the experience is quite encouraging, the other side of the enterprise – cinema distribution – is not too successful. As a rule these films do not make the first-run theatres, and their export figures are not impressive.

Thus, while the operation is proving financially viable, it wins no laurels for the producers.

In 1968 an entirely new conception of the television film emerged. It took shape in response to the problems encountered in the production of television serials. The order is usually for at least thirteen, and often for twenty-six or thirty-nine instalments, but it is dependent on the acceptance of a 'pilot' film. If the pilot instalment proves successful, the producers wins a contract for the entire series; if the film fails he loses his initial outlay, usually in the region of $600,000 to $700,000. There is not much one can do with the one-hour-long pilot film; it is not really suitable for the cinema, and, rejected by one television network, it is unlikely to be accepted by another. But recently the television companies have hit on an idea which lessens the producer's risk.

They suggest that the producer make a feature-length film for which they offer to pay $800,000. If successful, it will lead to an immediate contract for the entire television series, if not the producer's deficit should not exceed $400,000 to $500,000 (a full-length film of this sort involves an outlay of $1,200,000 to $1,500,000). In principle the losses can be easily recouped through a cinema release, or sales to TV stations outside the three big networks.

In theory the system seems excellent and occasionally it does produce practical results. The NBC series *Ironside*, with Raymond Burr as a retired police officer, was started in this manner. But one misses in this conception of a feature length 'pilot' some sort of artistic criteria. It seems that a sixty-minute idea has to be padded out to last 120 minutes. Only time can show whether such trial films can take a permanent place in the programme schedules of American television.

Both these methods of increasing the flow of feature films to the television screen, by initiating productions and through the operation of the long 'pilot' principle, have the same weakness: they produce pictures lacking in the Hollywood glamour and self-confidence. These are the poor relations of the comedies and dramas shot by oustanding directors, scripted by best-selling writers and with shining stars in their cast. Television companies are very conscious of this, and try to remedy the weakness by 'borrowing' from the cinema its plots and ready-made narrative formulas, or by signing up Hollywood stars to add glamour to the cast of television serials. In this way an acceptable substitute for the cinema film is evolved to fill gaps in the programme schedules and to compete more effectively with rival stations showing real films.

A characteristic feature of the majority of TV serials is their cinematic origin. It seems that the television success of cinema films has persuaded producers of serials to turn for inspiration to the big screen. If a hero has proved attractive to the cinema public, why not show him again, and again, at weekly intervals, on the small screen? Or, why not continue a story which has charmed cinema audiences? Television versions or continuations of earlier cinematic hits appear almost daily.

A few examples: ABC prides itself on a series called 'Nanny and the Professor', relating the adventures of a certain English governess endowed with magic powers. Does it ring a bell? Of course, it is a reincarnation of Disney's *Mary Poppins* with Julie Andrews. In another ABC serial, *The Brady Bunch*, we meet a widower with three children, marrying a widow with three more. It is almost a carbon copy of United Artists' *Yours, Mine and Ours*, directed by Melville Shavelson, with Henry Fonda and Lucille Ball. ABC's *Room 222*, about the problems of a black teacher (played by Lloyd Haynes) in a white school has been fathered by *To Sir, with Love* with Sidney Poitier. CBS has acquired from Paramount the television rights of a comedy, *Barefoot in the Park*, which as a film with Jane Fonda, Robert Redford and Charles Boyer was one of the great cinema successes of the 1967 season.

The practice of basing television serials on successful films is not new. It has existed almost as long as the American television networks. A new development is the sharp increase in these operations – an attempt to find in them a remedy for a marked fall of interest in conventional television fiction. Every third item is now of cinematic origin, and soon it may well be two out of every three filmed fiction programmes.

In the 1968–9 season several new cinema by-products made their appearance: the ABC family serial *Here Come the Brides* was a variation on Metro-Goldwyn-Mayer's *Seven Brides for Seven Brothers*; ABC also presented *The Ghost and Mrs Muir* after Joseph Mankiewicz's 1947 film with Gene Tierney and Rex Harrison – an outlandish comedy about the 'affair' of a certain widow with the ghost of the former owner of the house she is living in; CBS asked its viewers to take another look at the immortal 'Blondie'. Immortal, because this character of a smart, pretty and tastefully sexy blonde has been exploited to the death – as one would have thought – by all the mass media. Between 1938 and 1948 no less than twenty-three films appeared built around this character, played first by Penny Singleton, and later, towards the end of the series, by Rita Hayworth. 'Blondie' has also inspired comic strips and radio serials. Her first appearance on television, judging by the early reactions, has failed to raise much enthusiasm. Employing such played-out, hackneyed formulas may well prove to be misconceived.

There is nothing new under the sun, or at least, on the small screen hardly anything. The principle remains: if the cap fits, wear it. The thriller series *Mission Impossible* was inspired by Dassin's *Topkapi*, made in 1961 with Peter Ustinov and Melina Mercouri. Topkapi is the name of a museum in Istanbul where the opening act of the great spy affair was played out. Two popular children's serials, *Daktari* and *The Gentle Ben*, built around the animal characters of a lion and a bear, have been based on the films *Clarence, the Cross-eyed Lion* and *The Gentle Giant*. And *Lassie* (CBS), the dog, has been romping around the small screen for the last seventeen years. A family serial, *Bewitched*, which for several seasons now has been showing up well in the rating charts, can claim a progenitor in the person of Veronica Lake, the heroine of René Clair's *I Married a Witch*. Many other instances of such family relationships could be quoted.

The signing up of star personalities from the world of the cinema to adorn television serials swelled in 1971–2 to almost stampede proportions. This is undoubtedly a desperate measure to save the television genre which has been coming under increasing pressure. The appearance of Hollywood stars in various interminably drawn-out comedies of manners, comedy-thrillers and family dramas is designed to halt the slide and persuade the viewers to switch back to these basic television attractions. The opportunity for this operation has arisen because of the difficult financial position of the cinema industry, which has had to economize on the super-star casts, and the fashion among the younger directors of employing unknown actors, and sometimes even amateurs. Unemployed stars willingly turn to television, picking up far from negligible fees there.

Jim Garner receives $40,000 for each instalment of *Nichols*, produced by Warner Brothers for NBC. His contract guarantees that his total earnings for the series will not fall below $1 million. Rock Hudson gets more ($50,000) for a single instalment, but his NBC guarantee for the serial *McMillan* and *Wife* is less – half a million only. Anthony Quinn gets $700,000 for the starring part in *The Man and the City*, a serial produced by Universal for ABC. James Stewart gets $35,000 for a shorter, half-hour instalment, and Glenn Ford $32,000 for an instalment of *Cade's County* (Twentieth Century-Fox for CBS). Let us add that in the same 1971–2 season every Monday Doris Day appeared on the CBS network, and on Wednesday, under the auspices of ABC, Shirley MacLaine. In 1972–3 Julie Andrews got an hour for herself on Saturday night at ABC.

Television is holding on to film for dear life. It is afraid to part from it and strives to clear all obstacles threatening the continuation of this relationship. The big three, ABC, CBS and NBC, are agreed on this. And Hollywood is co-operating, seeking to remain the biggest centre of production for the television market. In this sense the relationship is a stable one, for as long, anyway, as commercial television, and the three big monopolists controlling it, remain in power. But in the last few years heavy clouds have been gathering on the horizon, threatening another revolution. The magnates cannot sleep calmly, and their film partners are watching intently for any signs of a wobble in the foundations on which the entire edifice of American television rests. One reads in the press with increasing frequency that the third revolution in the field of communications has already arrived, and its effects are likely to prove more important and far-reaching than those of the two earlier revolutionary inventions: film and television.

Cables and Cassettes

The third revolution, according to film and television journalists, is the appearance of cassettes, which make it possible to project at home, on the television screen, any pre-recorded audio-visual programme. This is a parallel development to hi-fi systems, with their gram and tape deck units; cassettes with their visual content play the part of gramophone records, or magnetic tapes. Some systems already have the facility of recording programmes directly from the television screen.

Cassettes are now talked and written about all over the world. However, the principle of cable transmission by means of a common aerial is of greatest interest in the United States and, to a lesser extent, in Canada. For the current institutional structure of commercial television, a cable transmission known as CATV (Community Antenna TV) poses a much more immediate and grave threat than the invention of cassettes; while for the cinema industry it is a vital opportunity to enlarge the market for its products. This is why these reflections on the third revolution must start with a discussion of cable transmission and the issues originating from it.

The abbreviation 'CATV' is hardly ever off the pages of the American press. Community Antenna Television was started as an innocent and useful method of improving TV reception or, in the majority of cases, of making it possible to receive TV programmes in 'blind' areas not reached by any television stations. The contractor puts up a single, powerful, tall, many-tiered antenna, plugging into it individual receivers joined to it by a cable. At the turn of the forties such community antennae were first put up in Oregon and Pennsylvania, in small, out-of-the-way settlements not served by television stations.

For the next ten or fifteen years cable television developed and prospered on the fringes of commercial television. Little was heard of it and no one felt menaced by its spread. Only in 1965 did a tumult arise when it came to the public notice that in the United States 1,325 cable systems already existed, and a million and a quarter houses were plugged into CATV. Significantly, antennae had been put up also in places without the excuse of being situated in 'blind' areas, for instance in New York.

Three factors explain the popularity of CATV. First, the image transmitted through the cable is greatly improved in comparison with sets serviced by a home aerial, especially – which has now become all important – the colour image. Second, a tall, community antenna, enlarges the service area and increases the number of channels available to the owner of an individual set, which can receive signals from remote stations as well as UHF – Ultra High Frequency waves. Theoretically CATV places at one's disposal up to 400 channels. (In practice the maximum number of available channels is twelve.) Third, cable television contractors can easily operate as transmitting stations, taking up any free channels. In 1971 – 1190 CATV companies were already transmitting their own programmes, competing with commercial television and, to a lesser extent, with the educational channel. A fourth factor no doubt also plays a part: CATV is not expensive. Plugging into it costs about $15, and then around $5 a month for the service. A luxury within the means of practically everyone.

No wonder cable television is becoming increasingly popular. In 1971 5,300,000 premises were enjoying the advantages of CATV. It is still a relatively minor percentage of the total: about 5 per cent in fact, but the growth of new installations is moving ahead, year after year, and an increasing number of contractors transmit their own programmes. At present the range of these programmes is very modest, consisting in most cases of time and weather information. In 1971 only 467 CATV systems supplied their subscribers with local live shows, tape or film, but in future the original programmes will undoubtedly become richer, more varied, and therefore more interesting.

This is the crux of the matter. The right to transmit has become the bone of contention between commercial and cable television. While the antennae had been used to receive only the existing signals everything was in order, but the moment some stations started transmitting the contractor's own programmes, the peace was shattered and cut-throat competition began. The National Association of Broadcasters saw fit to treat these transmissions as a *casus belli* and set up an elaborate campaign, looking for allies in the Senate and the White House, and also raising the alarm with FCC – the Federal Commission of Communications, an institution watching over this entire field. Film companies, disturbed about the possible infringement of their sacred producers' copyrights, also rose to defend them. A joint, tele-cinematic front came into existence, directed against the cable intruders. But the alliance proved short-lived. Hollywood soon arrived at the conclusion that the situation, far from being menacing, holds promise of another source of profit.

The future of cable television was made secure by the support of the Federal Government, who rightly saw in CATV a way to spread and enrich the programmes of educational television, and to afford the use of free channels to local municipal and state authorities. These obligations were made clear to CATV contractors in the 1971 FCC instructions; the principles governing local transmissions, for all systems serving over 3,500 subscribers, were formulated and made binding. These systems were required to originate a significant amount of programming. The requirement of programme origination was, in 1971, temporarily reversed by the U.S. Court of Appeals, and in 1972 finally reconfirmed by the U.S. Supreme Court.

As already stated, Hollywood at first opposed CATV,

accusing it of creating unfair competition. United Artists even started legal proceedings against one of the contractors but lost the case in the U.S. Supreme Court. The verdict was that cable transmission does not infringe a copyright. The case, however, concerned the transmission of received signals, not of local programmes. As the number of these was growing, Hollywood, seeing a fast-developing new market, shifted its position, looking for some kind of a peaceful, advantageous arrangement. A symposium was even organized in Hollywood to discuss the entire problem of CATV. Cable contractors were represented, as well as film trade unions. Suspicion on both sides prevented an agreement from being reached at the meeting, but this was before the FCC expressed its support for CATV.

With the cable firms officially free to expand and to operate their own programmes Hollywood saw the whole issue in a different light. Just as before, after the conflicts, bickering, and general opposition to television had stopped, and an era of co-operation between the cinema and the commercial TV companies began, so now the story was repeated with CATV. After a drawn-out period of inter-mittent, secret bartering and negotiations, on 14 June 1971 an agreement was signed between the cable television industry and the big seven Hollywood studios: Columbia, Universal (MCA), Metro-Goldwyn-Mayer, Paramount, Twentieth Century-Fox, Warner Brothers and United Artists. Cable firms are now obliged to pay licence copyright fees to the Hollywood companies for all films transmitted in the fifty areas of the highest television density. In all the other areas films can be shown without an additional payment.

This was the situation on the cable television front at the turn of 1972. The future is now clear: a growing number of American viewers are going to be serviced by CATV. According to the current estimates, by 1985 60 million houses will be plugged into it, and 80 per cent of the entire territory of the United States will be covered by the cable networks. There will be a proportionate increase in the number of transmitting stations, and in the choice of channels available to the viewers. And that means a steadily increasing demand for films of all kinds. Hollywood is counting on it.

Astronomical numbers of films will also be needed for television cassettes. But in this field all estimates and speculations are extremely difficult. All one knows is that a change of earthquaking proportions, of crucial significance for the future of both television and cinema, is coming. What its effect will be only time will show. At the moment, early in the eighth decade of the twentieth century, the third audio-visual revolution has only just begun.

The cassette phenomenon exploded on the scene towards the end of the sixties. Reputedly, the invention was first patented in West Germany by the Japanese firm, Sony Corporation, back in 1954, but at the time it was hardly noticed. By now its technical aspect has already been perfected. An attachment to a television set has been constructed which is loaded with cartridges – usually in the form of a reel of film, or magnetic tape – and a moving sound image, in colour, appears on the screen. Anyone can now set up a private video-library and, at his or her leisure, at all times of day or night, watch the pictures he feels like watching. Thus, as has already been observed, the pleasures and facilities of hi-fi have been extended into the field of vision. The cultural and technological consequences of this revolution are bound to be enormous. But in the early seventies they are still slow in coming, belonging to tomorrow, or the day after. Why is this so?

The first and foremost cause of the apparent deadlock is the variety and diversity of cassette systems. The two main rivals in the United States are Electro Video Recording, patented by the Columbia Broadcasting Corporation and manufactured by Motorola Corporation, Selecta Vision (owned by the National Broadcasting Corporation) and Disco Vision manufactured by MCA. CBS and NBC, two of the main competitors in commercial television, have thus extended their rivalry into the cassette field. But there are also other rivals, both native and foreign. In America Avco Industries and Norton Simon Inc., in Japan the powerful Sony electronics corporation and the Shibaden company, in

Germany Telefunken. These are only the leaders in this race. Behind them stretches an entire field of minor but very active and hopeful competitors. And each one urgently strives to persuade the potential customers that his system offers the greatest advantages and has the brightest future. But the customers wait for the situation to clarify itself.

It is outside our scope to weigh the advantages and weaknesses of the various systems, to compare the scale of prices and the respective production facilities. Anyway, it would have been a futile preoccupation: every day brings new technical innovations and the costs continuously fluctuate. One thing is certain: until first an internal, and then an international agreement is concluded about the standardization of equipment and inter-change of services among the existing systems, the cassette revolution is going to remain a theoretical proposition, with little practical impact. One thinks of historical precedents: the sound film gathered sufficient momentum to sweep away the silent cinema only when the patent owners had reached an agreement in two stages – the internal and the international. First the American systems of Western Electric and RCA, and then Klangfilm-Tobis and its American competitors agreed that whatever sound recording system had been used a film could be screened with any of the standardized sound projections equipment. This ended the situation where Western Electric films had had to be exhibited only in cinemas equipped with Western Electric projectors.

The cassette industry manufactures two different devices: attachments to television sets known as 'players', and cassettes or cartridges, with which the attachments are loaded. The first are popularly known as 'hardware', the second as 'software'. RCA 'players' cannot be loaded with CBS cassettes, or vice versa. And let us not forget there are other devices on the international market. In effect, no one is hurrying to buy either hardware or software. All wait for the finish of the race – which of the devices proves best and most competitively priced – and also for the expected moment of the international agreement on the standardization of equipment. Once the cassettes become like

Decca, Columbia or HMV records, fitting easily into any television player, orders are going to flow and the market will come to life.

A mood of uncertainty is not conducive to the setting up of large-scale production of software. In principle the possibilities are literally boundless. Everything, absolutely everything can be recorded and preserved in cassette form: feature films, documentaries, educational and instructional films, spectacles and TV programmes of all kinds, literary adaptations, concerts and recitals, readings from poetry and prose, etc. It is impossible to foresee the make-up and balance, or to set any limits on this enormously diverse, comprehensive and rich repertory. There will be collectors of cinematic classics, of jazz, of visualized literary master-pieces, of illustrated medicine and biology lectures – the list is endless. The producers must choose what to record, what rights to acquire, how long to continue waiting and when to start production for the mass market. In the early seventies the waiting attitude still predominates. Especially in Holly-wood.

For the cinema, or, to be exact, for the film production centres, the invention of the television cassette opens the door to the world of fantastic riches. Every film, old, new or just projected, becomes a potential candidate for cassette registration. But the mirage of the land of plenty cannot obstruct the very real problems of today. To offer contracts – to whom and on what terms? This is a key question. The film companies do not want to act recklessly, and almost blindly. To entrust cinematic treasure to a competitor who may ultimately lose? Or to sell at a relatively low current price which in a month, or a year, may rocket sky-high? Cassette industrialists also play it cannily, reluctant to go into mass production and commit themselves to large investments. 'Let's wait and see', is, in this field, the current motto of the entire cinema world. The single exception to this rule is Twentieth Century-Fox which has already signed away to CBS the rights of all its films more than five years old, to be loaded into the Electronic Video Recording cassettes. Perhaps Darryl Zanuck, responsible for the decision, remembered that William Fox had been proved right in going it alone and gambling on the sound film?

Getting ready for the forthcoming offensive are not only the film and television giants but also – a new phenomenon – the book publishers. Some of them believe that the days are drawing near when almost every book of value may have to be published not only in print but also as a cassette recording, either in a literal, word by word version – read aloud by an accomplished performer – or as a film adaptation. The length and time of projection are no longer the decisive factors. One could have a collection of fifty *War and Peace* cassettes, or *The Forsyte Saga*, and view a favourite chapter whenever one felt so disposed. With the illegal transfer of cassette recording made easy the problem of copyright will have to be re-opened and come under close scrutiny. Solutions that seem to be working well in the record industry may have to be adopted and introduced.

In the United States McGraw-Hill, the publishers, are already setting up their own stock of 'cartridges', loading them with visual material from the affiliated Contemporary Films Library. One of the first to be transferred was Roman Polanski's short Polish film *Two Men and a Wardrobe*. Europe has advanced much further in these preparatory operations. In February 1971 six of the largest publishing enterprises in Western Germany, Italy, France and Switzerland, Sweden and Holland came together to set up the International Publishers' Audiovisual Association. In September 1971 the 'club' whose founder members include Arnoldo Mondadori, Librairie Hachette and C. Bertelsmann Verlag, admitted a British member: the Thomson Organisation Ltd., employing 20,000 people and with considerable interests in the press (including control over *The Times* and *The Sunday Times*), television and the travel business. The Association lists among its aims an exchange of information and joint projects in the field of audio-visual communications.

It seems significant that in all the talk about television cassettes, as reflected in the press, radio, book publications and international exhibitions one is always referred to the speculative future. What will be the volume of 'players' on the market in a year or two, how many people will have access to the new invention, what will be its social impact in America when 115 million existing sets will be fitted with the wonderful gadgets. But nothing is coming through about the actual situation (in the early seventies): how many devices have already been sold, who is using them, of what make and what are the cassettes loaded with? Are there hundreds or thousands of them? But is that really important? It is worth remembering that in January of 1946 there were 6,400 television sets in the United States; a year later 250,000, and in 1971 115 million. (Ninety-five per cent of all households are equipped with at least one set.) We can expect this mad acceleration to be repeated, once the multiple technical, patent and production problems are successfully solved.

The Brave Tomorrow

By 1980 or 1985 a citizen of the United States on his way home from work will stop at the news stall or the drug store to buy a television cassette or two. It will cost him the price of a glossy magazine, or a paper-back book. At home, ready to take his seat in front of the set, he will have the choice of his own audio-visual library, or any of the great number of channels. Audio-visual paradise on earth – a technical paradise, at least, because no one can foresee the quality of those programmes. Quantity and diversity do not necessarily add up to high standards.

But cables and cassettes do not exhaust the stock of technical possibilities. Cinemas face dangerous competition not only from perfected television systems (cable and cassette), but also from new ways of film distribution. Private houses and clubs already hold a large number of 16 mm and 8 mm projectors. The visual and sound quality keeps improving, and on the 16 mm gauge it has reached the standard of 35 mm prints. Eight mm is also keeping up the pace, with a new leap forward represented by 'super-8 mm', where a ready cartridge is loaded into a projector, cutting out the messy re-winding. But, as with cassettes, the problem

H

of standardization exists with respect to the cartridge shape and sound track (magnetic or optical). Six rival companies, producing 8 mm projectors suitable for screening features, have been competing in the American market. They include some powerful industrial giants like Technicolor, Eastman, Kodak, and Bell and Howell. According to the experts, the annual distribution turn-over (from the sale and hire of films) will soon be six times the turn-over figure of 16 mm prints in 1970. It seems more than likely that 8 mm cartridges will be used extensively by cable television stations.

Hotel distribution offers another potential, non-cinema release. It may sound like a fringe activity, and it does lack the revolutionary potential of the cassettes or CATV systems, but if it is put into operation – and there is no reason to doubt that it will be – hotel distribution may come to play an important part in film production calculations. It means closed circuit television being installed in the hotel. On the set in each room – apart from the normal transmission – there is a choice of two films on reserved channels. A meter starts ticking whenever one of the film channels is switched on. A charge for the service is added to the bill.

The Computer Cinema company, acting in partnership with Twentieth Century-Fox, conducted in 1971 an experimental transmission in a hotel in Newark, New Jersey, a city of 378,000 inhabitants. Three recent colour hits were offered: *M.A.S.H.*, *Patton* and *Tora, Tora, Tora*. The price, depending on the choice of film, $2 or $3. Paul Klein, the director of Computer Cinema estimates that in the near future, perhaps even in 1974, a million hotel rooms (one-third of the United States total) can be equipped for meter film projection. Taking into account the quick turnover of hotel customers, the closed circuit run of the films can be extended over a considerable length of time. Twelve to twenty titles annually should prove quite sufficient. The takings would be divided as follows: 10 per cent for the hotel, 30 to 40 per cent for the film company providing the films, and the rest for Computer Cinema. On this basis a studio could earn, for the hire of one film, a sum of between $2–$3½ million – considerably more than the money available from commercial television, and about the same as the average income from a cinema release. And all this as an extra flow of revenue.[5]

The example given by Computer Cinema has in 1972 already been followed by nineteen companies, offering cinema closed-circuit television in hotels! Twentieth Century-Fox has its own subsidiary, Primary Entertainment Corporation, providing feature films for hotels, motels, hospitals and nursing homes. Trans-World Communications Inc., a subsidiary of Columbia Pictures, made a deal with ITT Sheraton Corporation to bring films to twelve key Sheraton Hotels in major cities of the United States and Canada.

Cassettes and cable television promise a thorough shake-up of the conventional cinema industry. They represent an adventure, a leap into the unknown. But an even greater surprise could be in the offing in the shape of a communications satellite, adapted to cinematic needs. This idea is being fostered for the film industry by the tireless Radio Corporation of America, or to be exact, its department of Global Communications. The project must be considered as real and plausible since the National Association of Theatre Owners saw fit to issue a special report to brief its members about expected developments. The general outlines have been set out, and the RCA scientists and technicians are working hard on the details.

A communications satellite, or perhaps two – main one and a standby – are to be placed in the stratosphere, 23,000 miles away from the surface of the earth. The image and sound signals for all the separate film frames will be bounced off the satellite, after travelling through space, and returned to earth to the receiving stations scattered all over the United States. In the initial stages of development eleven to thirteen such stations are planned. The stations are to feed the satellite signals through cable or existing telephone installations to cinemas within a radius of around fifty miles. In this way the same film could be simultaneously screened in hundreds of halls, without projection equipment, technicians or prints.

Technically the project is feasible, as satellite television has already demonstrated. At the moment the image and sound quality would be somewhat inferior to conventional projection from a good new print, but in time, no doubt, this drawback could be corrected. Practical realization of the entire project, provisionally costed at $200 million, is dependent on gaining the support of the Federal Communications Commission. According to RCA estimates, the satellite could start functioning within twenty-four months of the FCC's hoped-for approval. It would cost the cinemas $125,000 a month for the use of satellite reception, plus $5,000 for the services of the distributing station. The costs for a single cinema would of course depend on the number plugged into the station, but even at first glance it is clear that the sums involved are not prohibitive, and the project may prove highly profitable. Science fiction? Perhaps, but certainly less remote than space travels to Mars or to Venus. It will not be easy, there will be opposition from the cinema-owners to overcome and the FCC is not likely to move in haste, but in the end technical progress should win through.

Traditional cinema, in the shape made familiar to us from the experience of many decades, is getting ready to leap into the unknown. It is unlikely to result in the total disappearance of cinemas from the surface of the earth. Experience teaches us that past forms never entirely die out. The invention of cinema did not lead to a liquidation of the live theatre; radio and gramophone failed to close the concert halls. Television has not swallowed film, on the contrary it has led to its further expansion. One can forecast, with caution, that the same pattern is likely to be repeated when the expected wonders of the technological revolution become everyday reality. Changed and adapted, the old forms are still going to persist. But a violent impact on the essential format and the content of all the existing audio-visual media cannot be avoided.

All distant prophesies are dangerous and often wide of the mark. Several commentators, speculating about the forthcoming impact of television cassettes, have quoted Edison, who, when faced with a question about the possible uses of the gramophone, replied that it should be used to dictate a last will.[6] And it wasn't an example of the great inventor's caustic wit, but a reasoned attempt to answer a practical inquiry. Edison imagined that a dying man, no longer able to hold a pen in his hand, would speak his will with the mechanism recording it on a waxed cylinder. Concerts were not envisaged. Who can today forecast accurately the many uses of TV cassettes and guess which of them are going to predominate?

However, two aspects of the coming revolution, ushered in by the new technical inventions, appear to be beyond doubt. Firstly, television cassettes are going to introduce the principle of reproducible audio-visual transmissions, the frequency of the reproductions to be dictated not by the supplier, as at present, but by the viewer. In this sense a film, or a television cassette recording, is going to resemble a book or a gramophone record, to be returned to as often as one likes. This is a momentous change, because so far the programme policies of both film and television have always been based on the assumption that the product would be designed for a single viewing. Of course, if one sets one's mind on it, one can see a film twice, three times or more, but always in its entirety and often in rather unsatisfactory circumstances (in a remote cinema, with poor projection, a damaged print, etc.). On television repeats are still the exception rather than the rule. This situation cannot continue. The question is: how will this recurrent viewing affect the viewers' responses, will it change their criteria of value, and force the revision of producers' attitudes?

Secondly, the greatly increased range of choice, the number and variety of easily available films and television programmes, should sweep away the current principle, binding on both film and television, that any worth-while audio-visual fare must be acceptable to a popular audience of many millions. The spectre of the box office and of Nielsen ratings will haunt no longer. Local cable television stations will count the audience for its programmes in tens of thousands; for educational television, reaching a million viewers is an earth-shaking success. The break-up of the traditional distribution and exhibition patterns would force the producers to cater for different public tastes. And programme variety, shifting the onus for the choice from the supplier to the viewer, should open the door wider to creative talent, to distinct and diverse artistic personalities. The future holds out the promise of freeing us from conformist uniformity and obligatory formulas allegedly demanded by the millions. Obviously, the communications revolution cannot achieve all this at one sweep, but it will follow this clearly sign-posted way.

8

In Search of a Common Denominator

Mini, Midi, Maxi

A cartoon in the *New Yorker*, in July 1971 portrayed a couple of guests leaving a typical, suburban, middle-class home. The host, having bid them goodbye, stays behind in the doorway. The couple, in a clearly despondent mood, are walking towards their car, the husband remarking to the wife: 'It was when he started referring to his movies as "films" that I knew we were in for a bad night.'[1] Amateurs, making 8 mm home movies, now often aspire to higher things, believing their work to be 'real films'. One can easily become a victim of these false claims and affections, like that *New Yorker* couple. Had they wanted to see a film they could have had a night out in a cinema, or stayed at home and switched on their television set, rather than sit tight in front of a home screen, with the projector rattling behind their back.

This cartoon in a popular weekly is symptomatic of the new situation. 'Film', the word that used to denote the professional screen work of the Hollywood, or foreign, studios, has expanded its meaning to include practically everything that moves and elicits sounds on screens of whatever size or shape. There are mini-films, midi-films and maxi-films: one-minute, ten-minutes, one-hour or four-hours long. They may start from quite different premises but they all aspire to the realm of creative art. Nowadays 'film' means also 'the cinema as art'. The makers of cinematic miniatures and super-blockbusters all look upon themselves as creative artists.

It is extremely difficult to put all the diverse, creative film activities into the same scale. At one time, in the fifties and even in the early sixties, there were distinct distinguishing features facilitating classification or comparison between works falling into the same category. The Hollywood cinema and the *avant garde* cinema were worlds apart then. A fiction film and a documentary film embodied two different sets of aesthetic values. There were different criteria for evaluating the programmes on the small screen and the wide-screen Technicolor spectacle showing in the cinema. Today, in the seventies, the dividing lines have become blurred or erased, and homogeneous genres and categories no longer exist. Film has become a polymorphous, multi-purpose medium, and, as Ernest Callenbach, the editor of *Film Quarterly* has remarked, the disintegration process of what was once an entity, is accelerating.[2] Is it possible then, to look in those fragmentary and disjointed phenomena for common, integrating features? Can there be any cinematic essence peculiar to mini-, midi-, or maxi-films? Before answering this question it is worth recalling, very shortly, the sort of 'films' (with and without the inverted commas) that the average citizen of the United States sees.

The shortest thirty-second or one-minute-long films are television commercials. These single point, single 'blow' pictures appear on the screen, interrupting a programme whatever it may be: a variety show, serial, feature film, round table discussion, prize fight, or even news bulletins and weather reports. Can all this eulogizing over the marvellous qualities of Coca-Cola, a soap, a shirt, or, in the old days, cigarettes (banned in 1971) possibly have any connection with the art of the cinema? Superficially not much but when one looks closely at these sharp and aggressive moving ads, one is struck by the perfection of the cinematic technique employed. They demonstrate a degree of control often bordering on virtuosity. The power of montage associations and contrasts, the effectiveness of sound counterpoint, the fluidity of camera movements are all here. Is one really justified in dismissing the heretical assertion of Mr Marty Goldman, who directs commercials for Televideo Productions when he calls his one-minute-long movies 'a contemporary form of art'? And is it really just misplaced conceit to say, as he does: 'After TV commercials there's nothing you don't know about films?'[3]

For a long time all television was considered inherently uncinematic. Not the other way round, because cinema soon became a favourite television fare. But for the viewer the dividing line was still clear: he watched feature films on the small screen with a different attitude to normal television programmes. In the cinema one expected only films made especially for cinema exhibition. Until the time, that is, when Universal started production for NBC of long feature films, premiered on television but later appearing in small, second or third run provincial cinemas. Next came the 'pilot' idea – of an ostensibly cinematic feature film, initiating a television series. For instance *Kona Coast* directed by Lamont Johnson, a thriller set in Honolulu adapted from John D. Macdonald's short story. Everything happens here like in a real, conventional feature film. Only experts and keen fans can perceive the significance of the fact that Richard Boone, the television star, plays the principal male part, and the projection takes one hour and twenty minutes, quite a bit less than the current Hollywood standard. After all, the average cinema-goer, unaware of behind-the-scenes manipulations, is going to compare *Kona Coast* with other theatre films, not with television serials. And thus another clear dividing line is becoming blurred.

Documentary films used to be the poor relations of the Hollywood product. They were of no interest to the big distributors and were destined for extra-cinema existence. This was the situation fifteen, or even ten, years ago. Now an amateur film-maker can shoot a documentary feature, taking the risk of backing it with his own money, and then try to sell it to a big Hollywood distributor. *Woodstock* is not the only exception; its significance is rather that it has cleared the way for the commercial distribution of documentary features. Floyd Mutrix wrote and directed, with William Fraker at the camera, a report on Los Angeles drug addicts called *Dusty and Sweets McGee*. The production cost him just over $42,000. Drug-taking has become a problem of great social urgency, and the work of the amateur film-makers showed some of its aspects in a sensationally new light. Small wonder that *Dusty and Sweets McGee* was acquired by Warner Brothers for $800,000 plus a percentage of any profits. The film has been screened in hundreds of cinemas, and the audiences see it in the context not of amateur 16 mm productions, but of professional work on a similar subject, like Roger Corman's *The Trip*. And thus the gap between documentary and fiction, amateurs and professionals, is not really there any more.

Finally, the tip of the cinematic pyramid, the super-spectacles. As stated in the early chapters, they are diverse now, employing a range of different effects, similar only in their length and the size of their budgets. Twentieth Century-Fox's *Tora, Tora, Tora* took four years to complete. In the sacred cause of realism an old American navy destroyer was purchased and wrecked, with a convoy of lesser craft; also five B17 Flying Fortresses and forty Japanese aircraft of various types. The attack on Pearl Harbor was reconstructed, point by point, on location and eventually on the screen. Japanese aircraft, sowing death, fire and destruction, flew wave after wave, at the viewer who sat riveted to his seat. Long shots gave way to close-ups, detailing and magnifying the savage destruction. Cameras, placed in the cockpits of the planes, were literally dancing in the air. Technical virtuosity, brilliant camerawork and editing, were given full reign in *Tora, Tora, Tora*.[4]

It is worth recalling the words of Marty Goldman, the master of the television commercial, about its place in the field of contemporary art, and the opportunities for technical apprenticeship afforded by the production of commercials. In the final analysis, a super-spectacle and a minute-long commercial employ the same devices to elicit a response from a viewer. Falling back on conventional cinematic technique film-makers return to the basic aesthetic precepts of film that is essentially – to put it with naïve simplicity – the art of a moving photographic image. One can, with good effect, model it on a stage spectacle, a novel, an animated painting, a musical symphony, a ballet, a journalistic report, a lecture, but it doesn't change the basic substance of the cinema, which remains that of a moving photographic image, enriched with sound and colour. If any common features can be said to exist in the heterogeneous, diverse and fragmented American cinema of the seventies, they should be looked for first of all in the realm of technique. Both the cinema's technical origins, and the scientific-technical revolution currently gripping America, point in that direction.

Three Faces of Technique

The most significant feature of the American cinema's current situation is a continuous expansion of its activities and a dramatic increase in the number of active film-makers. This is related directly to the technical progress that has greatly simplified the handling of the camera and the recording of sound. In the old days these skills were surrounded by an air of professional mystery, jealously guarded by the few master practitioners of their magic craft. Now anyone can become a camera operator or a sound engineer. A lightweight 8 mm or 16 mm camera and a portable tape-recorder are easy to operate not only for young, untrained amateurs, but, positively, for children. Film-making has become a popular pastime, and what has been registered on a film strip or a sound track can be used as raw material for creative work, serious, or not so serious. 'Blowing up' facilities from the narrow gauge to 35 mm have also been greatly improved. There are, in fact, no obstacles of a technical nature that could prevent an amateur work being transformed into a 'proper' film, ready for release in a first-run cinema.

This opening up of the creative field, enabling even the most private and personal films to be taken up for wide public distribution, is, socially and artistically, the most significant result of technical progress in the cinema. The quantitative change produces the effect of obliterating the dividing lines between the different categories and streams of film-making and, eventually, leads to the devaluation of previously valid formal criteria. Undoubtedly the television moloch, consuming daily millions of feet of film, has accelerated the pace of this evolution. The surfeit of moving imagery has led to a shift of emphasis towards content, and a rather deprecating attitude towards purely formal visual values, especially in documentary reporting or in anything which is a direct treatment of actuality and not a staged fiction.

Technical progress has made the command of the film medium almost as accessible as that of the written word. The camera has replaced the pen or the typewriter. And it is no longer an isolated phenomenon but a mass one. Tens, or hundreds, of thousands of people are involved, if not millions. As with the written word a personal scribble can become a public property. Travel notes, journals, even philosophical reflections can just as well be committed to film as to paper, and distributed even more widely. But where is the dividing line between private, amateur, part-time activities and imaginative work, aspiring to the heights of art? *Cinéma-vérité* provides many difficult borderline cases and it was the Americans – Richard Leacock and D. A. Pennebaker – who pioneered direct cinema.

In 1967 Jim McBride tried to combine, in *David Holzman's Diary*, direct personal comment, in the form of an open cinematic 'notebook', with fictional narrative. David Holzman, the film's hero (played by L. M. Kit Carson), impressed by Godard's dictum that 'film is truth, 24 times a second', decides to clarify the meaning of his own existence by letting a camera observe an entire week of his life. The experiment ends in failure. People turn away from him, protesting against the intrusion, and the cinematic result is far from being the whole truth. David's friend comments: 'Some people's lives are good movies, some people's lives are bad movies. Your life is not a very good script.' The camera, as an instrument of psychological and philosophical penetration, turns out to be of limited value, especially when the author insists on being both the object and the subject of the study.

David Holzman's Diary can be seen as an argument against the euphoric belief that in film humanity has found both a new, universal art form and a universal language. During the 1970 New York Film Festival the Film Society of Lincoln Center distributed a booklet proclaiming that 'Suddenly films have become the meaningful way for all generations, all nations, to really talk each other's language,' and a bit farther on, 'Now movies are the core language of the young.' Undoubtedly this uncritical rapture, the intoxication with the allegedly unlimited potential of film, can also be traced back to technical progress, which has made cameras and tape-recorders easily available.

Technical progress is a dialectical process. Inventions and innovations, which have opened up film-making to any willing amateur, are countered at the other end of the scale by discoveries and experiments accessible only to experts with a high degree of professional skill. Developments in production techniques have put new meaning into the rather hackneyed old dictum that 'in film nothing is impossible'. Amateurs may compete with professionals in recording actuality, documenting the look and the mood of the day, but when the lens becomes trained on the past, or the future, the professionals take over. In this field the big Hollywood studios are still holding sway.

It is technique in the widest sense rather than traditional craftsmanship that gives Hollywood the advantage – though one doesn't underestimate its value. Science fiction films especially need the support of considerable technical resources. Without them a creative film-maker is unable to follow his imagination beyond the confines of today.

The undisputed leader in imaginative science fiction is still Stanley Kubrick's *2001: A Space Odyssey*. An important contribution to this success was the screenplay of Arthur C. Clarke, the writer and scientist. It was inspired by his own short story, *The Sentinel*. But Kubrick and Clarke could not have got very far with their brilliant vision without expert assistance, particularly from NASA (the National Aeronautics Space Administration) – the government agency in charge of the Apollo Moon project. An astronaut, Deke Slayton, was a permanent production consultant. NASA put the film-makers in touch with forty companies and institutes involved in the study of and preliminary preparations for inter-planetary space travels. For two years, 1964 and 1965, at the script-writing and production planning stage, an impression staff of expert advisers was working at full capacity. For the shooting Metro-Goldwyn-Mayer ordered from the British company, Vickers Armstrong Ltd, a huge centrifugal machine, 38 feet in diameter, revolving at a speed of three miles per hour. Inside this contraption a condition similar to a state of weightlessness could be produced. Actors were put into those uncannily realistic space flight conditions, with a camera usually shooting from the outside, and communications kept by means of closed circuit television. The process of production became so complex that to manage the crew, numbering 108 people, a special control tower was set up, as in an airfield, manned by four men. The shooting schedule took up all of 1966, and was succeeded by long months of special effect and laboratory work. The finished film contained around 200 special effects, most of them so perfectly conceived and executed that not only an average viewer but even a sophisticated film technician could not be aware, without previous knowledge, of all the complex technical processes employed.

Franklin Schaffner's *Planet of the Apes* is science fiction of a different kind, posing no problems of making space flights appear realistic. All the action takes place after the earth space ship's landing on an unknown planet. Difficulties, serious ones, were only encountered when the planet's inhabitants had to be introduced: apes of human intelligence and with a human range of feeling. Arthur Jacobs, the producer, acquired the film rights of Pierre Boulle's French novel in 1964, but the production commenced three years later. None of the big studios were at first keen to back this ape fantasy, and the producer himself was not at all certain that the make-up problem could be successfully overcome. Actors in ape costume, or, literally, in apes' skin, were not supposed to be funny. Indeed hilarity among the audience would have destroyed the desired effect. Thus the entire success of the project hung on the possibility of devising ape masks that would retain the sensitive mobility of human features.

Around a million dollars was spent on lab make-up research and preparations alone. Twentieth Century-Fox, judging the project to be promising, approached some eminent chemists, asking for help. It was imperative to devise a mask that was ape-like but fully responsive to the play of actors' features, and – by no means a small, unimportant detail – that made it possible for them to eat in the course of the working day. Initially the masks allowed only liquid food, with teeth rendered practically immobile. And the mask took six hours to fix on, and three more to take it off at the end of the day. It would have been hardly possible to shoot at all.

In the end all the technical problems were solved fairly satisfactorily. The experts produced masks of elastic, semi-liquid foam rubber, fitting tightly to the actor's face, and yet responding to his mimicry. Time for making up was cut down to just over an hour. On days when crowd artists in ape-masks were called for, 200 make-up experts had to work hard to cope. But the end-product vindicated the trouble taken: the story and the ape-creatures were taken seriously.

Planet of the Apes was a box office success. Almost at once a sequel, *Beneath the Planet of the Apes*, was made, and soon after, the third and the fourth film of the series, *Escape from the Planet of the Apes* and *The Conquest of the Planet of the Apes*. In this fourth film the clever apes land on planet Earth, after travelling back in time 2,000 years. The make-up problems were much easier – only three of the main characters needed ape-masks. The earth creatures are, after all, human. But one of the visitors, the child of the hero-ape and the heroine-ape, is played by an authentic baby chimp. Penelope Gilliat comments on this intrusion of real nature into the far-fetched fiction: 'And now, lying in the hairy arms of Kim Hunter's costume, there is an actual baby chimp who is amazingly like a baby human being. The little chimpanzee stares up at the film studio mask of its acted mother and blinks intelligently.'[5] The wonders of technique make it possible to integrate an artificial, invented narrative with a live fragment of existing reality – the animal partner in the game played by humans.

It is only a step from macrocosm to microcosm. The script-writers of *Planet of the Apes*, Michael Wilson and Rod

Sterling, have it on the literary authority of Pierre Boulle that the human race is going to be conquered, oppressed and annihilated by the descendants of today's orang-utans, chimpanzees and gorillas. According to Walon Green's *The Hellstrom Chronicle* it is the insects – the hard-working ants, the brilliantly organized bees – who are taking over the earth from the wayward humans. Eight camera crews, armed with special lenses, worked for two years in various corners of the globe. The result is most impressive: insects observed in huge close-ups, engaged in deliberate, seemingly intelligent tasks, almost convince us of their title to be considered serious, menacing rivals of the species known as *homo sapiens*. And the commentator, a fictional entomologist, Hellstrom, is generous with doom-laden prophecies. The viewer, mesmerized by what goes on on the screen, may seek refuge in smiling, sceptical disbelief, but deep down the Hellstrom omens leave their mark.

Thus the new American cinema provides popular, democratic techniques, available to the millions, but also super-techniques for the initiated few. But the picture would not be complete without a third aspect of the technical progress which is leaving its mark on almost every film produced in the early seventies: the enrichment of cinematic language with *avant garde* audio-visual devices, sometimes, it is true, somewhat moth-eaten, but also modern or modernized. In almost every review of recent films one meets with acknowledgement and approval of the camera work, editing, and use of sound, not to speak of the direction. After the period of theatrical immobility, and of intoxication with interminably long takes and movements within the frame, came the renaissance of dynamic cinema, almost baroque in the density and rich variety of its effects.

It seems obvious that this rediscovery of *avant garde* tricks, with violently clashing images, unusual angles of vision, frozen frames, shooting through gauze, negative prints, etc., has its origin in television commercials. Not only because many of the current directors served their apprenticeship there, but because the public took to the sharp and pointed style of screen narration. Add to this the cult of sheer speed, the pleasure of conquering space characteristic of the modern social climate, not only in America, and we are getting close to understanding the fashionable acrobatic technique of American film-makers. Take *Le Mans*, directed by Lee H. Katzin, a story of car racing in France. Everything is there – slow motion photography, split screen images, frozen frames, double exposure, and also a playing around with sound, stylizing the natural acoustic backgrounds, mixing them with music, or fading the sound out altogether at some climatic moments. Racing cars are of course most cinematic anyway, but in *Le Mans* the production crew really excelled themselves, creating, in the best sense of the word, a poetic, audio-visual symphony. Without taking anything away from the director, praise is due to the two cameramen: Robert H. Hauser and René Guissart Junior.

In *Little Fauss and Big Halsey*, a story of motor-cyclists directed by Sidney J. Furie, huge static close-ups of a part of the human face are suddenly introduced at the climax of a dangerous race. The eyes and mouths of the competitors form an effective contrast to the earlier general shots, full of pace and movement. In Alan Pakula's *Klute* Gordon Willis, the cameraman, employs the device of masking a part of the frame to emphasize some element of the composition.

Not all the critics approve of this new visual inventiveness. Even Haskell Wexler's *Medium Cool* has been censured for alleged 'gimmickry'. One often meets the same word 'gimmicks' applied to other new films. In this, also, the influence of commercials, always striving after a single, unusual effect of maximum impact, cannot be denied. The conservatives believe that these formal and technical games have gone too far, and that all these gimmicks tend to break up the flow of conventional cinematic narrative. This point of view is usually held by older critics, formed by the American cinema of the thirties and forties. They still regard the narrative manner of that time, logical and flowing, without unnecessary diversions or jarring notes, as definitive. Even Pauline Kael, whose general aesthetic position is by no means conservative, can be included in that group. In her own assertion: 'TV has destroyed the narrative quality of the old movies.'[6] But it seems that not Pauline Kael but the *Chicago Sun Times* reviewer touches on the truth when, writing about *Medium Cool*, he observes that 'Most of us are now so conditioned by the quick cutting and free association of ideas in TV commercials that we think faster than feature-length movies can move. We understand cinematic shorthand.'[7] This is the heart of the matter. Technical developments have taught the modern viewer to understand not only the cinematic vocabulary, but cinematic shorthand.

Hopes and Omens

The current American cinema has a number of new and clearly discernible features of its own: the diversification of film has become a fact, new screen genres have been developed and a new public has appeared. This is the situation as of today, but what about tomorrow? Do all these changes point to a single future direction? Doubts and uncertainties exist here. The question: where is the American cinema going, what kind of future is lying in wait for it, is not at all easy to answer. Speculations based on rational and logical precepts cannot hold ground against some fantastic prophesies.

In *Film 67/68*, published by the American Society of Film Critics, the final chapter contains answers by ten leading critics to an inquiry about the future of film.[8] The chapter, under the promising but as one soon learns misleading title of 'Symposium', lists the answers in alphabetical order. All the statements are autonomous, there are no arguments. The following five questions (listed here in a shortened form) were put to the critics: (1) Is film the most relevant art of our time, and if so, can it retain this role in future? (2) Are we entering a new cinematic era, anticipated by current phenomena like *cinéma vérité*, underground, and various technical innovations? (3) What does the future hold for commercial, Hollywood productions? (4) Is the traditional story structure going to disappear? (5) Is it possible to go even further in the screen presentation of violence and sex?

One is surprised to find only ten answers. Were these the

only critics invited, or did the others decide to ignore the questionnaire? One notes the absence of such eminent and influential critics as Pauline Kael of the *New Yorker* and Manny Farber of *New Republic*.

On the whole the answers show a remarkable reluctance to speculate about the future. This is not surprising. Reviewers writing in the daily or weekly press are concerned with immediate rather than general issues. One feels that they are loath to commit themselves, preferring to talk about peripheral issues rather than plunge deep into the unknown. The caution is understandable. After all film is not an isolated phenomenon, and should be examined in the immensely complex context of the entire American culture. Andrew Sarris of the *Village Voice* rightly observes that 'Movies are only a part of modern culture, and it is too early to tell how important they will seem in the next century.'[9]

The critics represented in 'Symposium' agreed that in the United States in 1968 film was the most relevant of all the arts. The one exception is Wilfrid Sheed of *Esquire* who supports the claims of the novel 'because it can use all the tricks of the other arts.'[10] A novelist, according to Sheed, can not only adapt screen writing techniques, but, more importantly, use to his advantage the cinematically trained, imaginative responses of his readers, their ability to visualize his story. Thus his praise of the novel becomes a backhand compliment to film for the way it has shaped the readers' modern sensibilities.

A point referring to the first item on the questionnaire, commented on by several of the critics, is the relationship between film and television. With cassettes and cables on the way in television is obviously going to play a most prominent part in the distribution of films. Joseph Morgenstern of *Newsweek* puts it simply: 'The future of film exhibition lies in the home.'[11]

Comments on current trends and their possible influence on the cinema of the future were long, varied and disjointed. *Cinéma vérité*, the New Wave and the underground, failed to generate great enthusiasm. Stanley Kaufmann observed that thanks to the introduction of *cinéma vérité* the element of journalism in film has been growing and, at the same time, journalism itself is developing certain characteristics of an art.[12] Perhaps Richard Schickel of *Life* has perceived the general direction of the changes most clearly, expecting the birth of a new, standard, cinematic manner, absorbing, among others, elements of 'direct cinema' and of the underground.[13]

There was general agreement about what the critics felt was going to be the successful survival of commercial, Hollywood production. Some conceded to it, expressing regret, others without comment. All ten of them also agreed that film could never completely jettison traditional story structures. In some guise and measure they would continue their ageless screen existence.[14]

Finally, sex and violence. Opinions differ here. Stanley Kaufmann believes that in the presentation of violence film has reached, or even already overstepped, the permitted limits. Andrew Sarris gives a serious and at the same time provocative reply. He points out that as far as sex is concerned literature is still ahead of film, and in the violence stakes politics are beyond reach.[15]

Such were the conclusions of the symposium about the future of the cinema. A 'conclusion' is of course a misleading word in this context. Sending out the questionnaire to just a few notable critics the organizers could hardly hope to get in return a comprehensible, plausible and coherent futuristic vision. For an operation of this type a different questionnaire would have been needed and, perhaps, a different set of experts. Ernest Callenbach, complaining in *Film Quarterly* that his colleagues, the film critics, show little interest in theory, postulates that any attempt to formulate a generally applicable set of rules has to take account of two basic problems: firstly, the range of relationships between the material and the form, and secondly, the relationship between the work of art and the recipient.[16] Some of the critics taking part in the symposium may have touched, here and there, on the first problem but they seem to be completely indifferent as far as the second one is concerned. And how does one speculate on the future of the cinema without an active concern for its expressive force and the responsiveness of the public?

A clear-eyed look at the cinematic future demands a much wider context. One has to step beyond the limits of the cinema to see it as an ingredient of contemporary culture, a part of modern American life. Gerald Sykes, a critic, novelist and lecturer at Columbia University of New York, taking part in a conference on technology and society in Los Angeles in 1966, opened his speech with the words: 'Man rushes first to be saved by technology, and then to be saved *from* technology. We Americans are front-runners in both races.'[17]

The expansion of technology and the threat of technology are two sides of the same coin. Not all the theoreticians see technology as a 'big, bad wolf'. Its unqualified enthusiasts are also numerous, with their spiritual leader, Professor Marshall McLuhan, proclaiming to the world the coming of a new era. According to this Canadian philosopher (this title probably fits him best) humanity is entering the electronic age, the age of telegraph, telephone, phonograph, radio, film, television and automation. The age of the book, of the printed page, which was, in McLuhan's opinion, the original cause of all manner of disasters, creating barriers between peoples, isolating them in closed, hermetic groups, has finally come to an end. Now, thanks to the electronic media, everything is going to change: the 'linear' culture of the printed word and image is being replaced by the culture of the living word; there will be a renaissance of 'tribal' consciousness, but on a much higher plane of development. The media, led by television, will transform the world into a 'global village' – a single unit, with all the inhabitants responding to the same set of impulses.[18]

McLuhan worships television. Not its programme and content, these, to him, are of no account. He likes the way it transmits messages. His motto is: 'the medium is the message'.[19] No wonder the professor is idolized by the big television companies, with generous fees always available for him to act as adviser or lecturer. McLuhan is right to perceive the almost magical power in television transmissions, but his haughty indifference to the content of the messages is difficult to accept. Also controversial is his insistence that television appeals to the senses of touch and hearing, and not, as once seemed incontestable, to the visual sense. But had the author of *The Gutenberg Galaxy* agreed to the primacy of the visual element in television, his entire thesis about the new age of the audio-tactile culture would have been rudely undermined. The prophet of the electronic age is never worried by logical gaps or contradictions. When, during one of his lectures, a listener took issue with him on that ground, a somewhat unexpected retort was: 'You're still thinking lineally.'[20] Logic belongs to the bygone, bookish era, and has no right in ours.

McLuhan's scorn for anything visual, that is, associated with reading, with the absorption of lines of printed signs, reduces film to a modest place among the electric, or electronic media ('electric' and 'electronic' are, for him, interchangeable terms). He treats film slightingly, and doesn't rate highly its chances of survival. According to him, film, in the early stages of its development had been not so much a reflection as a parody of life. At the height of its popularity film became permeated by the culture of the printed word. Typically, refusing to be drawn into any discussion of the content of television, McLuhan at the same time insists on talking about Hollywood pictures in terms of their content – or lack of it. On the other hand he is not really concerned with realities, even the realities of television which he likes to refer to. It is, after all, well known how popular feature films are on television, how readily viewers respond to them. For McLuhan films on television are a parody of the cinema. To put a medium into the context of another creates a grotesque effect.[21] Perhaps for the Toronto wizard, but clearly not for millions of television viewers.

Only those who share with McLuhan his belief that film is a disintegrating medium, to be replaced with the more progressive, not linear, not bookish, and, surprisingly, not visual, television, can draw any comfort from his theories. He has gained no disciples among film critics. None of them sees the future of film so bleakly. In some respects the position of synesthesists, both of the 'expanded cinema' and the 'mixed media' variety, seems relatively close to McLuhanists.

Gene Youngblood, the leading theoretician of 'expanded cinema', has been mentioned in a previous chapter. One would like to emphasize here the concept of synesthesia which, according to Youngblood, is going to replace current structural–dramaturgic, analytical attitudes to the cinema.[22] The viewer of the future, surrounded by sound and images, is going to be quite free to respond to them according to his individual sensibility, perceiving them in his own arbitrary ways, seeing sounds and listening to images. It will be made easier for him by the wide application of two technical devices, greatly valued by Youngblood: double exposure and non-synchronized sound. The cinema of the future will cease to exist as cinema; it will be life itself, becoming real in the perceptions of viewer-listeners. Ideally films should drop the use of film stock, with its fixed frame, and forgo cinema projection; they should be shown wherever possible. But, as has already been observed, such transformation of the current distribution system is unthinkable without the large resources of powerful companies to draw upon. It is extremely difficult to see how this 'expanded cinema' could ever offer a genuine freedom of opportunity to an individual, independent artist, as Youngblood postulates.

The 'mixed media' theory is somewhat similar, but easier to put into practice, and much less expensive. Its central point is, however, not a film, but a stage spectacle, uniting a number of diverse creative pursuits: music, dance, theatre, obviously, and also film – an important ingredient in this melting pot. This new theatre, more narrowly known as a 'happening', is another manifestation of the reaction against the culture of the written word, meant for people of the electronic, post-literary era.[23]

Film plays a prominent part in this 'theatre of mixed means'. The popular 'happening' play, Robert Whitman's *Prune Flat*, produced on the off-Broadway stage, was an interesting combination of 'live' performers with film projection, partly thrown on the screen, partly on the actors' own bodies. A peculiar flattening effect of the human figure was achieved by covering a performer with his own image. Film is used here both as a prop and as a means of commenting directly on the action, considerably enriching the viewer's range of responses. In another happening, devised by Claes Oldenburg, the scene is the interior of a cinema, with the watching audience lit by flashes of light coming off the screen. The title of this spectacle is *Movie House*.

'Expanded cinema' and the 'theatre of mixed means' grow out of the same technological frustrations. Some are no longer satisfied with traditional cinema, nor others with traditional theatre. The difference between the two is practical rather than theoretical. 'Expanded cinema' has found a practical application so far only in the great international expositions, in New York, Montreal, and Osaka. In some of the most expensive pavilions multi-screen projections of various optical-stereophonic and television-film combinations were drawing in crowds of enthralled visitors. But a pleasant half-hour, or one-hour attraction at Expo is not in itself sufficient to revolutionize an art, with several decades of established creative tradition behind it. American critics, participants in the 'symposium' already referred to, see 'Expanded cinema' becoming a big-city, circus-like attraction, a sort of local Disneyland. In the words of Wilfrid Sheed, 'a cross between Lincoln Center and a planetarium – to take the children to'.[24]

The 'theatre of mixed means' has a very small, if most enthusiastic, following. It is a fringe activity, rather like *élite* exhibitions of ultra-modern and as yet unknown artists. Richard Kostelanetz in his book *The Theatre of Mixed Means* estimates that in 1968 in New York the overall number of spectators at these shows did not exceed 1,000 – a drop in the New York ocean.[25] And when Robert Whitman's *Prune Flat* found a hospitable stage off-Broadway, it was showing as a weekend attraction to half-empty and not too enthusiastic houses. So far there are no signs that this revolutionary transformation of the conventional stage can succeed in originating a synthetic, film-cum-theatre spectacle.

The only theory that can boast of a growing following, is

the *auteur* theory, or the 'authors'' cinema. This is un-doubtedly related to the structural changes that have taken place in Hollywood. The end of the big, independent studios, ruled by their sovereign 'bosses', absorption of these studios into the operations of giant corporations with hundreds of diverse industrial and trade interests, and, on the other hand, the success of productions projected, set up and controlled by individual, creative film-makers, made cheaply and without the traditional Hollywood gloss – all this has tended to shift the attention towards the person of the 'author', usually a director, but sometimes an independent producer, or even an actor involved in the project from the first idea to the final stage of making an exhibition print.

Propagators of the *auteur* theory are to be found both in the underground and in the commercial cinema. Among the critics who lend their practical support to the theory Andrew Sarris is pre-eminent. His book, *The American Cinema*, subtitled *Directors and Directions*, 1929–68, is written entirely from this position.[26] In his next work, *Confessions of a Cultist*, Sarris' position is further clarified and developed.[27]

The assumption that a film, as much as a novel, is a personal statement of its author – usually, as has already been suggested, a director – ought to lead us straight to the question of content. When the content of films had been determined exclusively, or at least in a large part, by the studios, there seemed to be little point in inquiring into it, or in questioning its social impact. It was, after all, general knowledge that studios were moved by the profit motive. But now the position is somewhat different: in many cases the artists hold the upper hand and can, presumably, express themselves freely.

One notes with some amazement that the majority of film critics, absorbed with the formal aspects of a cinematic work, pay little regard to its social impact. Content, when it does get a mention in a review, is written about as if the author has created his work in total isolation, as if it was his personal affair, at best to be shared with a critic. Stanley Kaufmann, perhaps the most socially conscious of American reviewers, doesn't attempt to formulate a programme for creative

K

cinéastes, restricting himself to the assertion that a critic should single out for praise those works that are of the greatest value for the *existence* of an individual.[28] In other words, creative film-makers should assist people with the business of living. One might add: to help them to live decently, with some hope for the future.

It may seem, for all its correctness, a rather hollow statement. Let us, however, consider, how films, initially those exhibited on the large screen, can help one to live. They can, but they do not have to, and certainly, at the moment, they prevailingly do not try. Let us return for a moment to the television moloch, keeping millions of viewers under a constant bombardment of sound and images. Gerald Sykes, already quoted here, says that America is living in the continuous excitement of a permanent sale, with the disposal of the product becoming more important than its actual production.[29] Television, manipulated by Madison Avenue, is always exerting pressure to buy something, while at the same time trying to entertain and to inform.

How does the viewer react to this mounting pressure of advertising messages which, in their mass, are ambiguous and contradictory, and mutually exclusive? Jonathan Miller, a fiery critic of McLuhan, but not without a certain sympathy and even admiration for him, believes that under this pressure the viewer, feeling frustrated and confused, retreats into isolation.[30] What he sees on the small screen is remote from the tangible realities of his life, and therefore unimportant. Miller may exaggerate the effects of saturation, but he is right in asserting that for the viewer the right of a choice is increasingly difficult to exercise – whether it is the choice of a political position or of a moral attitude to the phenomena reported on the box. Marshall McLuhan is also conscious of this condition of saturation with television information of all kinds, but his diagnosis is different. He asserts that 'when man is overwhelmed by information, he resorts to myth. Myth is inclusive, time-saving and fast.'[31] Cinema, or at least films, often provide a way of escape from television. A viewer expects to find in them some kind of moral indication, perhaps one-sided and crude, but at least clear-cut. It may be a realistic assessment of an existing situation, or more easily assimilable – a myth.

A Fruitful Unrest

One must not forget this information-giving and myth-making role of the cinema when trying to divine, in the confusing variety of films, some kind of general trend. If one asked a fairly well-informed viewer in the United States, or in Western Europe – always excellently provided with the cinematic product of the American continent – what were typical American films, the answer would probably begin with titles like *The Godfather, Cabaret, Love Story, 2001: – A Space Odyssey, Patton, Five Easy Pieces, Easy Rider* or *Woodstock*, and not with *The Sound of Music* or *Hello, Dolly*. Expensive blockbusters made in the traditional Hollywood manner are no longer representative of the American cinema. Contemporary pictures have taken over the representative role.

The American press speedily finds a label for any group of films displaying certain similarities. Two of the most popular labels are 'Youth Movies' and – a more comprehensive term – 'Now Pictures'. These are the fashionable streams, and therefore treated as the most significant current trends. 'Youth Movies' and 'Now Pictures' are almost synonymous with the contemporary American cinema.

What are the characteristic features of this trend? Here are some broad definitions, specified in an arbitrary order. The stylistic manner has largely been formed under the influence of television commercials: a lot of technical 'gimmicks', a loose dramatic structure far removed from the classical models, a free flowing narrative, often fragmentary, apt to stray from its main course. The new actors, not even remotely like the former Hollywood stars, seem much closer to pop-idols or jazz musicians; not quite the hippies, but absorbing some elements of the hippy outlook. Peter Fonda, Dustin Hoffman, Jon Voight, Jack Nicholson – how far they appear to be from the world of Gary Cooper, Tyrone Power, or even Clark Gable and Humphrey Bogart! The new actors have grown up and matured not in the hot houses of Hollywood but in the more exposed heat of the university campuses. Some of them are not exactly strangers to the 'drug culture', to LSD and marijuana. Their career in the cinema usually started in third-rate Westerns, Roger Corman 'Youth Movies' about motor-cycling gangs, or television serials. Jack Nicholson, invited by the University of California to give a series of lectures at their department of journalistic studies in Irwine, opened with the theme of 'Anti-establishment film'. A significant choice!

Another characteristic feature of 'Now Pictures' is a symbiosis of fiction and documentary. The two streams intermingle and absorb each other's elements to a point where they become completely integrated. An American critic, Andrew Sarris, traces this symbiosis to the interaction of two separate traditions: underground cinema, animated by mainly documentary attitudes, and conventional film fiction, based on classic dramatic structures.[32] Contemporary film-makers (although Sarris refers to the European rather than the American directors) operate between those two poles, subjected to their contradictory pulls. The fusion of documentary and fiction is manifested in insistence on natural backgrounds, in movement out of the studios, scorning specially constructed sets and all artificial props. Haskell Wexler's *Medium Cool* is a masterful example of this marriage. In the Chicago Democratic Convention sequence it is quite impossible to separate fiction from reality.

What sort of attitudes are projected in 'Now Pictures' where the protagonists, not markedly different from any chance passer-by and moving in a familiar world, live through the 'ordinary' human dramas? Almost unnoticed, a new cinematic landscape of America has taken shape, populated by a new set of film characters. And as frequently happens in creative fiction, this image, solidly based in contemporary reality and feeding on social conflicts, is already moving into a mythical dimension. New American screen myths are becoming current, with an entire stock of symbolic signs and metaphors.

A leading audio-visual symbol is the motor-cycle – a device

for taming the world, a sign of personal freedom, offering the means of escape from the everyday, humdrum realities of life. Both underground and Hollywood heroes may set off into the world riding a motor-cycle. They are not different in this respect from four million of their compatriots, who every Sunday get out their steel mounts and ride off to get drunk on speed and to put as much physical space as possible between them and their homes. Sometimes a car replaces a motor-cycle. In *Two Lane Black-top* the heroes travel on four wheels, not two, but they are driven on by the same motive: to find something different, and, at the same time, to discover their own identities.

A contemporary American screen hero tends to be a wanderer, seeking the truth and hungry for it: the truth about the world and about himself. His life is dominated by the ritual of the journey – measured by milestones, roadside cafés and nameless, almost identical motels. Jack Nicholson, himself one of the seekers, describes their predicament: 'They reject what hems them in, and the rejection is in itself an act of escape. . . . These Americans always want to be somewhere else, in a place which is different. . . . America is a vast country, but they always find in it the same thing. And so their escape is hopeless, without an issue. . . .'[33]

There is another kind of escape, complementing the first – the journey into illusion, triggered off by drugs. A great number of 'Now Pictures' touch on the drug problem, on the social habit of seeking oblivion in the innocent (as some would have it) marijuana or the deadly (there can be no doubt about that) heroin. There are film-makers, usually from the *avant garde* circles of the 'psychedelic cinema', who approve of the use of drugs, believing that they bring freedom from inhibitions and open up new fields for artistic expansion. Others, treating the same subject within the commercial set-up, assume the position of an outside observer. They describe the phenomenon, trace its origin, and leave the judgement to the viewer. Jerry Schatzberg, the director of *Panic in Needle Park*, was right to point out in an interview that the drug problem should not be taken out of its social context. Drugs are most popular among the deprived, he says, because they can provide a momentary escape from the condition of poverty. And he concludes: 'It is society itself, rather than the drug pushers, which should have been put in the dock.'[34]

The American screen myth is tragic in substance. There is no real escape, neither outwardly into nature, nor inwardly into drug-induced hallucinations. In the end everything stays unchanged. Within this general scheme of things two contrasting and contradictory moods – sentimentality and cruelty – keep shifting and changing places. The heroes are responsive and emotional, perhaps not noble in the traditional sense but aspiring to a full and peaceful life. But they have to live within a society that is cruel and destructive. This is how painful conflicts arise, often leading to a disaster. However, the real world, appearing on the screen as the background to all those conflicts, is by no means uniformly black, hence the characteristic mixture of comedy and violent drama. Humorous scenes are succeeded by tragic ones, although these are sometimes lacking in real seriousness and depth of feeling. 'Black humour' is highly fashionable. Arthur Penn's admiration for Samuel Beckett is not without reason: in *Little Big Man* the master's influence is clearly evident.[35]

There was a time when the American screen was given over to the 'American dream', presented in hundreds of variations: the vision of a rich country, inhabited by prosperous, happy, go-ahead people. This optimistic fantasy has now been replaced by the 'American nightmare' – the essential content of the new mythology of the screen.

Myth and reality – the two contrasting concepts – are dialectically related and interdependent. There are always some purely opportunistic film-makers resolved to follow the prevailing fashion, and there are the sincere ones, with a compulsion to say what they feel and what they really believe in. Not the least difficulty in assessing the real artistic and social worth of the new American cinema is the fact that all of them have had a hand in fostering the myths. It is not always easy to delve into the motives behind a creative work, to gauge the exact degree of an author's true commitment.

How does one tell what was inspired by direct experience, and what by the currently established vogue?

Abraham Polonsky, a black-listed director who, after an enforced silence of twenty years, was allowed to return to active film-making, summed up most aptly the dialectical relationship between myth and reality: 'The best way to escape from reality is to start believing in the reality of a myth,' he said.[36] Have the American directors, repeating the same image of a man running away from the social reality, convinced themselves of the reality of the myth they have created? All sweeping generalizations tend to be wide of the mark, but it seems that those who are really concerned about the social progress of their country are not content to stay with the myth of a 'running American'. The most forcefully expressive description of the existing situation is not sufficient when it fails to indicate to the viewer some acceptable conclusion. Jack Nicholson is reserved in his comments, and the programme suggested by him is more than modest. Laudably, he limits himself to the proposition that 'we should now try to point to a way out of this mess by giving some glimpses of some solutions.'[37] The onus of responsibility is shifted on to the viewers: it is up to them to construct more coherent signposts out of those fragmentary glimpses. Let them turn the screen allusions and parallels (like the fashionable excursions into the Depression-ridden thirties) into clear lessons for the future. The American nightmare, unlike the rosy American dream that preceded it, offers no models to be followed. Even in negation it seems to be lacking in a sense of purpose. Those bitter yarns of evil times achieve, à rebours, the mood of a sad fairy-tale, at the other extreme from the old fairy-tales of the American Paradise.

Can the good, uplifting fairy-tales, those with a happy end, ever come back? It is significant that some persecuted minorities, fighting for their rights, create a new demand for optimistic films. The Red Indians, the remnants of the one-time master race of the American continent, may be satisfied with historical rehabilitation of the kind attempted by Arthur Penn in *Little Big Man*, and Ralph Nelson in *Soldier Blue*. For the Negro minority this would not be enough. The need for affirmation calls for black contemporary heroes, appearing in realistic situations, but in a halo of romantic glory, heroes like Shaft or Sweetback.

The Political Ferment

Pictures like *Shaft* or *Sweetback* would have been unthinkable at the time of McCarthy's witch hunts. Seen in this perspective, the change in the cinema has been conclusive, and, for all the remaining barriers and restrictions, undoubtedly progressive. Ferment in the country's political life has left its impact on the screen. The extent of creative freedom, both for the studios and for individual film-makers, has certainly been expanded, unlike television, where Pentagon and FBI pressures make life difficult for independently minded producers. Vice-President Spiro Agnew kept up his attacks on television, his favourite target, ignoring the cinema. Perhaps he regarded it as '*quantite negligeable*', or perhaps he never went near a cinema and had no idea what goes on there

Film-makers of the 'Hollywood ten', persecuted by the infamous UnAmerican Activities Committee, have been able to resume normal work, with Dalton Trumbo, Albert Maltz and Herbert Biberman (shortly before his death) among them. Abraham Polonsky's *Tell Them Willie Boy is Here* has reminded us of this director's existence. But, most importantly, documentary films are being produced, treating subjects excluded from television screens. Joseph Strick, the maker of the screen version of James Joyce's *Ulysses*, directed the twenty-minute-long *Interviews with My Lai Veterans*. Five ex-service men of different social backgrounds and living in different parts of the United States, talk about their complicity – or rather their alleged innocence – in the My Lai massacre. The film, photographed by Haskell Wexler, is a shattering exposure of the moral devastation caused by the war. The men on the screen are not aware of this cost, it would never occur to them to see themselves as murderers, and the only comment they throw out in passing is: Why so much noise about My Lai, when there were other similar incidents, before and after it. The Hollywood

Motion Pictures Academy, responsible for the annual Oscar awards, is often criticized for its decisions; but it surely deserves some credit for giving its 1970 award for the best documentary picture of the year to *Interviews with My Lai Veterans*.

Another example of a demonstrably political film is *The Murder of Fred Hampton*. In 1969 the Chicago police raided the Black Panthers' headquarters. It happened in the early hours of the morning, and the two leaders of the movement, Fred Hampton and his deputy, Mark Clark, still in their beds, were run through with a hail of bullets. The police asserted that they were acting in self-defence. Mike Gray, a documentary film-maker, was at the time engaged on a film about Hampton, with a considerable footage already shot. As soon as he learned about the murderous affair in Chicago he went to the spot and started a most thorough investigation of his own, recording on film everything that seemed of any possible consequence: shots of the scene of the crime, interviews with witnesses, with the friends and wife of the dead leader, etc. Not content with that, he acquired and included in his film the television documentation prepared by the police: a reconstruction of the alleged course of action in the Black Panthers' headquarters. In this way a unique cinematic document was born, constituting, apart from anything else, a persuasive indictment of the procedures and operational methods of the American forces of public order.

In 1972 several new political films appeared on American screens. It is worthwhile mentioning that one of them, independently produced by Marvin Worth and Arnold Perl, was released by one of the Hollywood Big Five, namely Warner Brothers. The film in question, a documentary entitled *Malcolm X*, is a biography of the black leader who was assassinated in 1965. His widow, Mrs Betty Shabazz, collaborated actively in the production of this screen memorial.

Winter Soldier, another political film, is a documentary about an investigation which took place in Detroit in the winter of 1971. Over 200 American war veterans testified about atrocities committed in Vietnam. The film, made by a team of eighteen film-makers, who preferred to remain anonymous, was shown for a short period on educational television in New York, and later at the Cannes Film Festival in May 1972. *Winter Soldier*, although not much of a film in the traditional sense, is a terrifying document of human degradation, a document one cannot easily forget.

The Trial of the Catonsville Nine is an adaptation of a play of the same name, written by Daniel Berrigan, one of the nine peace activists who burned their draft record cards in 1968 at Catonsville, Maryland. Gregory Peck produced a screen version of the play and Gordon Davidson directed it. Haskell Wexler was the cameraman. The film is, in parts, too theatrical, rather static and stagey, but its anti-war message carries a passionate conviction and is endowed with great dramatic force. Here again, a characteristic trait of the new American cinema trends: Gregory Peck and Haskell Wexler, two V.I.P's of Hollywood, assumed both artistic and financial responsibility for the venture; Cinema 5, in the heart of Manhattan, screened *The Trial of Catonsville Nine*.

The American cinema is like a gigantic pot, with ever-new ingredients being continuously poured into it. The pot is boiling, steaming, the pressure is rising. No one is sure what is inside, and it is not always the most interesting things that come to the surface. But, occasionally, among the froth and dregs, there is a glimpse of something that sticks in the mind, something of permanent worth.

NOTES

CHAPTER 1

1. 'Vote on Hollywood Angers Councilman', *Los Angeles Times*, 15 November 1967. 'Hollywood Retains its 30-Year Lines,' *Los Angeles Times*, 8 December 1967.
2. 'Dreams for Sale', *Newsweek*, 4 May 1970.
3. 'Recession Taught Gulf and Western Humility: Bluhdorn on Credibility', *Variety*, 29 March 1972.
4. 'Conglomerates under Probe', *Variety*, 6 August 1969.
5. 'See Government Choke of Biz', *Variety*, 11 June 1969.
6. 'Kinney W 7 Owners Approve Merger,' *Variety*, 11 June 1969.
7. 'Kinney W 7 Owners Approve Merger', *Variety*, 11 June 1969.
8. 'Hollywood S.O.S. and Subsidy', *Variety*, December 1970.
9. 'SAG to Nixon: Help Us Fast: Submits 4 Point Action Program', *Variety*, 4 October 1972.
10. 'Government to Ankle Film Production', *Variety*, 11 October 1972.
11. Jacques Lourcelle, 'Otto Preminger', *Cinéma d'aujourd'hui*, Editions Seghers, Paris, 1965, p. 105.

CHAPTER 2

1. Phil A. Konry, *Yes, Mr De Mille*, G. P. Putman's Sons, New York, 1969, p. 88.
2. Cecil B. de Mille, *Autobiography*, W. H. Allen, London, 1960, p. 235.
3. *Yes, Mr De Mille*, op. cit., p. 206.
4. Cecil B. De Mille, *Der Spiegel*, 28 January 1959.
5. *Yes, Mr De Mille*, op. cit., p. 59.
6. 'All Time Box Office Champions', *Variety*, 65th Anniversary Edition, 6 January 1971.
7. 'All Time Box Office Champs', *Variety*, 67th Anniversary Edition, 3 January 1973.
8. Bosley Crowther, 'Cleopatra is a Surpassing Film', *New York Times*, 13 June 1963.
9. 'Movie Cleopatra is called disappointing by Judith Crist', *New York Herald Tribune*, 13 June 1963.

10. ' "Sara una Bibbia ecumenica" annuncia Huston', *L'Unitá*, 15 January 1964.
11. Pauline Kael, *Kiss Kiss Bang Bang*, an Atlantic Monthly Press Book, Little Brown & Co., Boston, 1968, p. 135.
12. Thomas Quinn Curtis, 'A Plain in Spain goes Russian', *The New York Times*, 17 February 1965.
13. John Gillett, 'Patton: Lust for Glory', *Monthly Film Bulletin*, June 1970, p. 122–3.
14. J. M., 'Magnificent Anachronism', *Newsweek*, 16 February 1970.
15. C. V., *'L'homme qui aimait la guerre'*, *L'Express*, 20–6 April 1970.
16. Filmspiegel, *'Patton – Rebell in Uniform'*, *Neue Zürcher Zeitung*, 2 May 1970.
17. 'Beyond the Stars', *The New Yorker*, 24 April 1965.
18. Rich, 'Airport', *Variety*, 18 February 1970.
19. *Kiss Kiss Bang Bang*, op. cit., p. 176–7.
20. Pauline Kael, 'Keep Going', *The New Yorker*, 3 January 1970.

CHAPTER 3

1. Bob Thomas, King Cohn, *The Life and Times of Harry Cohn*, Barne and Rockliff, London, 1967, p. 19.
2. Norman Zierold, *The Hollywood Tycoons*, Hamish Hamilton, London, 1969, p. 286.
3. 'Zukor at 96', *Variety*, 26 November 1969.
4. A. D. Murphy, 'Adolph Zukor's 100th Birthday', *Variety*, 10 January 1973.
5. *Time*, 22 January 1973.
6. *The Hollywood Tycoons*, op. cit., p. 155.
7. Jack L. Rolls, '1776 With Legit Players', *Variety*, 6 October 1971.
8. *The Hollywood Tycoons*, op. cit., p. 244.
9. Leo Guild, *Zanuck: Hollywood's Last Tycoon*, Holloway Home Publishing Co., New York, 1970, p. 195.
10. Zanuck's Monday Relinquishment of Fox Chairmanship, *Variety*, 19 May 1971.
11. Abel Green. 'Elmo Williams in N.Y. As D F Z Shapes New Fox Films: "Around 20 a Year" ', *Variety*, 28 April 1971.
12. Gordon Irving, 'Zanuck in Edinburgh', *Variety*, 9 September 1970.

13. 'French Q. and A. with Zanuck', *Variety*, 14 May 1969.
14. Richard Zanuck, 'Don't Write Off the Film Biz', *Variety*, 20 January 1971.
15. 'Joe Hyams, Poured in the Mogul Mold', *Los Angeles Times West Magazine*, 11 June 1967.
16. Ibid.
17. 'Army Arched, Zukor Asks Bob Hope: How Did You Know It Was My 100th Birthday?', *Variety*, 10 January 1973.
18. Gene Arnel, Bob Evans, 'We Keep Control', *Variety*, 3 February 1971.
19. 'Only you, Jim Aubrey', *Newsweek*, 15 March 1965.
20. 'Among Aubrey's Aims: Ease Choke of Paper Work', *Variety*, 24 December 1969.
21. Ronald Gold, 'Picker on Flop Loss-Cutting', *Variety*, 26 August 1970.
22. Norman Zierold, *The Hollywood Tycoons*, op. cit., p. 299.
23. 'The New Movies', *Newsweek*, 7 December 1970.
24. Paul Mayersberg, *Hollywood – the Haunted House*, Allen Lane the Penguin Press, London, 1967, p. 51.
25. 'Add L. B. Mayer Anecdote', *Variety*, 24 February 1971.
26. Dick Adler, 'Ernest Lehman: Prolonging the Agony', *Los Angeles Times West Magazine*, 13 August 1967.
27. 'The New Movies', *Newsweek*, 7 December 1970.
28. *Hollywood – the Haunted House*, op. cit., p. 67.
29. 'Producer, Director, Writer Ought to Be Three Separate Persons: Manduke', *Variety*, 5 March 1969.
30. *Hollywood – the Haunted House*, op. cit., p. 69.
31. Charles Champlin, 'Hollywood – Changing of the Guard', *Los Angeles Times*, 19 March 1967.
32. Andrew Sarris, *The American Cinema: Directors and Directions, 1929–1968*, E. P. Dutton & Co., New York, 1968, p. 55.
33. Aubrey Tarbox, 'A Film Whose Parts He Never Made', *Variety*, 13 August 1969.
34. Gerald Pratley, *The Cinema of John Frankheimer* (International Film Guide Series), A. Zwemmer, Ltd, London, 1970, p. 30.
35. *The American Cinema*, op. cit., p. 193.
36. John Pratley, *The Cinema of John Frankheimer*, op. cit., p. 34.
37. Mary Blume, 'Carving Out New Territory in Old West', *International Herald Tribune*, 14–15 February 1970.

38. 'New Faces IV', *Saturday Review*, 24 December 1966.
39. Bob Rose, 'Movies for TV Produced by Director', *Los Angeles Times*, 17 June 1967.
40. *The Cinema of John Frankenheimer*, op. cit., p. 33.
41. Mary Blume, 'Mervyn Leroy Brooding About Bad Taste', *International Herald Tribune*, 24–25 October 1970.
42. Joseph Gelmis, *The Film Director as Superstar*, Doubleday & Company, Inc. New York, 1970, p. 180.
43. 'Man of the Future', *Newsweek*, 31 May 1971.
44. McCandlish Phillips, 'The Woman Barbara Loden Might Have Been', *International Herald Tribune*, 12 March 1971.
45. 'The New Movies', *Newsweek*, 7 December 1970.
46. Ibid.

CHAPTER 4

1. 'The New Movies', *Newsweek*, 7 December 1970.
2. 'The Troubled American: A Special Report on the White Majority', *Newsweek*, 6 October 1969.
3. Ibid.
4. Pauline Kael, 'Blood and Snow', *The New Yorker*, 15 February 1969.
5. 'The Duke at 60', *Time*, 9 June 1967.
6. 'War Films and Showmen', *Variety*, 2 July 1969.
7. Interview with Buck Henry about *CATCH 22*, *Film Quarterly*, Vol. XXIV, No. 1, Fall 1970.
8. Bob Rafelson, *The New Yorker*, 24 October 1970.
9. 'Alice's Restaurant's Children', *Newsweek*, 29 September 1969.
10. 'The New Movies', *Newsweek*, 7 December 1970.
11. Stephen Farber, 'Movies from behind the Barricades', *Film Quarterly*, Winter 1970.
12. '*Duro giudizio di Antonioni sull'America*', *L'Unitá*, 18 April 1968.
13. Marsha Kinder, '*Zabriskie Point*', *Sight and Sound*, Winter 1968, Vol. 38, No. 1.
14. Addison Verrill, 'Black Panther's Film Profits', *Variety*, 2 September 1970.
15. Hal Humphrey, 'Another Kind of Negro Stereotype', *Los Angeles Times*, 13 April 1967.
16. Bill Cosby, 'For a Touch of Color', *Los Angeles Times West Magazine*, 17 September 1967.

17. Brendan Gill, 'Current Cinema', *The New Yorker*, 25 December 1965.
18. Samuel Lachize, '*Cinéma, la Chronique*', *Humanité Dimanche*, 6–12 July 1970.
19. Valenti to Hyman Re Negro Director: 'You Honor Our Biz', *Variety*, 15 May 1968.
20. Ronald Gold, 'Gordon Park's Filming Credo', *Variety*, 3 March 1971.
21. 'Sweet Song of Success', *Newsweek*, 21 January 1971.
22. Peter Goldman, 'Black America Now', *Newsweek*, 19 February 1973.
23. Kevin Thomas, 'Cinematographer Who Pictures Responsibility', *Los Angeles Times*, 1 June 1967.
24. Ibid.
25. Ibid.
26. 'Medium Cool for the Medium Young', *Variety*, 13 August 1969.
27. Hank Werba, 'Agnew Echo at Italo Film Fest – USIA Chief Hits "Aberration" Pics', *Variety*, 7 October 1970.

CHAPTER 5

1. Louis Safir, '*America violente*', *Rinascita*, 11 June 1971.
2. Ibid.
3. Richard Goldstein, 'The Last Cowboy Saint', *Los Angeles Times West Magazine*, 5 February 1967.
4. 'The Duke at 60', *The Times*, 9 June 1967.
5. Richard Goldstein, 'The Last Cowboy Saint', op. cit.
6. Hans Werba, 'Leone Tags His *Once Upon a Time*, An American Western Filmed by an Italian', *Variety*, 17 July 1968.
7. 'Hi-ho, Denaro!' *Time*, 4 August 1967.
8. *Variety*, 28 May 1969.
9. *Variety*, 17 July 1968.
10. 'Press Violent about Film's Violence: Prod Sam Peckinpah Following *Bunch*', *Variety*, 2 July 1969.
11. Ibid.
12. 'Truth as Defense of *Soldier Blue*', *Variety*, 24 March 1971.
13. *Giornale dello Spettacolo*, 26 September 1970.
14. John Simon, *The Case for Inhumanity*, *Film 67/68*, Simon & Schuster.
15. 'Like Bonnie, Like Clyde', *Time*, 26 December 1967.

16. Penelope Gilliatt, 'The New Centurions', *The New Yorker*, 2 August 1972.

17. Penelope Houston, America's First Family, *New Statesman*, 1 September 1972.

18. Paul D. Zimmerman, 'Kubrick's Brilliant Vision', *Newsweek*, 3 January 1972.

19. Season's Greetings: Bang!', *Time*, 20 December 1971.

20. 'True Blue', *Newsweek*, 13 July 1970.

21. Judith Crist, 'Russ Meyer's Vixen', *New York Post*, 26 May 1969.

22. *Time*, 13 June 1969.

23. C. Herman Pritchett, *American Constitutional Issues*, McGraw Hill Book Co. Inc., p. 272–8.

24. 'Pornography Goes Public', *Newsweek*, 21 December 1970.

25. 'Pornography: The Oldest Debate', *Newsweek*, 12 October 1970.

26. 'Bipartisan Raps Strong; But Nixon Staff Shrillest', *Variety*, 7 October 1970.

27. 'Hollywood's Own Anti-Porno Rally Hits Russ Meyer', *Variety*, 27 January 1971.

28. Larry Michie, Nixon Court vs. Obscenity, *Variety*, 27 September 1972.

29. *The Australian*, 23 June 1973.

30. 'Year's Surprise: Family Films Did Best', *Variety*, 7 January 1971.

31. '*L'Express va plus loin avec Erich Segal*', *L'Express*, 29 March and 4 April 1971.

CHAPTER 6

1. Sheldon Renan, *An Introduction to the American Underground Film*, E. P. Dutton & Co. Inc., New York, 1967, p. 100.

2. Ibid., p. 103.

3. Ibid., *passim*.

4. Parker Tyler, *Underground Film: A Critical History*, Grove Press Inc., New York, 1970.

5. Ibid, p. 236.

6. *Film Culture Reader*, edited and with introduction by P. Adams Sitney, Praeger, New York, 1970.

7. 'Cinema Underground', *The New Yorker*, 13 July 1963.

8. *An Introduction to the American Underground*, op. cit., p. 82.

9. *The Village Voice*, 18 May 1961.

10. Gideon Bachman, '*Braught die "Dritte Alternative" eine Ideologie? Ein Gesprach mit Pier Paolo Pasolini and Jonas Mekas*', *Film*, Heft, 10 October 1967.

11. Jonas Mekas, 'The Experimental Film in America', *Film Culture*, Vol. 1, No. 3, May–June 1955.

12. Ed Emshwiller, 'Images from the Underground', *Dialogue*, Vol. 4, No. 1, 1971.

13. *New Cinema Club*, London, July–September 1970.

14. Tony Conrad, 'On the "Flicker" ', *Film Culture*, No. 41, Summer 1966.

15. Paul Sharitz, 'Notes on Films (1966–1968)', *Film Culture*, No. 47, Summer 1969.

16. *An Introduction to the American Underground Cinema*, op. cit., p. 109.

17. *Film Culture*, No. 48–9, Winter–Spring 1970.

18. *The Village Voice,* 21 August 1969.

19. Gregory Battcock, *The New American Cinema: A Critical Anthology*, E. P. Dutton & Co. Inc., New York, 1969, p. 205.

20. Clifford Terry, 'Second Chicago Film Festival Better than Last Year But Still No Great Success', *Chicago Tribune*, 26 November 1966.

21. *An Introduction to the American Underground Cinema*, op. cit., p. 195.

22. Susan Pike, 'The Chelsea Girls', *Film Culture*, No. 46, Summer 1967.

23. 'Nuts from Underground', *Time*, 30 December 1966.

24. Kent E. Carroll, 'Home on Range of Comedy', *Variety*, 28 May 1969.

25. Otto Hahn, Andy Warhol, '*Prêtre du cinéma souterrain*', *L'Express*, 14–20 November 1966.

26. New Cinema Club, London, July–September 1970.

27. *Newsweek*, 5 February 1973.

28. Parker Tyler, *Underground Film*, op. cit., p. 51.

29. *An Introduction to the American Underground Cinema,*

30. Op. cit., *Cinema Journal*, Vol. X, No. 2, Spring 1971. op. cit., p. 17.

31. Gideon Bachman, '*Protest wofür? Aus New Yorker Filmtage· buch*', *Film*, June 1968.

32. Jonas Mekas, 'The Experimental Film in America', op. cit.

33. Parker Tyler, *Underground Film*, op. cit., p. 10.

34. Jonas Mekas, 'A Language All Their Own', *Los Angeles Times Calendar*, 26 March 1967.

35. *An Introduction to the American Underground Cinema*, op. cit., p. 35.
36. Ibid., p. 37.
37. Gideon Bachman, '*Braucht die "Dritte Alternative" eine Ideologie?*', op. cit.
38. P. Adams Sitney, 'Structural Film', *Film Culture*, No. 47, Summer 1969.
39. Gene Youngblood, *Expanded Cinema*, E. P. Dutton & Co. Inc., New York, 1970.
40. 'Expanded Arts', *Film Culture*, No. 43, Winter 1966.
41. Gregory Battcock, *The New American Cinema*, op. cit., p. 137–8.

CHAPTER 7

1. *Variety*, 15 October 1969.
2. 'K. and E. Summary of 69–70 First Half', *Variety*, 23 December 1970.
3. Drob Knight, 'Dann Downbeat on TV Future of Pix', *Variety*, 14 January 1970.
4. 'Edited for Television', *Time*, March 1971.
5. Les Brown, 'Computer Cinema: How Feevee Fared in Newark Hotel Against Free TV', *Variety*, 29 September 1971.
6. Jindrich Brichta, *Edison ukázal cestu*, Orbis, Praha, 1959, p. 43–4.

CHAPTER 8

1. *The New Yorker*, 3 July 1971.
2. Ernest Callenbach, 'Recent Film Writing: A Survey', *Film Quarterly*, Vol. XXIV, No. 3, Spring 1971.
3. 'The Commercial', *The New Yorker*, 7 August 1971.
4. Pauline Kael, 'The Current Cinema, Numbing the Audience', *The New Yorker*, 3 October 1970.
5. Penelope Gilliatt, 'The Current Cinema, The Upstanding Chimp', *The New Yorker*, 5 June 1971.
6. Pauline Kael, 'The Current Cinema, Notes on Heart and Mind', *The New Yorker*, 23 January 1971.
7. Roger Ebert, 'Medium Cool', *Chicago Sun Times*, 21 September 1969.
8. *Film 67/68*, op. cit., p. 282–305.
9. Ibid., p. 298.

10. Ibid., p. 303.
11. Ibid., p. 297.
12. Ibid., p. 291.
13. Ibid., p. 300.
14. Ibid., p. 290.
15. Ibid., p. 299.
16. Recent Film Writing: A Survey, op. cit.
17. Gerald Sykes, 'A New Salvation – A New Supernatural, Technology and Human Values', Center for the Study of Democratic Institutions, New York, 1966, p. 6.
18. 'Understanding McLuhan', *Newsweek*, 28 February 1966.
19. *McLuhan: Hot and Cold* edited by Gerald Emanuel Stern. The New American Library, New York, 1969, p. 262.
20. Marshall McLuhan, *Understanding Media*, Routledge & Kegan Paul Ltd, London, 1964, p. 286.
21. *McLuhan, Hot and Cold*, op. cit., p. 262.
22. *Expanded Cinema*, op. cit.
23. Richard Kostelanetz, *The Theatre of Mixed Means*, Pitman Press, London, 1970, p. 33.
24. *Film 67/68*, op. cit., p. 303.
25. *The Theatre of Mixed Means*, op. cit., p. 47.
26. *The American Cinema*, op. cit.
27. *Confessions of a Cultist*, Simon and Schuster, New York, 1970.
28. Recent Film Writing: A Survey, op. cit.
29. 'A New Salvation – A New Supernatural', op. cit., p. 9.
30. Jonathan Miller, *McLuhan*, Fontana/Collins, London, 1971, p. 126.
31. *McLuhan: Hot and Cold*, op. cit., p. 273.
32. *Recent Film Writing: A Survey*, op. cit.
33. Jack Nicholson, '*Le Refus d'est parfois la fuite*', *Humanité Dimanche*, 14 March 1971.
34. Jerzy Schatzberg, '*Panique à Needle Park*', *Humanité Dimanche*, 15 June 1971.
35. Penn, 'Premier *cinéaste* Cheyenne', *L'Express* 5–11, April 1971.
36. Abraham Polonsky, 'Willie Boy *et la joie de survivre*', *Humanité Dimanche*, 28 December 1969.
37. 'Nicholson in N.Y.: End of "Riot Fad" in U.S. Features', *Variety*, 16 September 1970.

FILM INDEX

NAME INDEX

GENERAL INDEX